PROGRAMMING INTERVIEWS EXPOS
SECRETS TO LANDING YOUR NEXT J

D0600834

Programming Interviews Exposed

Third Edition

Programming Interviews Exposed

SECRETS TO LANDING YOUR NEXT JOB

Third Edition

John Mongan
Eric Giguère
Noah Kindler

John Wiley & Sons, Inc.

Programming Interviews Exposed: Secrets to Landing Your Next Job, Third Edition

Published by
John Wiley & Sons, Inc.
10475 Crosspoint Boulevard
Indianapolis, IN 46256
www.wiley.com

Copyright © 2013 by John Wiley & Sons, Inc., Indianapolis, Indiana

Published simultaneously in Canada

ISBN: 978-1-118-26136-1
ISBN: 978-1-118-28720-0 (ebk)
ISBN: 978-1-118-28340-0 (ebk)
ISBN: 978-1-118-28466-7 (ebk)

Manufactured in the United States of America

10 9 8 7 6 5

For general information on our other products and services please contact our Customer Care Department within the United States at (877) 762-2974, outside the United States at (317) 572-3993 or fax (317) 572-4002.

Wiley publishes in a variety of print and electronic formats and by print-on-demand. Some material included with standard print versions of this book may not be included in e-books or in print-on-demand. If this book refers to media such as a CD or DVD that is not included in the version you purchased, you may download this material at http://booksupport.wiley.com. For more information about Wiley products, visit www.wiley.com.

Library of Congress Control Number: 2012941787

For Thuy, the love of my life, who understands me.

—JOHN MONGAN

To my parents, Jean-Claude and Marie-Jolle, who encouraged and supported my love of programming.

—ERIC GIGUÈRE

To Mikey, Alex, and Teddy

—NOAH KINDLER

ABOUT THE AUTHORS

JOHN MONGAN is a self-taught programmer with professional experience as a consultant for several software and pharmaceutical companies. He has three patents on software testing technologies. He holds a B.S. degree from Stanford and an M.D. and a Ph.D. degree in bioinformatics from UC San Diego, where he worked on supercomputer simulations of protein dynamics. He currently conducts research in medical informatics as a resident radiologist at UC San Francisco.

ERIC GIGUÈRE started programming in BASIC on a Commodore VIC-20 (a long time ago) and was hooked. He holds BMath and MMath degrees in computer science from the University of Waterloo, has extensive professional programming experience, and is the author of several programming books. He currently works as a software engineer at Google.

NOAH KINDLER is VP Technology at the security technology company Avira. He leads software design and development teams across several products with a user base of over 100 million.

ABOUT THE TECHNICAL EDITORS

MICHAEL GILBERT is a long-time systems programmer for various engineering firms. He got his start developing games for the Atari ST, and was a frequent contributing editor for *STart* magazine. Over the years, he's developed gaming software on the PC and Mac for clients worldwide. He's also an expert Flash Actionscript programmer and has produced a popular internet gaming environment called HigherGames, you can check it out at www.highergames.com. He now enjoys developing games for the iPhone and iPad, and currently has four games in the AppStore (Woridgo, Jumpin' Java, Kings Battlefield, and Set Pro HD). In his spare time, he enjoys trying to defeat his wife Janeen in a friendly game of Scrabble. You can follow him on Twitter at mija711.

JUSTIN VOGT is an experienced software development professional with a unique blend of skills (technical, architectural, design, communication, creative, management, and development leadership). He has over 15 years of diverse experience in software development and has worked on projects that include embedded software, mobile development, web development, commercial software development, device communications, medical application development, and non-profit organization solution development.

CREDITS

EXECUTIVE EDITOR
Carol Long

PROJECT EDITOR
Maureen Spears

TECHNICAL EDITOR
Justin J. Vogt

PRODUCTION EDITOR
Kathleen Wisor

COPY EDITOR
Apostrophe Editing

EDITORIAL MANAGER
Mary Beth Wakefield

FREELANCER EDITORIAL MANAGER
Rosemarie Graham

ASSOCIATE DIRECTOR OF MARKETING
David Mayhew

MARKETING MANAGER
Ashley Zurcher

BUSINESS MANAGER
Amy Knies

PRODUCTION MANAGER
Tim Tate

**VICE PRESIDENT AND
EXECUTIVE GROUP PUBLISHER**
Richard Swadley

VICE PRESIDENT AND EXECUTIVE PUBLISHER
Neil Edde

ASSOCIATE PUBLISHER
Jim Minatel

PROJECT COORDINATOR, COVER
Katie Crocker

COMPOSITOR
Craig Johnson, Happenstance Type-O-Rama

PROOFREADER
Nancy Carrasco

INDEXER
Jack Lewis

COVER DESIGNER
Ryan Sneed

COVER IMAGE
© Andrew Rich / iStockPhoto

ACKNOWLEDGMENTS

THE PREPARATION OF THIS EDITION followed an unusual path, and we appreciate the extensive efforts of the staff at Wiley to bring it to a timely and successful completion. The contributions of our editor, Maureen Spears, who can rapidly overcome any obstacle that arises, and the personal attention of our publisher, Jim Minatel, and our senior acquisitions editor, Carol Long, were especially key, and we thank them for their time, work, and assistance.

The quality of this edition has been greatly improved by Wayne Heym's thoughtful comments and detailed review, and we thank him for his generous contributions.

In addition, John is deeply grateful for Michael J. Mongan's help in facilitating his participation with this edition.

No third edition would have been possible without the two that preceded it, however, and the many people who contributed to them. For this reason, we also thank our original editors, Margaret Hendrey and Marjorie Spencer, for their patience and helpfulness. We are also grateful to our original reviewers and advisors, Dan Hill, Elise Lipkowitz, Charity Lu, Rob Maguire, and Tom Mongan. Dan's contributions in particular were tremendous—the quality of the first edition was vastly improved by his careful and meticulous reviews.

CONTENTS

PREFACE

THE MOST IMPORTANT THING WE HAVE TO TELL YOU is the same as in the first edition: You will get as much out of this book as you put into it. If you read this book cover to cover, you will learn something, but not nearly as much as you would if you take some time trying to work through the problems before you read the answers.

That said, many of the other things we have to tell you *have* changed over the period of more than a decade since the first edition was published, so it was thrilling to have another opportunity to revise *Programming Interviews Exposed*.

This edition represents the largest update yet. In addition to revising, expanding, and updating the material from the previous edition, chapters on the important topics of sorting and design patterns are added. The non-programming parts of the book were revised to reflect the realities of today's job market. Throughout all this, we maintain the approachable style and step-by-step thought process developed for the original edition.

Code samples are largely in C, C++, or Java, but in most cases the focus is on the data structures and algorithms, and the language choice is entirely secondary. All the examples should be easily understandable for an experienced programmer.

One of us (Eric) recently interviewed for and landed his dream job at Google, which has given him additional perspective on programming interviews, reflected in this revision. We're pleased that Google seems to be leading a shift away from the use of trivial puzzles in interviews, something we've complained about since the first edition (see the following original preface).

We hope you enjoy the third edition of *Programming Interviews Exposed* and that it helps you get the job you've always wanted. We'd love to hear your thoughts on the book and your interview experiences. You can contact us at authors@piexposed.com. Be sure to visit the official *Programming Interviews Exposed* site at http://www.piexposed.com for updates and more information.

PREFACE TO THE FIRST EDITION

If you're like us, you don't usually read prefaces. This one has some useful information in it, though, so we hope you'll make an exception. If you're still tempted to skip the preface, here's what you really need to know: You'll get as much out of this book as you put into it. If you read this book cover to cover, you'll learn something, but not nearly as much as you would if you take some time trying to work through the problems on your own before you read the answers.

This book will help prepare you for the interviews you will face when seeking a job in programming, development, technical consulting, or any other field that warrants a programming interview. Programming interviews bear little resemblance to those described in traditional job-hunting and interview books. They consist almost entirely of programming problems, puzzles, and technical questions about computers. This book discusses each of the kinds of problems you are likely to encounter and illustrates how they are best approached using questions from real interviews as examples.

At this point you may be wondering who we are and what gives us the authority to write this book. We're both recent graduates who've been through a lot of interviews in the past few years. We've interviewed for jobs ranging from technical consulting with large established companies to writing device drivers for startups. This book is based on the experiences and observations we've taken from those interviews — what yielded offers and what didn't. We believe that this is the best possible basis for a book like this. Rather than give you some HR exec's idea of how interviewing should be done or a head hunter's impression of how it might be done, we will tell you what interviews are really like at America's top software and computer companies and what you need to do to get the job you want.

> **NOTE** *For the record, we don't think that the way interviewing is done today is necessarily the way it should be done. The current paradigm puts too much emphasis on the ability to solve puzzles and familiarity with a relatively limited body of knowledge, and it generally fails to measure a lot of the skills that are critical to success in industry.*

To that end, we haven't made up any of the questions in this book. Every last one of them has been lifted from a recent interview. The distributions of problem type and difficulty are similar to what you should expect to encounter in your interviews. We must emphasize that the problems presented in this book are a representative sample of the questions asked in interviews, not a comprehensive compilation. Reading this book straight through and memorizing the answers would completely miss the point. You may be asked some of the questions that appear in this book, but you should not expect that. A large and constantly changing body of questions is asked, and any intelligent interviewer who has seen this book will never again use any of the questions that appear here. On the other hand, interview questions encompass relatively few topic areas and types of questions, and these rarely change. If you work on learning to solve not just the specific problems we present, but the types of problems we present, you'll be able to handle anything they throw at you in an interview.

We've taken a couple of steps to facilitate the objective of improving your problem-solving skills. First, where appropriate, we provide reviews of important topics before we present questions on those topics. Second, instead of merely giving answers to the problems, we illustrate the problem-solving process from beginning to solution. We've found that most textbooks and nearly all puzzle books take a different approach to examples: They begin with a problem, go immediately to the answer, and then explain why the answer is correct. In our experience, the result is that the reader may under-stand the particular answer and why it's right, but is left with no clue as to how the author came up with that solution or how a similar problem might be solved. We hope that our step-by-step approach to solutions will address this issue, helping you to understand not only the answers but also how you arrive at the answers.

Learning by watching is never as effective as learning by doing. If you want to get the most out of this book, you will have to work out the problems yourself. We suggest the following method:

1. After you read a problem, put the book down and try to work out the solution.

2. If you get stuck, start reading the solution. We never blurt out the answer at the beginning, so you don't have to worry that we're going to give away the entire solution.

3. Read just far enough to get the hint you need, and then put down the book and keep working.

4. Repeat this as necessary.

The more of the solution you work out yourself, the better your understanding will be. In addition, this method closely resembles the actual interview experience, where you will have to solve the problems yourself, but the interviewer will give you hints when you get stuck.

Programming is a difficult and technical art. It would be impossible to teach everything you need to know about computers and programming in one book. Therefore, we've had to make some assumptions about who you are. We assume that you have a background in computers equivalent to at least the first year or two of a computer science degree. Specifically, we expect that you are comfortable with programming in C, that you've had some experience with object-oriented programming in C++ or perhaps Java, and that you know the fundamentals of computer architecture and computer science theory. These are effectively the minimum requirements for a general development job, so most interviewers will have similar expectations. If you find yourself lacking in any of these areas, you should seriously consider seeking more education before starting your job search and interviews.

It's also possible that you have a great deal more computer knowledge and experience than what we've described as the minimum requirements. If so, you may be particularly interested in some of the more advanced topics included. However, don't ignore the basic topics and questions, no matter how much experience you have. Interviewers tend to start with the fundamentals regardless of what's on your résumé.

We have made every effort to ensure that all of the information in this book is correct. All of the code has been compiled and tested. Nevertheless, as you probably know all too well from your own programs, a few bugs and errors are inevitable. As we become aware of such problems, we will post corrections at `http://www.piexposed.com`.

We're confident that you'll find this book useful in getting the job you want. We hope that you may also find it an entertaining exploration of some clever puzzles in your chosen profession. If you'd like to tell us about your reaction to our book, share your thoughts on any particular problem or topic, or provide a problem from one of your recent interviews, we'd love to hear from you. Please e-mail us at `authors@piexposed.com`.

Go find a killer job!

INTRODUCTION

LANDING A GREAT PROGRAMMING JOB isn't a matter of luck; it's a matter of preparation. The programming interview process that most software firms use today is designed to determine whether you can actually code. It can be a grueling process, especially because the limitations imposed by the interview format make the process almost completely different from anything you experience in school or on the job. If you've never encountered it before, it can be quite a shock. Even great programmers who are inexperienced with programming interviews often struggle if they are unprepared for what they will face.

This book was written to prepare you for the technical interview process so that you have no problem demonstrating how great a programmer you are. It doesn't teach you how to program; it shows you how to use the programming skills you have to shine in a programming interview. As you read this book, keep in mind that programming interviews (for the most part) are not factual recall tests, so this book isn't a cheat sheet of all the facts you need to know for your interview. Instead, it teaches by example the techniques and thought processes you need to succeed. The best way to internalize these is to take time to work through and understand the problems. If you do, you'll approach your interviews with confidence because you'll be prepared to solve any problem you're given, putting you that much closer to landing the job you want.

WHY PROGRAMMING INTERVIEWS?

Why do software firms use programming interviews? They want to hire great programmers who can work well with others to successfully produce great products. Unfortunately, bitter experience has taught employers that a substantial portion of applicants for programming jobs simply cannot code. You might expect that these applicants could be screened out by careful review of résumés, experience, course work, and degrees, but in practice this often fails. There are a surprisingly large number of applicants with sparkling résumés and years of apparently relevant industry experience who cannot accomplish even the simplest of programming tasks. Many of them have picked up enough terminology that they can appear competent in conversations about programming and technology. Hiring one of these "developers" who can't code can easily sink a department (or even a small company).

Recognizing that traditional interviews are ineffective to identify applicants who can't code, employers took a logical step: Ask applicants to do some coding during the interview. Thus the programming interview was born. Programming interviews are extremely effective at separating those who can code from those who can't, which is why they are a nearly universal part of the technical interview process.

The difficulty with programming interviews is that employers don't just want to screen out people who can't code. Employers want to distinguish the *best* programmers from those who are merely competent. This is a more difficult distinction to make. Typically, interviewers try to measure an applicant's ability by posing difficult programming challenges and noting how quickly and accurately the applicant solves them.

The problem with this approach is that due to the time restriction inherent to an interview, the skills that can be tested in a programming interview only partially overlap the skills that are relevant to real-world development. By necessity, programming interviews evaluate your ability to solve problems on the spot, with someone watching you, without the benefit of any of the references you would typically have available. There isn't time to write a lot of code, so problems must have short solutions. Most problems with short solutions would be trivial, so to avoid this many interview problems involve unusual algorithmic tricks, absurd restrictions, or obscure language features. Because these types of problems don't typically arise in real-world development, an excellent programmer who is unprepared for the peculiarities of the interview experience may appear to be unqualified.

Conversely, there are many skills essential to development in a professional environment that programming interviews don't assess well (or at all). These include communicating and working as part of a team; architecture, and management of large codebases; time management and discipline to consistently produce reliable code on schedule; and the ability to tackle a large project, identify all the component parts, and carry the project through to completion.

Clearly, programming interviews do not provide a perfect measure of an applicant's worth as a future employee. But to paraphrase Churchill's assessment of democracy, it's the worst form of technical interview except for all the other forms that have been tried. More to the point, programming interviews are the way employers choose who they will hire, so you need to perform well in them regardless of whether they are an ideal form of assessment. This book is devoted to teaching you how to adapt your programming skills to the peculiarities of interview problems and gives you the preparation and practice you need to shine in interviews so that you get the job you want.

HOW TO USE THIS BOOK

Preparation is the key to mastering the programming interview process. The following are some general guidelines on how to effectively use this book to prepare for programming interviews:

➤ **Give yourself enough time to prepare.** Start your preparations as early as possible, ideally weeks or even months ahead of your interviews. You need that time to practice the concepts presented here. (If you don't have the luxury of that much time, try to put aside some blocks of uninterrupted time to study the material.)

➤ **Practice answering problems.** Don't just read through the solutions. Work through the problems using the solutions for a hint when you get stuck and to verify your answer. Try to simulate the interview experience. Most of the time you'll be writing code on paper or a whiteboard; practice this! It sounds silly, but it takes some practice to get the programming part of your brain engaged through a pen instead of a keyboard.

➤ **Make sure you understand the underlying concepts.** Understanding the concepts that underlie the problems is the key to your success. Don't skip or gloss over the material you don't understand. This book provides enough of an explanation to refresh your memory of topics you've learned before, but if you encounter something you've completely forgotten or never learned, you may need to read more about it in another reference.

➤ **Don't bother memorizing the answers to the problems.** Interviewers are unlikely to present you with any of the problems in this book. Even if they do, they may change the problem in any number of small ways. If you answer it by rote, your answer may be incorrect.

➤ **Keep practicing.** Your preparation doesn't stop after finishing this book. Keep working on programming problems; they're easy to find on the Internet. Find additional reference material, especially in your areas of expertise, and keep reading.

Your health and well-being is your most important asset; it affects how well you learn and how well you interview. Remember to get enough sleep — especially close to an interview date — and to exercise and eat properly. Take regular breaks to help your mind integrate the material. Don't try to cram at the last minute — when it's time for your interview, you'll be a much more effective problem solver if you go in relaxed with a clear mind than if you stress yourself by cramming right up until the interview.

As part of your preparation, be sure to visit `http://www.piexposed.com` to sign up for our mailing list and learn about the special smartphone app we've prepared to help you with your interviews.

Now, let's get started!

1

Before the Search

Before starting your job search, you need to prepare yourself. You shouldn't apply for jobs without knowing what kind of job you want. Just being a good coder isn't enough; you must understand what the market wants and how you can improve and package your own skills to make sure that the company with the job you want will want you.

KNOW YOURSELF

Stereotypes to the contrary, all programmers are *not* alike. Knowing what kind of programmer you are is crucial to finding the right kind of job. Although you can probably do many different kinds of programming tasks, you probably don't find them all equally engaging. Doing something you don't enjoy is fine on a short-term basis, but you need to be interested in and excited by what you're doing for it to sustain you over the long term. The best programmers are passionate about their work, and you can't truly be passionate about something that's only moderately interesting to you.

If you're not sure what you like or dislike, ask yourself some questions:

➤ **Are you a systems programmer or an application developer?** Systems programmers work on the code that keeps computer systems running: frameworks, tools, compilers, drivers, servers, and so on. Other programmers are their primary audience, so little interaction occurs with non-programmers — and usually the job involves little or no user interface work. Application developers, on the other hand, work on the pieces that those non-programmers use to do their own work, and often more interaction occurs with non-technical people. Many programmers find interacting with non-technical people about technical topics to be frustrating; on the other hand, you may enjoy creating applications that are seen and used by an audience that extends beyond other programmers.

➤ **Do you like coding user interfaces?** User interface design — also referred to as *user experience (UX)* or *human computer interaction (HCI)* — is a role that draws on a diverse set of skills, including programming, graphic design, and psychology. This work is high profile because the user interface is the most visible part of any application. User interface design is particularly important in mobile application development, where the restrictions of the device require even greater creativity and innovation. If you have the necessary skills and enjoy this work, you're in elite company: Many programmers find it finicky, hard to do well, and easy to criticize, especially when you take internationalization and accessibility issues into account.

➤ **Are you a good debugger?** If you think finding problems in your own code is difficult, imagine what it's like to fix problems with someone else's code. It requires strong analytical and problem-solving skills. Finding and fixing bugs can be extremely rewarding in its own right. You need to know if you'd be happy doing primarily maintenance work. (Of course, you should always expect to maintain your own code — all programmers need debugging skills.) In many cases, particularly in older companies, maintenance programming jobs involve working primarily with older technologies now considered outdated or no longer in fashion. Developing your experience and skills with older technologies may narrow the range of jobs that you're suited for, but because expertise in older technologies is hard to find, you may be highly sought after by the smaller number of companies dependent on older programs.

➤ **Do you like testing?** Testing — also referred to as *quality assurance* or QA for short — requires a combination of meticulous attention to detail to ensure that tests cover every conceivable use of a program and outside-the-box creativity to find bugs in the program by generating combinations of inputs that the program's developers never considered. Skilled testers are hard to find, and good programming skills are required to write tools and automated test cases.

➤ **Are you an architect or a coder?** Every coding job includes some kind of design aspect, but certain jobs lean more one way than the other. If you enjoy designing, particularly designing the large-scale structure of big projects, a position as a software architect might be more appealing than a coding-focused job. Although you need a good understanding of how to code to be an effective architect, architecture positions can involve a lot of meetings and interpersonal interactions and little or no coding. Unless you have formal training in software architecture, the usual route to becoming an architect is to code first and to then display an aptitude for designing and fitting together different pieces of a project.

The preceding questions deal with different kinds of programming, but you should also consider non-programming responsibilities that might interest you and the work environment that you prefer:

➤ **Does management interest you?** Some coders have a long-term goal to become a manager, but others shiver at the very thought. If management is your goal, you need to develop leadership skills and demonstrate that you can manage the human parts of the software development equation as well as the technical pieces. If management is *not* your goal, look for companies with good *technical* career paths, so you're not forced to manage people to be promoted. (You still need leadership skills to get promoted no matter which career path you choose, but leadership skills are separate from people management skills.)

➤ **Do you want to work for a big company?** There are advantages and disadvantages to working at big companies. For example, a large company may offer more job stability (although layoffs during downturns are common) and some kind of career path. It may also have a name brand that non-techies recognize. On the other hand, you may feel stifled by the bureaucracy, rigidness, and intracompany rivalry often found in bigger companies.

➤ **Do you want to work for a small company?** The pay may be less, but getting in on the ground floor at a new company can create opportunities for future advancement (and possibly substantial remuneration) as the company grows and succeeds. Also, the work environment at small companies is often more informal than at larger organizations. The downside, of course, is that most new ventures fail, and you may be out of a job within a year or two, most likely without the kind of severance package you might expect from a large company.

➤ **Do you want to work on open source projects?** The vast majority of programming jobs have historically involved proprietary, closed-source projects, which some programmers don't like. A shift has occurred in some companies in favor of more open software development, which provides opportunities for people to work on open-source projects and still be paid for that participation. If it's important to you that your work project is open source, it's best to seek out companies already involved in open source. Trying to champion open source in traditional software companies is often a frustrating and fruitless undertaking.

➤ **Do you want long-term or short-term projects?** Some programmers crave change, spending a few months at most on each project. If you like short-term projects and don't mind traveling, a gig with a consulting company might make more sense than a more conventional corporate job.

Realize that there are no universal answers to these questions, and no right or wrong way to answer them. The more truthful you are in answering them, the more likely you'll find the kind of programming job you truly enjoy.

KNOW THE MARKET

Knowing what you'd like to do is great, but don't box yourself in too narrowly. You also need to understand the current job market and how it constrains your search for the "ideal" job, especially during an economic downturn like the one that burst the Internet bubble of the late '90s or the global real estate and banking meltdown of the late 2000s.

Basic Market Information

A number of sources of information exist about what's hot and what's not in the developer job market, including the following:

➤ **Social networks** — The tremendous growth of social networks, such as LinkedIn, Facebook, and Google+, have transformed social networks into virtual recruiting grounds for all types and sizes of organizations. LinkedIn is particularly important. The other social networks can provide an indirect "pulse" of the market and also valuable leads for new and even unannounced job postings.

➤ **Online job sites** — Visit two kinds of job sites as part of your research. Job listing sites such as Dice (which specializes in technology-related career listings) and Monster (a general job listing site) enable you to see what kinds of jobs are currently in demand. Review sites such as Glassdoor and CareerBliss discuss working conditions, salaries, bonuses, perks, and other information useful for finding the right kind of company for you.

➤ **Bookstores** — Even though more and more programmer documentation is available online, professionally published books are still important, whether printed or downloadable. The number of books published on any given topic is a good indication of the level of interest the programming community has in that topic. Look especially for niche topics that are suddenly going mainstream, but beware that in most companies, mainstream use of technologies lags the interest levels represented in books by a few years.

➤ **Professional development courses** — Colleges and universities try to keep abreast of what companies want and create professional development courses around those needs.

If you're not in college or university, find out what languages and technologies the local institutions and your alma mater require of their computer science students; although academic needs don't always coincide with what employers want, educational institutions try to graduate students with practical skills that employers can use.

What About Outsourcing?

Outsourcing and *offshoring* — contracting tasks to other companies or foreign divisions or companies — is an important part of the technical employment landscape. Outsourcing of ancillary business activities such as payroll administration and property maintenance has been around for decades. More recently, this has expanded to programming, driven by the advent of inexpensive computers, cheap long distance communication provided by the Internet, and the recognition of technically educated workforces in low-wage developing countries. There was a flurry of outsourcing, particularly offshoring, in the mid-2000s. This has become less topical in the past several years because most companies that intend to outsource have already outsourced whatever they can. In addition, the costs of offshoring have risen as wages rise in the developing world, particularly in India and China. This coupled with recognition of the hidden costs of coordination with workforces from different cultures on very different schedules have led some companies to insource roles they previously outsourced. Nevertheless, outsourcing and offshoring remain a possibility for expanding companies that think they may cut costs, as well as established companies wondering if they're paying too much by keeping their work local.

If outsourcing (and offshoring in particular) is something that worries you, consider taking steps to avoid landing a job that might be outsourced at some point in the future. The following are some suggestions:

➤ **Work for software development firms** — A software firm's *raison d'être* is the intellectual property it develops. Although medium and large firms may open development centers in other parts of the world, the smart ones are unlikely to move their entire operations to other countries or entrust their future to outside firms. That said, some companies outsource all or substantial parts of a project to other countries for cost or other reasons, so it pays to research a company's behaviors and policies.

➤ **Work for an outsourcer** — Oddly enough, many outsourcing firms hire personnel in countries such as the United States.

> ➤ **Move up the programmer food chain** — Design-oriented jobs are less likely to be outsourced. Coders are relatively cheap and plentiful, but good designers are much harder to find. (This assumes that your company recognizes that good design skills are separate from good coding skills.) Another way to make yourself more difficult to replace is to acquire *domain specific knowledge*: expertise related to the programs you write but outside of the field of programming. For example, if you develop financial software, it's much more difficult to outsource your job if it involves the application of accounting skills in addition to programming than if you're purely a coder.

> ➤ **Take a management job** — Management can be a refuge from outsourcing, so a management-oriented career path is one option to consider.

Of all these options, moving up the food chain is usually the best approach. The more non-programming knowledge your job requires, or the more interaction with customers, the less likely you are to be outsourced. There's no *guarantee* you'll never be outsourced, of course, or that you'll always keep your job. Your company may shutter or downsize the project you're working on at any point, after all, and put you back on the street. This is why developing reusable and marketable skills throughout your career is extremely important.

DEVELOP MARKETABLE SKILLS

In the appendix we discuss your résumé as a *marketing tool* to get you job interviews. The easiest thing to sell is something that people want, so it's important that you have *marketable skills* to offer a prospective employer.

To stand out from the crowd both on paper and in the interviews you need to develop skills and accomplishments, especially if you're entering the job market for the first time. The following are some approaches you can take:

> ➤ **Upgrade your credentials** — Companies such as Google are well known for favoring job applicants with graduate degrees. Getting a master's or doctorate degree is one way to upgrade your credentials. You can upgrade your credentials in other ways, such as taking university or professional development courses or participating in programming contests.

> ➤ **Get certified** — Certification is a contentious issue in the software development profession, but some jobs either prefer or require candidates to be certified in specific technologies, especially IT jobs. Consider surveying job listings to see whether certifications are required for the jobs that interest you before you invest time and money in certifications.

> ➤ **Work on a side project** — A great way to expand your skill set is to work on a project not directly related to your primary work or study focus. Starting or joining an open-source development project is one way to go. Or if you work at a company, see if it will let you spend time on an ancillary project.

> ➤ **Do well in school** — Although grades aren't everything, they are one measure that companies use to rank new graduates with little job experience. The better your grades, especially in computer science and mathematics courses, the more you can impress a potential employer.

➤ **Keep learning** — The end of formal education doesn't mean you should stop learning, especially when so much information about programming is available from a wide variety of sources. Whether it's books or blogs, there's always a way to keep current, no matter what type of programming you do. It's also a great way to expand your horizons and discover other areas of interest. This kind of learning doesn't show up on your résumé, but it's something you can highlight in your technical interviews.

➤ **Be an intern** — New graduates who manage to secure employment during their non-school terms — especially those that participate in cooperative education programs — have a huge advantage over their peers who haven't yet ventured into the real world. Software development in the field is often different from software development in an academic setting, and potential employers are cognizant of this.

The key is to *keep learning*, no matter the stage of your career. You can't develop marketable skills overnight; they take some effort and initiative on your part but can have long-lasting effects on your career.

GET THINGS DONE

Companies look for software developers who *get things done*. You may look great on paper in terms of skills and education, but credentials and knowledge don't make products or services that a company can sell. It's your ability to *accomplish something* that truly sets you apart from the other candidates.

Getting an advanced degree such as a Ph.D., becoming a trusted contributor to a widely used open source project, or carrying a product through from start to launch are all big accomplishments. But small accomplishments can be just as important, such as adding a feature to a product, making a measurable improvement to the product's performance, starting and completing a side project, or creating a useful application for a class project. These all show that you can get things done.

Recruiters and hiring committees like to see that you have multiple accomplishments — a pattern of getting things done. This is especially true for more senior and experienced developers. You need to show those accomplishments on your résumé and your online profile. Whether your accomplishments are big or small, always be ready to talk intelligently and confidently about each one. This is incredibly important! Make sure you can clearly and succinctly describe the underlying problem and how your project solved it, even to a non-technical person. Displaying a passion for programming is always positive; clearly communicating how your passion produces products and services that other people can use makes you really stand out from the other candidates.

MANAGE YOUR ONLINE PROFILE

Your online profile — everything public about you online — is just as important as your résumé. Recruiters use online profiles to find desirable candidates. Screeners use them to weed out undesirable applicants. Interviewers use them to prepare in-depth interview questions when résumés lack details.

An online profile consists of any or all these things:

- ➤ **LinkedIn profile** — LinkedIn is a social network for tracking professional connections. It's free to join, and you can create a detailed profile about yourself, including your jobs and your education — essentially an online résumé. Colleagues and customers can publicly endorse you or your work, which can be quite valuable.

- ➤ **Other social network profiles** — Other social networks such as Facebook or Google+, depending on your privacy settings.

- ➤ **Personal website** — This is a potential source of more in-depth information about you.

- ➤ **Articles and blog posts** — If you write about programming-related topics, this is a good way for recruiters to assess your experience.

- ➤ **Comments and forum posts** — These provide another way to gain some insight into your programming skills and your general attitude toward technology and technology companies.

The impression employers get from your online profile can affect your chances of being hired. If your résumé lists extensive experience with C# but they find a forum posting you made only 6 months ago asking how to open a file in C#, they'll probably conclude that you're exaggerating your experience level, putting your whole résumé into doubt. Or if they see disturbing or inflammatory material that they think you've authored, they may decide to pass you over for an interview, no matter how well your résumé reads or how long ago you wrote those things. No one's proud of everything they ever did in high school or college, but those who have grown up in the post-Internet era see things follow them that they'd rather forget about, something the older generations rarely had to contend with.

At some point before you apply for a job, take a good look at your online profile. Put yourself in a company's shoes to see how much information — good or bad — they can find about you, or link to you. If your online profile is possibly going to prevent you from being hired, take some steps to sanitize your profile. If possible, remove questionable material from the web and from the search engines.

Spend some time developing the positive aspects of your profile. This is particularly important if there's unfavorable material about you on the web that you're unable to remove. You may want to read a little about search engine optimization (SEO) and apply some of these techniques to get the positive aspects of your profile to appear before older, less favorable items in search results. If you don't have a LinkedIn profile, create one, and make it as detailed as possible; if you already have one, make sure it's up to date. Consider creating a profile on Stack Overflow or a similar Q&A site, and spend some time answering questions relating to your areas of expertise.

> **WARNING** *One caveat about updating your LinkedIn profile: By default, all your contacts are notified of your updates. Many people have learned to interpret these notifications as de facto announcements that someone is looking for a new job. That might help you get the word out, but if your contacts include people at your current company and you don't want them to know you're looking for a new job, disable these notifications before you make your updates.*

Develop an online profile that doesn't throw any red flags in front of the screeners and shows you in the best possible light. Finding a good job is hard enough — why make it harder?

SUMMARY

What you do *before* a formal job search is critical to finding the right kind of job. With that in mind, you should consider the following things:

➤ Know your likes and dislikes as a programmer and a prospective employee.

➤ Understand the market to find and apply for the best jobs.

➤ Develop the marketable skills that employers look for and that can enhance your career.

➤ Manage your public profile to show you in the best possible light and make sure there are no surprises to turn off potential employers.

Once you've worked through all these points, you're ready to begin your job search.

2

The Job Application Process

Interviewing and recruiting procedures are similar at most tech companies, so the more prepared you are for what you will encounter, the more successful you will be. This chapter familiarizes you with the entire job-search process, from contacting companies to starting your new job, so you won't need to write off your first few application attempts as learning experiences. Hiring procedures at technical companies are often substantially different from those followed by more traditional firms, so you may find this information useful even if you've spent some time in the working world.

FINDING AND CONTACTING COMPANIES

The first step to getting a job is to find and make contact with companies you're interested in working for. Although referrals are the best way to land a job, you can also work with headhunters or contact a company directly.

Finding Companies

You can better target your search if you know which companies you're most interested in working for. Big companies are easy to find — you can probably name a dozen national and international tech companies off the top of your head. You can identify candidate medium-sized (as well as large) companies through articles in trade and local business press. Many magazines and newspapers regularly compile lists of successful companies and rankings of the best places to work. (Take these rankings with a grain of salt: There's often a lot of variation in quality of work life across large companies.) Most companies of this size also advertise at least some of their job openings on online job boards; these postings can help you identify companies to investigate even if the specific job posted isn't right for you.

Small companies, especially early-stage startups, can be much more challenging to find. Often these companies are too small, too new, or too secretive to get much press. They may lack the resources to advertise their openings beyond their own website, which you can't find unless you know the name of the company. One good way to find these companies is asking friends and acquaintances if they know of startups that are hiring. Another technique is to use online social networks. You can use some sites, such as LinkedIn, to search for people by profession within a region. Most people on these sites list the name of their company, so you can build a list of companies in a particular region by going through the results of this search. This can be laborious, but part of the payoff is that if you can't find these companies any other way, neither can anyone else, so you're likely to be competing with fewer applicants.

Getting Referrals

Referrals are the best way to find a job. Tell all your friends about what kind of job you're looking for. Even if they don't work for the kinds of companies that might hire you, they may know people who do. Coming from "Susan's friend" or "Bill's neighbor," your résumé is sure to receive more careful consideration than the hundreds (or thousands) of anonymous résumés that come flooding in from online postings, job fairs, and other recruitment activities. Be sure to use your social networks, both real and virtual, to identify potential job opportunities.

Don't feel you're imposing on your friends and acquaintances. Companies often reward employees with big bonuses — as much as several thousand dollars — for successful referrals of talented software engineers. Your friends have a financial incentive to submit as many résumés as possible! (This is why referral bonuses are paid only *after* the referred person has been hired and has started working for the company.)

After you have a contact at a company, it's up to you to make the most of it. Your approach depends on how well you know the contact.

If the contact is not a close friend, e-mail the person to arrange a time to speak. When you speak to the person, ask about the company and the work environment. Then ask about any existing job openings. The person might not know of any — many employees know only about job openings in their immediate workgroup — but if you know jobs are available, point the person to the job listings. Explain why you'd be a good match for one of those openings. Then ask the person to submit your résumé. Before you end your conversation, always thank people for their time.

If the contacts are close friends, you can be more casual and just ask about job openings and if they'd refer you.

The best referrals are from people who have worked with you before. A current employee who vouches for your skills and accomplishments is the strongest type of referral. That's why you need to keep track of former co-workers — you might want to work with them again one day.

Working with Headhunters

Particularly when labor markets are tight, some firms use outside recruiters known as *headhunters* to help them find candidates. In addition, you may find it useful to seek out a headhunter and provide her with your information.

If you list yourself with a headhunter, she can assist you with your job search and call you when she learns of an opening that matches your skill set. It may take a while, so don't be discouraged.

Some headhunters are more helpful than others, so ask around to see if anyone you know has recommendations. If you can't locate a headhunter this way, you can search the web for headhunters, recruiters, or staffing services. You can check out a prospective headhunter by asking for references, but be aware that headhunters deal with so many people that even those who frequently do a poor job probably have 5 or 10 satisfied clients who serve as references.

When you work with headhunters, you must understand their motivation: headhunters are paid only when an applicant they've referred is hired. It is therefore in a headhunter's interest to put as many people as possible into as many jobs as possible as quickly as possible. A headhunter has no financial incentive to find you the best possible job — or to find a company the best possible applicant, for that matter. If you recognize that a headhunter is in business for the purpose of making a living and not for the purpose of helping you, you are less likely to be surprised or disappointed by your experiences. This is not to suggest that headhunters are bad people or that as a rule they take advantage of applicants or companies. Headhunters can be helpful and useful, but you must not expect them to look out for your interests above their own.

When you get a potential lead from a headhunter, she will usually send you a job description and a vague description of the type of company but not the name of the company. This is to make sure that if you apply for the job, you do it through the headhunter so that she gets her commission. It's unethical to independently apply for a job that comes to you through a headhunter, but sometimes you might like to have more information about the job or company before you proceed. For example, you may determine that it's a job you've already applied for, or at a location that would involve too long of a commute. The job description that the headhunter sends you is often copied verbatim from the company's website so by pasting it into your favorite search engine you can often find the original job listing.

Some companies don't work with headhunters in any capacity, so don't limit yourself by conducting your entire job search through a headhunter. As a corollary of this, avoid working with any headhunter who insists on being your exclusive representative. Finally, be aware that "headhunter" is a widely used term by people outside of this profession, but considered pejorative by most of the people who do this work, so it's best not to use the word "headhunter" when you speak to one of them.

Contacting the Company Directly

You can also try contacting companies directly. The Internet is the best medium for this approach. Most companies' web pages have instructions for submitting résumés. If the website lists specific openings, read through them and submit your résumé specifically for the openings that interest you. If you don't have a contact within the company, it's best to look for specific job openings: In many companies, résumés targeted at a specific job opportunity are forwarded directly to the hiring manager, whereas those that don't mention a specific opening languish in the human resources database. A tech-oriented job site is a good place to start your search if you don't have a specific company already in mind.

If a site doesn't provide any directions for submitting your résumé, look for an e-mail address to which you can send it. Send your résumé as both plain text in the body of the e-mail (so the recipient can read it without having to do any work) and, unless there are instructions to the contrary, as an attached file so that the recipient can print a copy. A PDF file is ideal; otherwise, attach a Microsoft Word file. Do not send a file in any other format unless specifically requested. Be sure to convert the file so that it can be read by older versions of Word, and scan it with an antivirus program (you can easily do this by mailing the resume to yourself as an attachment) to be absolutely certain that your résumé isn't carrying any macro viruses.

Approaching a company directly like this is a bit of a long shot, especially when the résumé is sent to a generic human resources e-mail address. Many companies use automated screening software to filter incoming résumés, so if your résumé lacks the right buzzwords, a human probably won't even see it. Consult the appendix for tips to get your résumé past automated screeners. With a good résumé in hand it takes so little time and effort to apply that you have nothing to lose.

Job Fairs

Job fairs are an easy way to learn about and make contact with a lot of companies without much effort. Your chances of success with any one particular company at a job fair are low because each company sees so many applicants. However, given the number of companies at a job fair, your over-all odds may still be favorable. If you collect business cards at the job fair and follow up with people afterward, you can separate yourself from the rest of the job fair crowd.

In addition, if they are available to you, college career centers, alumni organizations, and professional associations can also be helpful in finding jobs.

THE INTERVIEW PROCESS

If someone is sufficiently impressed by your résumé to want to talk to you, the next step is one or more screening interviews, usually followed by an on-site interview. Here, we prepare you for the stages of the interview process and help you dress for success.

Screening Interviews

Screening interviews are usually conducted by phone and last anywhere from 15 minutes to an hour. You should take the interview in a quiet room with no distractions and keep pen and paper handy to take notes. Screening interviews may also take place on the spot at a job fair or on campus as part of a college recruiting process.

The initial screening interview is with a company recruiter or human resources representative. The recruiter wants to make sure that you're interested in doing the job the company is hiring for, that you have the skills needed for the position, and that you're willing to accept any logistical requirements of the position, such as relocation or travel.

If you make it past the recruiter, there's normally a second screening interview in which a technical person asks you a few knowledge-based questions. These questions are designed to eliminate applicants who have inflated their résumés or are weak in skills that are key to the position. During the technical interview you may be asked to write some code using some kind of cloud-based document-sharing tool such as Google Docs. This gives the interviewer a firsthand look at your coding skills.

You should treat the phone interview as seriously as an on-site interview. It *is* an interview.

If the feedback from the technical interviewer is positive, the recruiter will get back to you, usually within a week, to schedule an on-site interview at the company's office.

On-Site Interviews

Your performance in *on-site interviews* is the biggest factor in determining whether you get an offer. These interviews consist mostly of a variety of technical questions: problems requiring you to implement a simple program or function; questions that test your knowledge of computers, languages, and programming; and sometimes even mathematics and logic puzzles. The majority of this book focuses on helping you answer these questions to succeed in your interviews.

Your on-site interviews usually last either a half day or a full day and typically consist of three to six interviews of 30 to 60 minutes each. Arrive early and well rested at the company's office, and take a restroom break if at all possible before any of the interviewing starts. Turn off any phones or pagers you carry. Under no circumstances should you interrupt your interview to read or answer a text, page, or call. You'll likely be greeted by either the recruiter you've been dealing with or the hiring manager. You may get an informal tour before the actual interviewing starts, which is a good way to see what the working conditions are like at that location.

Your interviewers may be the members of the team you'll work with if you are hired, or they may be engineers chosen at random from other groups within the company. Most companies have a rule that any interviewer can block an applicant from being hired, so all your interviews are important. Sometimes you may interview with two separate teams on the same day. Usually each group you interview with makes a separate decision about giving you an offer.

The company usually takes you out for lunch midway through your interview day. A free lunch at a nice restaurant or even at the company cafeteria is certainly enjoyable, but don't let your guard down completely. If you make a negative impression at lunch, you may lose your offer. Be polite, and avoid alcohol and messy foods. These general guidelines apply to all company outings, including evening recruiting activities. Moderate drinking is acceptable during evening outings, but show restraint. Getting drunk isn't likely to improve your chances to get an offer.

At the end of the day, you may meet with the boss; if he or she spends a lot of time trying to sell you on working for the company, it's a pretty strong indication that you've done well in your interviews and an offer will follow.

Dress

Job applicants traditionally wear suits to interviews. Most tech companies, though, are business casual — or even just casual. The running joke at some of these companies is that the only people who wear suits are job candidates and salespeople.

This is one area in which it's critical to do some research. It's probably not to your advantage to wear a suit if nobody else at the company is wearing them, not even the salespeople. On the other hand, if you wear jeans and a T-shirt, interviewers may feel you're not showing sufficient respect or seriousness, even though they may be wearing jeans. Ask around to see what's appropriate for the company. Expectations for dress vary by location and nature of business. For example, programmers working for a bank or brokerage may be expected to wear suits. You should aim to dress as well as or slightly more formally than you would be expected to dress for the job you're interviewing for.

In general, though, a suit or even a jacket and tie is overkill for most technical job interviews. A standard technical interviewing outfit for men consists of non-denim cotton pants, a collared shirt, and loafers (no sneakers or sandals). Women can dress similarly to men. No matter what your sex, go light on the perfume or cologne.

A RECRUITER'S ROLE

Your interviews and offer are usually coordinated by a company recruiter or human resources representative. The recruiter is responsible for the scheduling and logistical aspects of your interview, including reimbursing you for travel or lodging expenses. Recruiters aren't usually involved in the hiring decision but may pass on information about you to those who are. They are also usually the ones who call you back about your offer and handle compensation negotiations.

Recruiters are usually good at what they do. The vast majority of recruiters are honorable people deserving of your respect and courtesy. Nevertheless, don't let their friendliness fool you into thinking that their job is to help you; their job is to get you to sign with their company as quickly as possible for as little money as possible. As with headhunters, you need to understand the position recruiters are in so that you understand how they behave:

➤ **Recruiters may focus on a job's benefits or perks to draw attention away from negative aspects of a job offer.** They generally tell you to come to them with any questions about your offer. This is fine for benefit and salary questions, but ill-advised when you have questions about the job. The recruiter usually doesn't know much about the job you're being hired to do. When you ask a specific question about the job, the recruiter has little incentive to do the work to find the answer, especially if that answer might cause you to turn down the offer. Instead, recruiters are likely to give you a vague response along the lines of what they think you want to hear. When you want straight answers to your questions, it's best to go directly to the people you'll be working for. You can also try going directly to your potential manager if you feel the recruiter is being unreasonable with you. This is a somewhat risky strategy — it certainly won't win you the recruiters' love — but often the hiring manager has the authority to overrule decisions or restrictions that a recruiter makes. Hiring managers are often more willing to be flexible than recruiters. You're just another applicant to recruiters, but to the hiring manager, you're the person she chose to work with.

➤ **After the decision is made to give you an offer, the recruiter's job is to do everything necessary to get you to accept the offer at the lowest possible salary.** A recruiter's pay is often tied to how many candidates he signs. To maneuver you, a recruiter sometimes might try to play career counselor or advisor by asking you about each of your offers and leading you through a supposedly objective analysis to determine which is the best offer. Not surprisingly, this exercise always leads to the conclusion that the offer from the recruiter's company is clearly the best choice.

➤ **Some recruiters are territorial enough about their candidates that they won't give you your prospective team's contact information.** To protect against this possibility, collect business cards from your interviewers during your interviews, particularly from your prospective managers. Then you'll have the necessary information without having to go through the recruiter.

OFFERS AND NEGOTIATION

When you get an offer, you've made it through the hardest part: You now have a job, if you want it. However, the game isn't over yet. You're looking for a job because you need to make money; how you play the end game largely determines how much you get.

When your recruiter or hiring manager makes you an offer, she may also tell you how much the company plans to pay you. Perhaps a more common practice, though, is for the recruiter or hiring manager to tell you that the company would like to hire you and ask you how much you want to make. Answering this question is covered in detail in Chapter 17.

After you've been given a specific offer that includes details about salary, signing bonus, and stock options, you need to decide whether you're satisfied with it. This shouldn't be a snap decision — never accept an offer on the spot. Always spend at least a day thinking about important decisions such as this; it's surprising how much can change in a day.

Dealing with Recruiter Pressures

Recruiters often employ a variety of high-pressure tactics to get you to accept offers quickly. They may tell you that you must accept the offer within a few days if you want the job, or they may offer you an exploding signing bonus: a signing bonus that decreases by a fixed amount each day. Don't let this bullying rush your decision. If the company wants you (and it probably does if it made you an offer), these limits and terms are negotiable, even when a recruiter claims they aren't. You may have to go over the recruiter's head and talk to your hiring manager if the recruiter refuses to be flexible. If these conditions are non-negotiable, you probably don't want to work for a rigid company full of bullies anyway.

Negotiating Your Salary

If, after careful consideration, the offer meets or exceeds your expectations, you're all set. On the other hand, if you're not completely happy with your offer, you should try to negotiate. All too often, applicants assume that offers are non-negotiable and reject offers without negotiation or accept offers they're not pleased with. Almost every offer is negotiable to some extent.

You should never reject an offer for monetary reasons without trying to negotiate. When you negotiate an offer that you would otherwise reject, you hold the ultimate high card. You're ready to walk, so you have nothing to lose.

Even when an offer is in the range you were expecting, it's often worthwhile to negotiate. As long as you are respectful and truthful in your negotiations and your requests are reasonable, you'll almost never lose an offer just because you tried to negotiate it. In the worst case, the company refuses to change the offer, and you're no worse off than before you tried to negotiate.

If you decide to negotiate your compensation package, here's how you do it:

➤ **Figure out exactly what you want.** You may want a signing bonus, better pay, or more stock options.

➤ **Arrange a phone call with the appropriate negotiator, usually the recruiter.** Your negotiator is usually the same person who gave you the terms of your offer. Don't call the negotiator blind because you may catch him at an inconvenient time.

➤ **Explain your case.** Say you appreciate receiving the offer and explain why you're not completely happy with it. For example, you could say, "I'm pleased to have received the offer, but I'm having a hard time accepting it because it's not competitive with my other offers." Or you could say, "Thank you again for the offer, but I'm having trouble accepting it because I know from discussions with my peers and from talking with other companies that this offer is below market rates." If the negotiator asks you to go into greater detail about which other companies have offered you more money and how much, or where your peers work, you're under no obligation to do so. You can easily say, "I keep all my offers confidential, including yours, and feel that it's unprofessional to give out that sort of information."

➤ **Thank the negotiator for his time and help and say that you' re looking forward to hearing from him again.** Negotiators rarely change an offer on the spot. The company's negotiator may ask you what you had in mind or, conversely, tell you that the offer is non-negotiable. Claiming that the offer is non-negotiable is often merely a hardball negotiation tactic, so in either case you should respond by politely and respectfully spelling out exactly what you expect in an offer and giving the negotiator a chance to consider what you've said.

Many people find negotiation uncomfortable, especially when dealing with professional recruiters who do it every day. It's not uncommon for someone to accept an offer as close enough just to avoid having to negotiate. If you feel this way about negotiation, try looking at it this way: You rarely have anything to lose, and even modest success in negotiation can be rewarding. If it takes you a 30-minute phone call to get your offer increased by $3,000, you've made $6,000 per hour. Even lawyers aren't paid that much.

Remember that the best time to get more money is *before* you accept the job. When you're an employee, the company holds all the power.

Accepting and Rejecting Offers

At some point, your negotiations will be complete, and you will be ready to accept an offer. After you inform a company you're accepting its offer, be sure to keep in touch to coordinate start dates and paperwork. The company may do a background check on you at this point to verify your identity and your credentials.

Be professional about declining your other offers. Contacts are important, especially in the computer business where people change jobs frequently. You've no doubt built contacts at all the companies that made you offers. It's foolish to squander your contacts at other companies by failing to inform them of your decision. If you had a recruiter at the company, you should e-mail her with your decision. (Don't expect her to be overjoyed, however.) You should also personally call the hiring managers who made you an offer to thank them and let them know what you decided. For example, you can say, "I want to thank you again for extending me the offer. I was impressed with your company, but I've decided it's not the best choice for me right now. Thank you again, and I appreciate your confidence in me." Besides simply being classy, this approach can often get a response such as, "I was pleased to meet you, and I'm sorry that you won't be joining us. If things don't work out at that company, give me a call, and maybe we can work something out. Best of luck."

This gives you a great place to start the next time you look for work.

SUMMARY

You can find prospective jobs in various ways, but networking through friends and acquaintances is usually the best method. If that's not possible, find and contact companies directly. You may also engage the services of a headhunter; be aware that the headhunter's motivations aren't always aligned with yours.

The interviews are the most important part of the job application process. There are one or two screening interviews, usually by phone, to ensure that you're applying for the right job and that you are actually qualified. After the screening interviews, there are usually a series of on-site technical interviews that ultimately determine whether a job offer comes your way. Be sure to dress appropriately for the interviews, and turn off any electronic gadgets you might have with you.

During the interview process you'll frequently interact with one of the company's recruiters, especially if a job offer is made. Be sure to understand the recruiter's role during this process.

When an offer is made, don't accept it immediately. Give yourself time to consider it. Look over the offer, and try to negotiate a better deal because most offers aren't fixed in stone, no matter what the recruiter says. After accepting a job offer, be sure to contact anyone else who has made you an offer to thank them for their interest in you.

3

Approaches to Programming Problems

Coding questions are the meat of a programming interview and your opportunity to demonstrate that you can do the job. These questions are the heart of the process that most computer and software companies use to decide who to hire. Many companies make offers to less than 10 percent of the people who interview with them. How a candidate performs during the programming interviews is the main determinant of whether an offer is made.

The programming questions are generally difficult. If everyone (or even most people) answered a particular question quickly, the company would stop asking it because it wouldn't tell them anything about the applicants. Many of the questions are designed to take up to an hour to solve, so don't get frustrated if you don't see the answer right away. It's not unusual for each interview to explore just a single question.

> **NOTE** *These problems are hard! Some of the questions are designed to see how you handle a problem when you don't immediately see the solution.*

THE PROCESS

The point of coding questions is to determine how well you can code. It's the most important part of the interview because the code you write and the answers you give to the interviewer largely determine whether he recommends you for the job.

The Scenario

You usually work one-on-one with your interviewer. He will give you a marker and a whiteboard (or pen and paper) and ask you to write some code. The interviewer usually wants you to talk through the question before you start writing. Generally, you are asked to code a function or method, but sometimes you need to write a class definition or a sequence of related code modules. In any case, you write code, either in an actual programming language or in some form of pseudo-code. (The closer you can get to actual working code, the better.)

The Problems

The problems the interviewers give you have specific requirements. They must be short enough to be explained and solved reasonably quickly, yet complex enough that not everyone can solve them. Therefore, it's unlikely that you'll be asked any real-world problems. Almost any worthy real-world problem would take too long to explain, let alone solve. That isn't an option in an interview. Instead, many of these problems require algorithmic tricks or uncommonly used features of a language.

The problems often prohibit you from using the most-common way to do something or from using the ideal data structure. For example, you might be given a problem such as this: "Write a function that determines whether two integers are equal without using any comparison operators."

This is an outright silly and contrived problem. Almost every language that ever existed has some way to compare two integers. However, you're not off the hook if you respond, "This is a stupid question; I'd always use the equality operator. I'd never have this problem." You would flunk if you answer this way. The interviewer is looking for a different way to compare two integers. (Hint: Try using bit operators.)

Instead, describe the better way to solve the problem and then solve it as it was asked. For example, if you are asked to solve a certain problem with a hash table, you might say, "This would be easy with a binary search tree because it's much easier to extract the largest element, but let's see how I can solve this with a hash table."

> **NOTE** *Many problems involve ridiculous restrictions, use obscure features of languages, and seem silly and contrived. Play within the rules. Real-world programming is rarely done in a vacuum. The ability to work within the particular constraints of a situation is an important skill to develop.*

Problems are generally presented in ascending order of difficulty. This is not a hard-and-fast rule, but you can expect them to get more difficult as you answer more of them correctly. Often, different interviewers communicate with each other about what they asked you, what you could answer, and what you couldn't answer. If you solve all the problems in your early interviews but are stumped by harder problems later, this may indicate that earlier interviewers were impressed with your responses.

Which Languages to Use

If you apply for a job with specific language requirements, you should know those languages and expect to use them to solve the problems. If you apply for a general programming or development position, a thorough knowledge of a mainstream language such as C#, Java, and/or C++ is enough to get by. Your interviewer may permit you to use other popular languages, such as JavaScript, PHP, or Python. If you are given a choice, select the language you know best, but expect to be required to solve some problems in a specific language. Interviewers are less likely to be amenable to you using languages such as Lisp, Tcl, Prolog, Lua, or Fortran, but if you are particularly expert in one of these, there's no harm in asking.

Before you go to your interview, make sure you are completely comfortable with the use and syntax of any language you plan to use. If it has been a few years since you've done any C++ programming, for example, you should at least thumb through a good C++ reference guide and refamiliarize yourself with the language.

Interactivity Is Key

The code you write in the interview is probably the only example of your code that your interviewer sees. If you write ugly code, your interviewer will assume you always write ugly code. This is your chance to shine and show your best code. Take the time to make your code solid and pretty.

> **NOTE** *Brush up on the languages you expect to use and always write your best code!*

Programming questions are designed to see both how well you can code and how you solve problems. If all the interviewer wanted to do were measure your coding ability, she could give you a piece of paper with problems and come back an hour later to evaluate how you did, as they do in programming contests. What the interviewer wants is to see your thought processes as you work through each stage of the programming problem.

The problem-solving process in these interviews is interactive, and if you have difficulty, the interviewer generally guides you to the correct answer via a series of hints. Of course, the less help you need to solve the problem, the better you look, but showing an intelligent thought process and responding well to the hints you are given is also important. If you don't respond well to guidance, your interviewer might suspect that you won't work well in a team environment.

Even when you immediately know the answer to a problem, don't just blurt it out. Break the answer down into discrete steps and explain the thought processes behind each step. The point is to show the interviewer that you understand the underlying concepts, not that you've managed to memorize the answer to a programming puzzle.

If you know any additional information pertaining to the problem, you may want to mention it during the process to show your general knowledge of programming, even if it's not directly applicable to the problem at hand. In answering these problems, show that you're not just a propeller-head coder. Demonstrate that you have logical thought processes, are generally knowledgeable about computers, and can communicate well.

> **NOTE** *Keep talking! Always explain what you are doing. Otherwise, the interviewer has no way to know how you tackle complex programming problems.*

SOLVING THE PROBLEMS

When you begin solving a problem, don't start writing code immediately. First, make sure you completely understand the problem. It may help to work through a simple, concrete example and then try to generalize the process to an algorithm. When you're convinced you have the right algorithm, explain it clearly. Writing the code should be one of your final steps.

The Basic Steps

The best way to solve an interview problem is to approach it methodically.

1. **Make sure you understand the problem.** Your initial assumptions about the problem may be wrong, or the interviewer's explanation may be brief or difficult to follow. You can't demonstrate your skills if you don't understand the problem. Don't hesitate to ask your interviewer questions about the problem. Don't start solving the problem until you understand it. The interviewer may be deliberately obscuring things to determine whether you can find and understand the actual problem. In these cases, asking the right clarifying questions is an important part of the correct solution.

2. **When you understand the question, try a simple example.** This example may lead to insights about how to solve the general problem or bring to light any remaining misunderstandings that you have. Starting with an example also demonstrates a methodical, logical thought process. Examples are especially useful if you don't see the solution right away.

> **NOTE** *Make sure you understand the problem before you start solving it, and then start with an example to solidify your understanding.*

3. **Focus on the algorithm and data structures you will use to solve the problem.** This can take a long time and require additional examples. This is to be expected. *Interactivity is important during this process.* If you stand quietly staring at the whiteboard, the interviewer has no way to know whether you're making productive headway or are simply clueless. Talk to your interviewer and tell him what you are doing. For example, you might say something like, "I'm wondering whether I can store the values in an array and then sort them, but I don't think that will work because I can't quickly look up elements in an array by value." This demonstrates your skill, which is the point of the interview, and may also lead to hints from the interviewer, who might respond, "You're close to the solution. Do you really need to look up elements by value, or could you...."

It may take a long time to solve the problem, and you may be tempted to begin coding before you figure out a complete solution. Resist this temptation. Consider who you would rather work with: someone who thinks about a problem for a long time and then codes it correctly the first time or someone who hastily jumps into a problem, makes several errors while coding, and doesn't have any idea where he is going. Not a difficult decision, is it?

4. **After you figure out your algorithm and how you can implement it, explain your solution to the interviewer.** This gives her an opportunity to evaluate your solution before you

begin coding. Your interviewer may say, "Sounds great, go ahead and code it," or something like, "That's not quite right because you can't look up elements in a hash table that way." Another common response is "That sounds like it will work, but there's a more efficient solution." In any case, you gain valuable information about whether you should move on to coding or go back to working on the algorithm.

5. **While you code, explain what you're doing.** For example, you might say, "Here, I'm initializing the array to all zeroes." This narrative enables the interviewer to follow your code more easily.

> **NOTE** *Explain what you are doing to your interviewer before and while coding the solution. Keep talking!*

6. **Ask questions when necessary.** You generally won't be penalized for asking factual questions that you might otherwise look up in a reference. You obviously can't ask a question such as, "How do I solve this problem?" but it is acceptable to ask a question such as, "I can't remember — what format string do I use to print out a localized date?" Although it's better to know these things, it's okay to ask this sort of question.

7. **After you write the code for a problem, immediately verify that the code works by tracing through it with an example.** This step demonstrates clearly that your code is correct in at least one case. It also illustrates a logical thought process and your intention to check your work and search for bugs. The example may also help you flush out minor bugs in your solution.

8. **Make sure you check your code for** *all* **error and special cases, especially boundary conditions.** Programmers might overlook many error and special cases; forgetting these cases in an interview indicates you might forget them on the job. If time does not allow for extensive checking, at least explain that you should check for such failures. Covering error and special cases can impress your interviewer and help you correctly solve the problem.

> **NOTE** *Try an example, and check all error and special cases.*

After you try an example and feel comfortable that your code is correct, the interviewer may ask you questions about what you wrote. These questions often focus on running time, alternative implementations, and complexity. If your interviewer does not ask you these questions, you should volunteer the information to show that you are cognizant of these issues. For example, you could say, "This implementation has linear running time, which is the best possible because I need to check all the input values. The dynamic memory allocation will slow it down a little, as will the overhead of using recursion."

When You Get Stuck

Getting stuck on a problem is expected and an important part of the interviewing process. Interviewers want to see how you respond when you don't recognize the answer to a question immediately. Giving up or getting frustrated is the worst thing to do if this happens to you. Instead, show interest in the problem and keep trying to solve it:

➤ **Go back to an example.** Try performing the task and analyzing what you are doing. Try extending your specific example to the general case. You may have to use detailed examples. This is okay, because it shows the interviewer your persistence in finding the correct solution.

> **NOTE** *When all else fails, return to a specific example. Try to move from the specific example to the general case and from there to the solution.*

➤ **Try a different data structure.** Perhaps a linked list, an array, a hash table, or a binary search tree can help. If you're given an unusual data structure, look for similarities between it and more-familiar data structures. Using the right data structure often makes a problem much easier.

➤ **Consider the less-commonly used or more-advanced aspects of a language.** Sometimes the key to a problem involves one of these features.

> **NOTE** *Sometimes a different data structure or advanced language feature is key to the solution.*

Even when you don't feel stuck, you may have problems. You may miss an elegant or obvious way to implement something and write too much code. Almost all interview coding questions have short answers. You rarely need to write more than 30 lines of code and almost never more than 50. If you start writing a lot of code, you may be heading in the wrong direction.

ANALYZING YOUR SOLUTION

After you answer the problem, you may be asked about the efficiency of your implementation. Often, you have to compare trade-offs between your implementation and another possible solution and identify the conditions that make each option more favorable. Common questions focus on run time and memory usage.

A good understanding of Big-O analysis is critical to make a good impression with the interviewer. *Big-O analysis* is a form of runtime analysis that measures the efficiency of an algorithm in terms of the time it takes for the algorithm to run as a function of the input size. It's not a formal benchmark, just a simple way to classify algorithms by relative efficiency when dealing with very large input sizes.

Most coding problem solutions in this book include a runtime analysis to help you solidify your understanding of the algorithms.

Big-*O* Analysis In Action

Consider a simple function that returns the maximum value stored in an array of non-negative integers. The size of the array is n. There are at least two easy ways to implement the function.

In the first alternative, you keep track of the current largest number as the function iterates through the array and return that value when you are done iterating. This implementation, called CompareToMax, looks like:

```
/* Returns the largest value in an array of non-negative integers */
int CompareToMax(int array[], int n)
{
    int curMax, i;

    /* Make sure that there is at least one element in the array. */
    if (n <= 0)
        return -1;

    /* Set the largest number so far to the first array value. */
    curMax = array[0];

    /* Compare every number with the largest number so far. */
    for (i = 1; i < n; i++) {
        if (array[i] > curMax) {
            curMax = array[i];
        }
    }

    return curMax;
}
```

The second alternative compares each value to all the other values. If all other values are less than or equal to a given value, that value must be the maximum value. This implementation, called CompareToAll, looks like:

```
/* Returns the largest value in an array of non-negative integers */
int CompareToAll(int array[], int n)
{
    int  i, j;
    bool isMax;

    /* Make sure that there is at least one element in the array. */
    if (n <= 0)
        return -1;

    for (i = n-1; i > 0; i--) {
        isMax = true;
        for (j = 0; j < n; j++) {
            /* See if any value is greater. */
            if (array[j] > array[i]) {
                isMax = false; /* array[i] is not the largest value. */
                break;
            }
        }
```

```
            /* It isMax is true, no larger value exists; array[i] is max. */
            if (isMax) break;
    }

    return array[i];
}
```

Both of these functions correctly return the maximum value. Which one is more efficient? You could try benchmarking them, but this would tie your measure of efficiency to the particular system you used for benchmarking. It's more useful to have a means of comparing the performance of different algorithms that depends only on the algorithm. Big-O analysis enables you to do exactly that: Compare the predicted relative performance of different algorithms.

How Big-O Analysis Works

In Big-O analysis, input size is assumed to be an unknown value n. In this example, n simply represents the number of elements in an array. In other problems, n may represent the number of nodes in a linked list, the number of bits in a data type, or the number of entries in a hash table. After determining what n means in terms of the input, you must determine how many operations are performed for each of the n input items. "Operation" is a fuzzy word because algorithms differ greatly. Commonly, an operation is something that a real computer can do in a constant amount of time, like adding an input value to a constant, creating a new input item, or deleting an input value. In Big-O analysis, the times for these operations are all considered equivalent. In both CompareToMax and CompareToAll, the operation of greatest interest is comparing an array value to another value.

In CompareToMax, each array element was compared once to a maximum value. Thus, the n input items are each examined once, resulting in n examinations. This is considered $O(n)$, usually referred to as linear time: The time required to run the algorithm increases linearly with the number of input items.

You may notice that in addition to examining each element once, there is a check to ensure that the array is not empty and a step that initializes the curMax variable. It may seem more accurate to call this an $O(n + 2)$ function to reflect these extra operations. Big-O analysis, however, is concerned with the asymptotic running time: the limit of the running time as n gets very large. The justification for this is that when n is small, almost any algorithm will be fast. It's only when n become large that the differences between algorithms are noticeable. As n approaches infinity, the difference between n and $n + 2$ is insignificant, so the constant term can be ignored. Similarly, for an algorithm running in $n + n^2$ time, the difference between n^2 and $n + n^2$ is negligible for a very large n. Thus, in Big-O analysis you eliminate all but the highest-order term: the term that is largest as n gets very large. In this case, n is the highest-order term. Therefore, the CompareToMax function is $O(n)$.

The analysis of CompareToAll is a little more difficult. First, you need to make an assumption about where the largest number occurs in the array. For now, assume that the maximum element is at the end of the array. In this case, this function may compare each of n elements to n other elements. Thus there are $n \cdot n$ examinations so this is an $O(n^2)$ algorithm.

The analysis so far has shown that CompareToMax is $O(n)$ and CompareToAll is $O(n^2)$. This means that as the array grows, the number of comparisons in CompareToAll becomes much larger than in `CompareToMax`. Consider an array with 30,000 elements. `CompareToMax` compares on the order of 30,000 elements, whereas `CompareToAll` compares on the order of 900,000,000 elements. You would expect `CompareToMax` to be much faster because it examines 30,000 times fewer elements. In fact, one benchmark timed `CompareToMax` at less than .01 seconds, whereas `CompareToAll` took 23.99 seconds.

Best, Average, and Worst Cases

You may think this comparison was stacked against `CompareToAll` because the maximum value was at the end. This is true, and it raises the important issues of best-case, average-case, and worst-case running times. The analysis of `CompareToAll` was a worst-case scenario: The maximum value was at the end of the array. Consider, the average case, in which the largest value is in the middle. You end up checking only half the values n times because the maximum value is in the middle. This results in checking $n(n/2) = n^2/2$ times. This would appear to be an $O(n^2/2)$ running time. Consider what the 1/2 factor means. The actual time to check each value is highly dependent on the machine instructions that the code translates to and then on the speed at which the CPU can execute the instructions. Therefore, the 1/2 doesn't mean much. You could even come up with an $O(n^2)$ algorithm that was faster than an $O(n^2/2)$ algorithm. In Big-O analysis, you drop all constant factors, so the average case for `CompareToAll` is no better than the worst case. It is still $O(n^2)$.

The best-case running time for `CompareToAll` is better than $O(n^2)$. In this case, the maximum value is at the beginning of the array. The maximum value is compared to all other values only once, so the result is an $O(n)$ running time.

In `CompareToMax`, the best-case, average-case, and worst-case running times are identical. Regardless of the arrangement of the values in the array, the algorithm is always $O(n)$.

Ask the interviewer which scenario he is most interested in. Sometimes there are clues to this in the problem. Some sorting algorithms with terrible worst cases for unsorted data may nonetheless be well suited for a problem if the input is already sorted. These kinds of trade-offs are discussed in more detail in Chapter 8, which discusses general sorting algorithms.

Optimizations and Big-O Analysis

Algorithm optimizations do not always yield the expected changes in their overall running times. Consider the following optimization to `CompareToAll`: Instead of comparing each number to every other number, compare each number only with the numbers that follow it in the array. In essence, every number before the current number has already been compared to the current number. Thus, the algorithm is still correct if you compare only to numbers occurring after the current number.

What's the worst-case running time for this implementation? The first number is compared to n numbers, the second number to $n-1$ numbers, the third number to $n-2$, resulting in a number of comparisons equal to $n + (n-1) + (n-2) + (n-3) + ... + 1$. This is a common result, a mathematical series with a sum of $n^2/2 + n/2$. But because n^2 is the highest-order term, this version of the algorithm still has an $O(n^2)$ running time in the average case! For large input values, this optimization of the algorithm has no significant effect on its running time.

How to Do Big-O Analysis

The general procedure for Big-O runtime analysis is as follows:

1. Figure out what the input is and what n represents.

2. Express the number of operations the algorithm performs in terms of n.

3. Eliminate all but the highest-order terms.

4. Remove all constant factors.

For the algorithms you'll encounter in interviews, Big-O analysis should be straightforward as long as you correctly identify the operations that are dependent on the input size.

If you'd like to learn more about runtime analysis, you can find a more extensive, mathematically rigorous discussion in the first chapters of any good algorithms textbook. This book defines Big-O as it is most commonly used by professional programmers.

Which Algorithm Is Better?

The fastest-possible running time for any runtime analysis is $O(1)$, commonly referred to as *constant running time*. An algorithm with constant running time always takes the same amount of time to execute, regardless of the input size. This is the ideal run time for an algorithm, but it's rarely achievable.

The performance of most algorithms depends on n, the size of the input. The algorithms can be classified as follows from best-to-worse performance:

➤ $O(\log n)$ — An algorithm is said to be *logarithmic* if its running time increases logarithmically in proportion to the input size.

➤ $O(n)$ — A *linear algorithm*'s running time increases in direct proportion to the input size.

➤ $O(n \log n)$ — A *superlinear algorithm* is midway between a linear algorithm and a polynomial algorithm.

➤ $O(n^c)$ — A *polynomial algorithm* grows quickly based on the size of the input.

➤ $O(c^n)$ — An *exponential algorithm* grows even faster than a polynomial algorithm.

➤ $O(n!)$ — A *factorial algorithm* grows the fastest and becomes quickly unusable for even small values of n.

The run times of different orders of algorithms separate rapidly as n gets larger. Consider the run time for each of these algorithm classes with $n = 10$:

➤ $\log 10 = 1$

➤ $10 = 10$

➤ $10 \log 10 = 10$

➤ $10^2 = 100$

➤ $2^{10} = 1,024$

➤ $10! = 3,628,800$

Now double it to n = 20:

➤ $\log 20 = 1.30$

➤ $20 = 20$

➤ $20 \log 20 \approx 26.02$

➤ $20^2 = 400$

➤ $2^{20} = 1,048,576$

➤ $20! = 2.43 \times 10^{18}$

Finding an algorithm that works in superlinear time or better can make a huge difference in how well an application performs.

Memory Footprint Analysis

Runtime analysis is not the only relevant metric for performance. A common request from interviewers is to analyze how much memory a program uses. This is sometimes referred to as the *memory footprint* of the application. Memory use is sometimes as important as running time, particularly in constrained environments such as mobile devices.

In some cases, you will be asked about the memory usage of an *algorithm*. For this, the approach is to express the amount of memory required in terms of *n*, the size of the input, analogous to the preceding discussion of Big-O runtime analysis. The difference is that instead of determining how many operations are required for each item of input, you determine the amount of storage required for each item.

Other times, you may be asked about the memory footprint of an *implementation*. This is usually an exercise in estimation, especially for languages such as Java and C# that run in a virtual machine. Interviewers don't expect you to know to the byte exactly how much memory is used, but they like to see that you understand how the underlying data structures might be implemented. If you're a C++ expert, don't be surprised if you're asked how much memory a struct or class requires — the interviewer may want to check that you understand memory alignment and structure packing issues.

There is usually a trade-off between optimal memory use and runtime performance. The classic example of this is the Unicode string encodings discussed in Chapter 6, which enable more compact representations of strings while making it more expensive to perform many common string operations. Be sure to mention any trade-offs to the interviewer when discussing memory footprint issues.

SUMMARY

How you solve programming problems during your interviews can determine whether you get a job offer, so you need to answer them as correctly and completely as you can. The problems usually get progressively harder as the day progresses, so don't be surprised if you need an occasional hint from the interviewer. You normally code in a mainstream programming language, but the choice of language is ultimately dictated by the requirements of the job for which you apply, so be familiar with the right languages.

Interact with your interviewer as much as possible as you attempt each problem. Let her know what you're thinking at each point in your analysis of the problem and your attempts at coding an answer. Start by making sure you understand the problem, and then try some examples to reinforce that understanding. Choose the algorithm and make sure it works for those examples. Don't forget to test for special cases. If you're stuck, try more examples or choose a different algorithm. Keep obscure or advanced language features in mind when looking for alternative answers.

If asked to comment on the performance of a solution, a Big-O run time analysis is usually sufficient. Algorithms that run in constant, logarithmic, linear or superlinear time are preferred. You should also be prepared to comment on the memory footprint of an algorithm.

4

Linked Lists

The linked list, a deceptively simple data structure, is the basis for a surprising number of problems regarding the handling of dynamic data. Questions about efficient list traversal, list sorting, and the insertion or removal of data from either end of a list are good tests of basic data structure concepts, which is why an entire chapter is devoted to linked lists.

WHY LINKED LISTS?

The simplicity of linked list questions appeals to interviewers who want to present at least two or three problems over the course of a 1-hour interview, because they must give you problems that you can be reasonably expected to answer in only 20 to 30 minutes. You can write a relatively complete implementation of a linked list in less than 10 minutes, leaving you plenty of time to solve the problem. In contrast, it might take you most of the interview period to implement a more complex data structure such as a hash table.

Also, little variation exists in linked list implementations, which means that an interviewer can simply say "linked list" and not waste time discussing and clarifying implementation details.

Perhaps the strongest reason is that linked lists are useful to determine whether a candidate understands how pointers and references work, particularly in C and C++. If you're not a C or C++ programmer, you may find the linked list problems in this chapter challenging. Still, linked lists are so basic that you need to be familiar with them before moving to more complicated data structures found in the chapters that follow.

> **NOTE** *In real-world development, you don't usually write your own linked lists; you use the implementation in your language's standard library. In a programming interview, you're expected to be able to create your own implementation to demonstrate that you fully understand linked lists.*

KINDS OF LINKED LIST

There are three basic kinds of linked list: singly linked lists, doubly linked lists, and circular linked lists. Singly linked lists are the variety most commonly encountered in interviews.

Singly Linked Lists

When an interviewer says "linked list" he or she generally means a linear *singly linked list,* where each data element in the list has a link (a pointer or reference) to the element that follows it in the list, as shown in Figure 4-1. The first element in a singly linked list is referred to as the *head* of the list. The last element in such a list is called the *tail* of the list and has an empty or null link.

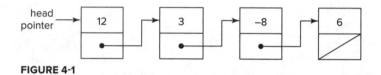

FIGURE 4-1

Singly linked lists have a host of special cases and potential programming pitfalls. Because the links in a singly linked list consist only of next pointers (or references), the list can be traversed only in the forward direction. Therefore a complete traversal of the list must begin with the first element. In other words, you need a pointer or reference to the first element of a list to locate all the elements in the list. It's common to store that pointer or reference in a separate data structure.

In C, the simplest singly linked list element is a struct with a pointer to a struct of the same type as its only member:

```
// The simplest singly linked list element
typedef struct ListElement {
  struct ListElement *next;
} ListElement;
```

Because it has no data, it's not a particularly useful list element. A more useful struct has at least one data member in addition to the pointer:

```
// A more useful singly linked list element
typedef struct IntElement {
    struct IntElement *next;
    int               data;
} IntElement;
```

The next pointer can be anywhere in the struct, but placing it at the beginning makes it easier to write generic list-handling routines that work no matter what data an element holds by casting the pointer to be of the generic list element type.

In C++ you could define a class for the list element:

```
// A singly linked list in C++
class IntElement {
  public:
    IntElement( int value ): next( NULL ), data( value ) {}
```

```cpp
    ~IntElement() {}

    IntElement *getNext() const { return next; }
    int value() const { return data; }
    void setNext( IntElement *elem ) { next = elem; }
    void setValue( int value ) { data = value; }

  private:
    IntElement *next;
    int         data;
};
```

However, it usually makes more sense to define a template for the list element:

```cpp
// A templated C++ singly linked list
template <class T>
class ListElement {
  public:
    ListElement( const T &value ): next( NULL ), data( value ) {}
    ~ListElement() {}

    ListElement *getNext() const { return next; }
    const T& value() const { return data; }
    void setNext( ListElement *elem ) { next = elem; }
    void setValue( const T &value ) { data = value; }

  private:
    ListElement *next;
    T            data;
};
```

> **NOTE** *When defining classes in C++, particularly in template form, it's always best to explicitly add copy constructors and assignment operators so you don't depend on the compiler-generated versions. In an interview, however, you'll generally skip these additional details as we've done here, but it doesn't hurt to mention them in passing to the interviewer.*

A Java implementation using generics is similar, but of course uses references instead of pointers:

```java
// A templated Java singly linked list
public class ListElement<T> {
  public ListElement( T value ) { data = value; }

  public ListElement<T> next() { return next; }
  public T value() { return data; }
  public void setNext( ListElement<T> elem ) { next = elem; }
  public void setValue( T value ) { data = value; }

  private ListElement<T> next;
  private T              data;
}
```

Doubly Linked Lists

A doubly linked list, as shown in Figure 4-2, eliminates many of the difficulties of using a singly linked list. In a *doubly linked list*, each element has a link to the *previous* element in the list as well as to the *next* element in the list. This additional link makes it possible to traverse the list in either direction. The entire list can be traversed starting from any element. A doubly linked list has head and tail elements just like a singly linked list. The head of the list has an empty or null previous link, just as the tail of the list has a null or empty next link.

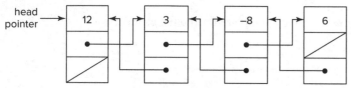

FIGURE 4-2

Doubly linked lists are not frequently seen in interview problems. Many problems involve singly linked lists specifically because they are more difficult that way; they would be trivial with a doubly linked list. Other problems are difficult whether the list is singly or doubly linked, so there's no point in using a doubly linked list, which adds complexity irrelevant to the problem.

Circular Linked Lists

The final variation on the linked list theme is the circular linked list, which comes in singly and doubly linked varieties. *Circular linked* lists have no ends — no head or tail. Each element in a circular linked list has non-null next (and previous, if it's also doubly linked) pointers or references. A list with one element merely points to itself.

The primary traversal problem for these lists is cycle avoidance — if you don't track where you start, you'll cycle infinitely through the list.

You may encounter circular linked lists from time to time, but they rarely appear in interview problems.

BASIC LINKED LIST OPERATIONS

Successfully solving linked list problems requires a thorough understanding of how to operate on linked lists. This includes tracking the head element so that the list doesn't get lost, traversing the list, and inserting and deleting list elements. These operations are much more straightforward with a doubly linked list, so we focus on the pitfalls of implementing these operations for singly linked lists.

Tracking the Head Element

The head element of a singly linked list must always be tracked; otherwise, the list will be lost — either garbage collected or leaked, depending on the language. This means that the pointer or reference to the head of the list must be updated when a new element is inserted ahead of the first element or when the existing first element is removed from the list.

Tracking the head element becomes a problem when you alter the list inside a function or method, because the caller must be made aware of the new head element. For example, the following Java code is incorrect because it fails to update the reference to the head of the list:

```java
public void insertInFront( ListElement<Integer> list, int data ){
    ListElement<Integer> l = new ListElement<Integer>( data );
    l.setNext( list );
}
```

The correct solution is to return the new head element from the method:

```java
public ListElement<Integer> insertInFront( ListElement<Integer> list, int data ){
    ListElement<Integer> l = new ListElement<Integer>( data );
    l.setNext( list );
    return l;
}
```

The caller updates its reference to the head element accordingly:

```java
int data = ....; // data to insert
ListElement<Integer> head = ....; // reference to head

head = insertInFront( head, data );
```

In C or C++ it's easier to make mistakes with pointer misuse. Consider this C code (that uses C++ features such as the `bool` datatype that are now available in C as part of the C99 standard) for inserting an element at the front of a list:

```c
bool insertInFront( IntElement *head, int data ){
    IntElement *newElem = malloc( sizeof(IntElement) );
    if( !newElem ) return false;

    newElem->data = data;
    newElem->next = head;
    head = newElem; // Incorrect! Updates only the local head pointer
    return true;
}
```

The preceding code is incorrect because it updates only the local copy of the head pointer. The correct version passes in a pointer to the head pointer:

```c
bool insertInFront( IntElement **head, int data ){
    IntElement *newElem = malloc( sizeof(IntElement) );
    if(!newElem) return false;

    newElem->data = data;
    newElem->next = *head;
    *head = newElem;
    return true;
}
```

This function uses the return value to indicate the success or failure of the memory allocation (because there are no exceptions in C), so it can't return the new head pointer as the Java function did. In C++, the head pointer could also be passed in by reference, or the function could return the new head pointer.

Traversing a List

Often, you need to work with list elements other than the head element. Operations on any but the first element of a linked list require traversal of some elements of the list. When traversing, you must always check that you haven't reached the end of the list. The following traversal is unsafe:

```
public ListElement<Integer> find( ListElement<Integer> head, int data ){
    ListElement<Integer> elem = head;
    while( elem.value() != data ){
        elem = elem.next();
    }

    return elem;
}
```

This method works fine as long as the data to find is actually in the list. If it isn't, an error occurs (a null reference exception) when you travel past the last element. A simple change to the loop fixes the problem:

```
public ListElement<Integer> find( ListElement<Integer> head, int data ){
    ListElement<Integer> elem = head;
    while( elem != null && elem.value() != data ){
        elem = elem.next();
    }

    return elem;
}
```

With this implementation, the caller must detect an error condition by checking for a null return value. (Alternatively, it may make more sense to throw an exception if the end of the list is reached and the element cannot be found.)

> **NOTE** *Always test for the end of a linked list as you traverse it.*

Inserting and Deleting Elements

Because links in a singly linked list are maintained exclusively with next pointers or references, any insertion or deletion of elements in the middle of a list requires modification of the previous element's next pointer or reference. If you're given only the element to delete (or before which to insert), this requires traversal of the list from the head because there's no other way to find the preceding element. Special care must be taken when the element to be deleted is the head of the list.

This C function deletes an element from a list:

```
bool deleteElement( IntElement **head, IntElement *deleteMe )
{
```

```
        IntElement *elem;

        if (!head || !*head || !deleteMe ) /* Check for null pointers */
            return false;

        elem = *head;
        if( deleteMe == *head ){ /* special case for head */
            *head = elem->next;
            free(deleteMe);
            return true;
        }

        while( elem ){
            if( elem->next == deleteMe ){
                /* elem is element preceding deleteMe */
                elem->next = deleteMe->next;
                free(deleteMe);
                return true;
            }
            elem = elem->next;
        }
        /* deleteMe not found */
        return false;
    }
```

> **NOTE** *Deletion and insertion require a pointer or reference to the element imme-
> diately preceding the deletion or insertion location.*

Performing deletions raises another issue in languages without garbage collection, like C or C++.
Suppose you want to remove all the elements from a linked list. The natural inclination is to use a
single pointer to traverse the list, freeing elements as you go. A problem arises, however, when this
is implemented. Do you advance the pointer first or free the element first? If you advance the pointer
first, then the freeing is impossible because you overwrote the pointer to the element to be freed. If
you free the element first, advancing the pointer is impossible because it involves reading the next
pointer in the element that was just freed. The solution is to use two pointers, as in the following
example:

```
    void deleteList( IntElement **head )
    {
        IntElement *deleteMe = *head;

        while( deleteMe ){
            IntElement *next = deleteMe->next;
            free(deleteMe);
            deleteMe = next;
        }

        *head = NULL;
    }
```

> **NOTE** *Deletion of an element always requires at least two pointer variables. Insertion requires two pointer variables as well, but because one of them is used for an element in the list and the other for the pointer returned by the memory allocation call, there's little danger of forgetting this in the insertion case.*

LINKED LIST PROBLEMS

The solutions to the linked list problems that follow can be implemented in any language that supports dynamic memory, but because you rarely implement your own linked lists in languages like Java and C#, these problems make most sense in C.

Stack Implementation

> **PROBLEM** *Discuss the stack data structure. Implement a stack in C using either a linked list or a dynamic array, and justify your decision. Design the interface to your stack to be complete, consistent, and easy to use.*

This problem is designed to determine three things:

1. Your knowledge of basic data structures

2. Your ability to write routines to manipulate these structures

3. Your ability to design consistent interfaces to a group of routines

A stack is a *last-in-first-out* (*LIFO*) data structure: Elements are always removed in the reverse order in which they were added, much in the same way that you add or remove a dish from a stack of dishes. The add element and remove element operations are conventionally called *push* and *pop*, respectively. Stacks are useful data structures for tasks that are divided into multiple subtasks. Tracking return addresses, parameters, and local variables for subroutines is one example of stack use; tracking tokens when parsing a programming language is another.

One of the ways to implement a stack is by using a *dynamic array*, an array that changes size as needed when elements are added. (See Chapter 6, "Arrays and Strings," for a more complete discussion of arrays.) The main advantage of dynamic arrays over linked lists is that arrays offer random access to the array elements — you can immediately access any element in the array if you know its index. However, operations on a stack always work on one end of the data structure (the top of the stack), so the random accessibility of a dynamic array gains you little. In addition, as a dynamic array grows, it must occasionally be resized, which can be a time-consuming operation as elements are copied from the old array to the new array.

Linked lists usually allocate memory dynamically for each element. Depending on the overhead of the memory allocator, these allocations are often more time consuming than the copies required by a dynamic array, so a stack based on a dynamic array is usually faster than one based on a linked list. Implementing a linked list is less complicated than implementing a dynamic array, so in an interview, a linked list is probably the best choice for your solution. Whichever choice you make, be sure to explain the pros and cons of both approaches to your interviewer.

After explaining your choice, you can design the routines and their interfaces. If you take a moment to design your code before writing it, you can avoid mistakes and inconsistencies in implementation. More important, this shows you won't skip right to coding on a larger project where good planning is essential to success. As always, talk to the interviewer about what you're doing.

Your stack will need push and pop routines. What will the prototype for these functions be? Each function must be passed the stack it operates on. The push operation will be passed the data it is to push, and pop will return a piece of data from the stack.

The simplest way to pass the stack is to pass a pointer to the stack. Because the stack will be implemented as a linked list, the pointer to the stack will be a pointer to the head of the list. In addition to the pointer to the stack, you could pass the data as a second parameter to push. The pop function could take only the pointer to the stack as an argument and return the value of the data it popped from the stack.

To write the prototypes, you need to know the type of the data that will be stored on the stack. You should declare a struct for a linked list element with the appropriate data type. If the interviewer doesn't make any suggestion, storing void pointers is a good general-purpose solution:

```
typedef struct Element {
    struct Element *next;
    void *data;
} Element;
```

The corresponding prototypes for push and pop follow:

```
void push( Element *stack, void *data );
void *pop( Element *stack );
```

Now consider what happens in these routines in terms of proper functionality and error handling. Both operations change the first element of the list. The calling routine's stack pointer must be modified to reflect this change, but any change you make to the pointer that is passed to these functions won't be propagated back to the calling routine. You can solve this problem by having both routines take a pointer to a pointer to the stack. This way, you can change the calling routine's pointer so that it continues to point at the first element of the list. Implementing this change results in the following:

```
void push( Element **stack, void *data );
void *pop( Element **stack );
```

What about error handling? The push operation needs to dynamically allocate memory for a new element. Memory allocation in C is an operation that can fail, so remember to check that the allocation succeeded when you write this routine. (In C++ an exception is thrown when allocation fails, so the error handling is somewhat different.)

You also need some way to indicate to the calling routine whether the push succeeded or failed. In C, it's generally most convenient to have a routine indicate success or failure by its return value. This way, the routine can be called from the condition of an if statement with error handling in the body. Have push return true for success and false for failure. (Throwing an exception is also an option in C++ and other languages with exception support.)

Can pop fail? It doesn't have to allocate memory, but what if it's asked to pop an empty stack? It should indicate that the operation was unsuccessful, but it still has to return data when it is successful. A C function has a single return value, but pop needs to return two values: the data it popped and an error code.

This problem has a number of possible solutions, none of which are entirely satisfactory. One approach is to use the single return value for both purposes. If pop is successful, have it return the data; if it is unsuccessful, return NULL. As long as your data is a pointer type and you never need to store null pointers on the stack, this works. If you have to store null pointers, however, there's no way to determine whether the null pointer returned by pop represents a legitimate element that you stored or an empty stack. Another option is to return a special value that can't represent a valid piece of data — a pointer to a reserved memory block, for example, or (for stacks dealing with non-negative numbers only) a negative value. Although restricting the values that can be stored on the stack might be acceptable in some cases, assume that for this problem it is not.

You must return two distinct values. How else can a function return data? The same way the stack parameter is handled: by passing a pointer to a variable. The routine can return data by using the pointer to change the variable's value, which the caller can access after popping the stack.

There are two possibilities for the interface to pop that use this approach to return two values. You can have pop take a pointer to an error code variable as an argument and return the data, or you can have it take a pointer to a data variable and return an error code. Intuitively, most programmers would expect pop to return data. However, using pop is awkward if the error code is not its return value: Instead of simply calling pop in the condition of an if or while statement, you must explicitly declare a variable for the error code and check its value in a separate statement after you call pop. Furthermore, push would take a data argument and return an error code, whereas pop would take an error code argument and return data. This may offend your sense of symmetry (it does ours).

Neither alternative is clearly correct; there are problems with either approach. In an interview, it wouldn't matter much which alternative you chose as long as you identified the pros and cons of each and justified your choice. We think error code arguments are particularly irksome, so this discussion continues by assuming you chose to have pop return an error code. This results in the following prototypes:

```
bool push( Element **stack, void *data );
bool pop( Element **stack, void **data );
```

You also want to write createStack and deleteStack functions, even though neither of these is absolutely necessary in a linked list stack implementation: You could delete the stack by calling pop until the stack is empty and create a stack by passing push a null pointer as the stack argument. However, writing these functions provides a complete, implementation-independent interface to the stack. A stack implemented as a dynamic array would need createStack and deleteStack functions to properly manage the underlying array. By including these functions in your implementation, you create the possibility that someone could change the underlying implementation of the stack without needing to change the programs that use the stack — always a good thing.

With the goals of implementation independence and consistency in mind, it's a good idea to have these functions return error codes, too. Even though in a linked list implementation neither createStack nor deleteStack can fail, they might fail under a different implementation, such as if createStack couldn't allocate memory for a dynamic array. If you design the interface with no way for these functions to indicate failure, you severely handicap anyone who might want to change your implementation.

Again, you face the same problem as with pop: createStack must return both the empty stack and an error code. You can't use a null pointer to indicate failure because a null pointer is the empty stack for a linked list implementation. In keeping with the previous decision, we write an implementation with an error code as the return value. Because createStack can't return the stack as its value, it must take a pointer to a pointer to the stack. Because all the other functions take a pointer to the stack pointer, it makes sense to have deleteStack take its stack parameter in the same way. This way you don't need to remember which functions require only a pointer to a stack and which take a pointer to a pointer to a stack — they all work the same way. This reasoning gives you the following prototypes:

```
bool createStack( Element **stack );
bool deleteStack( Element **stack );
```

When everything is designed properly, the coding is fairly simple. The createStack routine sets the stack pointer to NULL and returns success:

```
bool createStack( Element **stack ){
    *stack = NULL;
    return true;
}
```

The push operation allocates the new element, checks for failure, sets the data of the new element, places it at the top of the stack, and adjusts the stack pointer:

```
bool push( Element **stack, void *data ){
    Element *elem = malloc( sizeof(Element) );
    if( !elem ) return false;

    elem->data = data;
    elem->next = *stack;
    *stack = elem;
    return true;
}
```

The pop operation checks that the stack isn't empty, fetches the data from the top element, adjusts the stack pointer, and frees the element that is no longer on the stack, as follows:

```
bool pop( Element **stack, void **data ){
    Element *elem;
    if( !(elem = *stack) ) return false;

    *data = elem->data;
    *stack = elem->next;
    free( elem );
    return true;
}
```

Although `deleteStack` could call `pop` repeatedly, it's more efficient to simply traverse the data structure, freeing as you go. Don't forget that you need a temporary pointer to hold the address of the next element while you free the current one:

```
bool deleteStack( Element **stack ){
    Element *next;
    while( *stack ){
        next = (*stack)->next;
        free( *stack );
        *stack = next;
    }
    return true;
}
```

Before the discussion of this problem is complete, it is worth noting (and probably worth mentioning to the interviewer) that the interface design would be much more straightforward in an object-oriented language. The `createStack` and `deleteStack` operations become the constructor and destructor, respectively. The `push` and `pop` routines are bound to the stack object, so they don't need to have the stack explicitly passed to them, and the need for pointers to pointers evaporates. An exception can be thrown when there's an attempt to pop an empty stack or a memory allocation fails, which enables you to use the return value of `pop` for data instead of an error code. A minimal C++ version looks like the following:

```
class Stack
{
public:
    Stack() : head( NULL ) {};
    ~Stack();
    void push( void *data );
    void *pop();
protected:
    class Element {
    public:
        Element( Element *n, void *d ): next(n), data( d ) {}
        Element *getNext() const { return next; }
        void *value() const { return data; }
    private:
        Element    *next;
        void       *data;
    };

    Element *head;
};


Stack::~Stack() {
    while( head ){
        Element *next = head->getNext();
        delete head;
        head = next;
    }
}
```

```
void Stack::push( void *data ){
  //Allocation error will throw exception
  Element *element = new Element(head,data);
  head = element;
}

void *Stack::pop() {
  Element *popElement = head;
  void *data;

  /* Assume StackError exception class is defined elsewhere */
  if( head == NULL )
    throw StackError( E_EMPTY );

  data = head->value();
  head = head->getNext();
  delete popElement;
  return data;
}
```

A more complete C++ implementation should include a copy constructor and assignment operator, because the default versions created by the compiler could lead to multiple deletes of the same `Element` due to inadvertent sharing of elements between copies of a `Stack`.

Maintain Linked List Tail Pointer

> **PROBLEM** head *and* tail *are global pointers to the first and last element, respectively, of a singly linked list of integers. Implement C functions for the following prototypes:*
>
> ```
> bool delete( Element *elem );
> bool insertAfter( Element *elem, int data );
> ```
>
> *The argument to* delete *is the element to be deleted. The two arguments to* insertAfter *give the element after which the new element is to be inserted and the data for the new element. It should be possible to insert at the beginning of the list by calling* insertAfter *with* NULL *as the element argument. These functions should return a boolean indicating success.*
>
> *Your functions must keep the head and tail pointers current.*

This problem seems relatively straightforward. Deletion and insertion are common operations on a linked list, and you should be accustomed to using a head pointer for the list. The requirement to maintain a tail pointer is the only unusual aspect of this problem. This requirement doesn't seem to fundamentally change anything about the list or the way you operate on it, so it doesn't look as if you need to design any new algorithms. Just be sure to update the head and tail pointers when necessary.

When do you need to update these pointers? Obviously, operations in the middle of a long list do not affect either the head or tail. You need to update the pointers only when you change the list such that a different element appears at the beginning or end. More specifically, when you insert a new element at either end of the list, that element becomes the new beginning or end of the list. When you delete an element at the beginning or end of the list, the next-to-first or next-to-last element becomes the new first or last element.

For each operation you have a general case for operations in the middle of the list and special cases for operations at either end. When you deal with many special cases, it can be easy to miss some of them, especially if some of the special cases have more specific special cases of their own. One technique to identify special cases is to consider what circumstances are likely to lead to special cases being invoked. Then, you can check whether your proposed implementation works in each of these circumstances. If you discover a circumstance that creates a problem, you have discovered a new special case.

The circumstance where you are instructed to operate on the ends of the list has already been discussed. Another error-prone circumstance is a null pointer argument. The only other thing that can change is the list on which you are operating — specifically, its length.

What lengths of lists may be problematic? You can expect somewhat different cases for the beginning, middle, and end of the list. Any list that doesn't have these three distinct classes of elements could lead to additional special cases. An empty list has no elements, so it obviously has no beginning, middle, or end elements. A one-element list has no middle elements and one element that is both the beginning and end element. A two-element list has distinct beginning and end elements, but no middle element. Any list longer than this has all three classes of elements and is effectively the general case of lists — unlikely to lead to additional special cases. Based on this reasoning, you should explicitly confirm that your implementation works correctly for lists of length 0, 1, and 2.

At this point in the problem, you can begin writing `delete`. As mentioned earlier, you need a special case for deleting the first element of the list. You can compare the element to be deleted to `head` to determine whether you need to invoke this case:

```
bool delete( Element *elem ){
    if (elem == head) {
        head = elem->next;
        free( elem );
        return true;
    }
    ...
```

Now write the general middle case. You need an element pointer to keep track of your position in the list. (Call the pointer `curPos`.) Recall that to delete an element from a linked list, you need a pointer to the preceding element so that you can change its next pointer. The easiest way to find the preceding element is to compare `curPos->next` to `elem`, so `curPos` points to the preceding element when you find `elem`.

You also need to construct your loop so you don't miss any elements. If you initialize curPos to head, then curPos->next starts as the second element of the list. Starting at the second item is fine because you treat the first element as a special case, but make your first check before advancing curPos or you'll miss the second element. If curPos becomes NULL, you have reached the end of the list without finding the element you were supposed to delete, so you should return failure. The middle case yields the following (added code is bolded):

```
bool delete( Element *elem ){

    Element *curPos = head;

    if (elem == head) {
        head = elem->next;
        free( elem );
        return true;
    }


    while( curPos ){
        if( curPos->next == elem ){
            curPos->next = elem->next;
            free( elem );
            return true;
        }
        curPos = curPos->next;
    }

    return false;
    ...
```

Next, consider the last element case. The last element's next pointer is NULL. To remove it from the list, you need to make the next-to-last element's next pointer NULL and free the last element. If you examine the loop constructed for middle elements, you see that it can delete the last element as well as middle elements. The only difference is that you need to update the tail pointer when you delete the last element. If you set curPos->next to NULL, you know you changed the end of the list and must update the tail pointer. Adding this to complete the function, you get the following:

```
bool delete( Element *elem ){
    Element *curPos = head;

    if( elem == head ){
        head = elem->next;
        free( elem );
    }

    while( curPos ){
        if( curPos->next == elem ){
            curPos->next = elem->next;
            free( elem );
            if( curPos->next == NULL )
                tail = curPos;
            return true;
        }
```

```
            curPos = curPos->next;
        }

        return false;
    }
```

This solution covers the three discussed special cases. Before you present the interviewer with this solution, you should check behavior for null pointer arguments and the three potentially problematic list length circumstances.

What happens if `elem` is NULL? The `while` loop traverses the list until `curPos->next` is NULL (when `curPos` is the last element). Then, on the next line, evaluating `elem->next` dereferences a null pointer. Because it's never possible to delete NULL from the list, the easiest way to fix this problem is to return `false` if `elem` is NULL.

If the list has zero elements, then `head` and `tail` are both NULL. Because you'll check that `elem` isn't NULL, `elem == head` will always be false. Further, because `head` is NULL, `curPos` will be NULL, and the body of the `while` loop won't be executed. There doesn't seem to be any problem with zero-element lists. The function simply returns `false` because nothing can be deleted from an empty list.

Now try a one-element list. In this case, `head` and `tail` both point to the one element, which is the only element you can delete. Again, `elem == head` is true. `elem->next` is NULL, so you correctly set `head` to NULL and free the element; however, `tail` still points to the element you just freed. As you can see, you need another special case to set `tail` to NULL for one-element lists.

What about two-element lists? Deleting the first element causes `head` to point to the remaining element, as it should. Similarly, deleting the last element causes `tail` to be correctly updated. The lack of middle elements doesn't seem to be a problem. You can add the two additional special cases and then move on to `insertAfter`:

```
bool delete( Element *elem ){
    Element *curPos = head;


    if( !elem )
        return false;

    if( elem == head ){
        head = elem->next;
        free( elem );

        /* special case for 1 element list */
        if( !head )
            tail = NULL;
        return true;
    }

    while( curPos ){
        if( curPos->next == elem ){
            curPos->next = elem->next;
            free( elem );
```

```
            if( curPos->next == NULL )
                tail = curPos;
            return true;
        }
        curPos = curPos->next;
    }

    return false;
}
```

You can apply similar reasoning to writing insertAfter. Because you allocate a new element in this function, you must take care to check that the allocation is successful and that you don't leak any memory. Many of the special cases encountered in delete are relevant in insertAfter, however, and the code is structurally similar:

```
bool insertAfter( Element *elem, int data ){
    Element *newElem, *curPos = head;

    newElem = malloc( sizeof(Element) );
    if( !newElem )
        return false;
    newElem->data = data;

    /* Insert at beginning of list */
    if( !elem ){
        newElem->next = head;
        head = newElem;

        /* Special case for empty list */
        if( !tail )
            tail = newElem;
        return true;
    }

    while( curPos ){
        if( curPos == elem ){
            newElem->next = curPos->next;
            curPos->next = newElem;

            /* Special case for inserting at end of list */
            if( !(newElem->next) )
                tail = newElem;
            return true;
        }
        curPos = curPos->next;
    }

    /* Insert position not found; free element and return failure */
    free( newElem );
    return false;
}
```

This problem turns out to be an exercise in special cases. It's not particularly interesting or satis-fying to solve, but it's good practice. Many interview problems have special cases, so you should expect to encounter them frequently. In the real world of programming, unhandled special cases represent bugs that may be difficult to find, reproduce, and fix. Programmers who identify special cases as they are coding are likely to be more productive than those who find special cases through debugging. Intelligent interviewers recognize this and pay attention to whether a candidate identifies special cases as part of the coding process or needs to be prompted to recognize special cases.

Bugs in removeHead

> **PROBLEM** *Find and fix the bugs in the following C function that is supposed to remove the head element from a singly linked list:*
>
> ```c
> void removeHead( ListElement *head ){
>     free( head );          // Line 1
>     head = head->next;     // Line 2
> }
> ```

Bug-finding problems occur with some frequency, so it's worthwhile to discuss a general strategy that you can apply to this and other problems.

Because you will generally be given only a small amount of code to analyze, your bug-finding strategy will be a little different from real-world programming. You don't need to worry about interactions with other modules or other parts of the program. Instead, you must do a systematic analysis of every line of the function without the help of a debugger. Consider four common problem areas for any function you are given:

1. **Check that the data comes into the function properly.** Make sure you aren't accessing a variable that you don't have, you aren't reading something as an `int` that should be a `long`, and you have all the values you need to perform the task.

2. **Check that each line of the function works correctly.** The function is intended to perform a task. Verify that the task is executed correctly at each line and that the desired result is produced at the end.

3. **Check that the data comes out of the function correctly.** The return value should be what you expect. In addition, if the function is expected to update any caller variables, make sure this occurs.

4. **Check the common error conditions.** Error conditions vary depending on the specifics of a problem. They tend to involve unusual argument values. For instance, functions that operate on data structures may have trouble with empty or nearly empty data structures; functions that take a pointer as an argument may fail if passed a null pointer.

Starting with the first step, verify that data comes into the function properly. In a linked list, you can access every element given only the head. Because you are passed the list head, you have access to all the data you require — no bugs so far.

Now do a line-by-line analysis of the function. The first line frees head — okay so far. Line 2 then assigns a new value to head but uses the old value of head to do this. That's a problem. You have already freed head, and you are now dereferencing freed memory. You could try reversing the lines, but this would cause the element after head to be freed. You need to free head, but you also need its next value after it has been freed. You can solve this problem by using a temporary variable to store head's next value. Then you can free head and use the temporary variable to update head. These steps make the function look like the following:

```
void removeHead( ListElement *head ){
    ListElement *temp = head->next;    // Line 1
    free( head );                      // Line 2
    head = temp;                       // Line 3
}
```

Now, move to step 3 of the strategy to make sure the function returns values properly. Though there is no explicit return value, there is an implicit one. This function is supposed to update the caller's head value. In C, all function parameters are passed by value, so functions get a local copy of each argument, and any changes made to that local copy are not reflected outside the function. Any new value you assign to head on line 3 has no effect — another bug. To correct this, you need a way to change the value of head in the calling code. Variables cannot be passed by reference in C, so the solution is to pass a pointer to the variable you want to change — in this case, a pointer to the head pointer. After the change, the function should look like this:

```
void removeHead( ListElement **head ){
    ListElement *temp = (*head)->next;    // Line 1
    free( *head );                        // Line 2
    *head = temp;                         // Line 3
}
```

Now you can move on to the fourth step and check error conditions. Check a one-element and a zero-element list. In a one-element list, this function works properly. It removes the one element and sets the head to NULL, indicating that the head was removed. Now take a look at the zero-element case. A zero-element list is simply a null pointer. If head is a null pointer, you would dereference a null pointer on line 1. To correct this, check whether head is a null pointer and be sure not to dereference it in this case. This check makes the function look like the following:

```
void removeHead( ListElement **head ){
    ListElement *temp;
    if( head && *head ){
        temp = (*head)->next;
        free( *head );
        *head = temp;
    }
}
```

You have checked that the body of the function works properly, that the function is called correctly and returns values correctly, and that you have dealt with the error cases. You can declare your debugging effort complete and present this version of `removeHead` to the interviewer as your solution.

*M*th-to-Last Element of a Linked List

> **PROBLEM** *Given a singly linked list, devise a time- and space-efficient algorithm to find the* mth-to-last *element of the list. Implement your algorithm, taking care to handle relevant error conditions. Define* mth *to last such that when* m = 0 *the last element of the list is returned.*

Why is this a difficult problem? Finding the *m*th element from the beginning of a linked list would be an extremely trivial task. Singly linked lists can be traversed only in the forward direction. For this problem you are asked to find a given element based on its position relative to the *end* of the list. While you traverse the list, however, you don't know where the end is, and when you find the end, there is no easy way to backtrack the required number of elements.

You may want to tell your interviewer that a singly linked list is a particularly poor choice for a data structure when you frequently need to find the *m*th-to-last element. If you were to encounter such a problem while implementing a real program, the correct and most efficient solution would probably be to substitute a more suitable data structure (such as a doubly linked list) to replace the singly linked list. Although this comment shows that you understand good design, the interviewer still wants you to solve the problem as it was originally phrased.

How, then, can you get around the problem that there is no way to traverse backward through this data structure? You know that the element you want is *m* elements from the end of the list. Therefore, if you traverse *m* elements forward from an element and that places you exactly at the end of the list, you have found the element you were searching for. One approach is to simply test each element in this manner until you find the one you're searching for. Intuitively, this feels like an inefficient solution because you will traverse over the same elements many times. If you analyze this potential solution more closely, you can see that you would be traversing *m* elements for most of the elements in the list. If the length of the list is *n*, the algorithm would be approximately $O(mn)$. You need to find a solution more efficient than $O(mn)$.

What if you store some of the elements (or, more likely, pointers or references to the elements) as you traverse the list? Then, when you reach the end of the list, you can look back *m* elements in your storage data structure to find the appropriate element. If you use an appropriate temporary storage data structure, this algorithm is $O(n)$ because it requires only one traversal through the list. Yet this approach is far from perfect. As *m* becomes large, the temporary data structure would become large as well. In the worst-case scenario, this approach might require almost as much storage space as the list itself — not a particularly space-efficient algorithm.

Perhaps working back from the end of the list is not the best approach. Because counting from the beginning of the list is trivial, is there any way to count from the beginning to find the desired element? The desired element is m from the end of the list, and you know the value of m. It must also be l elements from the beginning of the list, although you don't know l. However, $l + m = n$, the length of the list. It's easy to count all the elements in the list. Then you can calculate $l = n - m$, and traverse l elements from the beginning of the list.

Although this process involves two passes through the list, it's still $O(n)$. It requires only a few variables' worth of storage, so this method is a significant improvement over the previous attempt. If you could change the functions that modify the list such that they would increment a count variable for every element added and decrement it for every element removed, you could eliminate the count pass, making this a relatively efficient algorithm. Again, though this point is worth mentioning to the interviewer, he or she is probably looking for a solution that doesn't modify the data structure or place any restrictions on the methods used to access it.

Assuming you must explicitly count the elements in the current algorithm, you must make almost two complete traversals of the linked list. A large list on a memory-constrained system might exist mostly in paged-out virtual memory (on disk). In such a case, each complete traversal of the list would require a large amount of disk access to swap the relevant portions of the list in and out of memory. Under these conditions, an algorithm that made only one complete traversal of the list might be significantly faster than an algorithm that made two traversals, even though they would both be $O(n)$. Is there a way to find the target element with a single traversal?

The counting-from-the-beginning algorithm obviously demands that you know the length of the list. If you can't track the length so that you know it ahead of time, you can determine the length only by a full-list traversal. There doesn't seem to be much hope for getting this algorithm down to a single traversal.

Try reconsidering the previous linear time algorithm, which required only one traversal but was rejected for requiring too much storage. Can you reduce the storage requirements of this approach?

When you reach the end of the list, you are actually interested in only one of the m elements you've been tracking — the element that is m elements behind your current position. You are tracking the rest of the m elements merely because the element m behind your current position changes every time your position advances. Keeping a queue m elements long, where you add the current element to the head and remove an element from the end every time you advance your current position, ensures that the last element in the queue is always m elements behind your current position.

In effect, you are using this m element data structure to make it easy to implicitly advance an m-behind pointer in lock step with your current position pointer. However, this data structure is unnecessary — you can explicitly advance the m-behind pointer by following each element's next pointer just as you do for your current position pointer. This is as easy as (or perhaps easier than) implicitly advancing by shifting through a queue, and it eliminates the need to track all the elements between your current position pointer and your m-behind pointer. This algorithm seems to be the one you've been looking for: linear time, a single traversal, and negligible storage requirements. Now you just need to work out the details.

You need to use two pointers: a current position pointer and an *m*-behind pointer. You must ensure that the two pointers are actually spaced *m* elements apart; then you can advance them at the same rate. When your current position is the end of the list, *m*-behind points to the *m*th-to-last element. How can you get the pointers spaced properly? If you count elements as you traverse the list, you can move the current position pointer to the *m*th element of the list. If you then start the *m*-behind pointer at the beginning of the list, they will be spaced *m* elements apart.

Are there any error conditions you need to watch for? If the list is less than *m* elements long, then there is no *m*th-to-last element. In such a case, you would run off the end of the list as you tried to advance the current position pointer to the *m*th element, possibly dereferencing a null pointer in the process. Therefore, check that you don't hit the end of the list while doing this initial advance.

With this caveat in mind, you can implement the algorithm. It's easy to introduce off-by-one errors in any code that spaces any two things *m* items apart or counts *m* items from a given point. You may want to refer to the exact definition of "*m*th to last" given in the problem and try a simple example on paper to make sure you get your counts right, particularly in the initial advancement of the current pointer.

```
ListElement *findMToLastElement( ListElement *head, int m ){
    ListElement *current, *mBehind;
    int i;
    if (!head)
        return NULL;
    /* Advance current m elements from beginning,
     * checking for the end of the list
     */
    current = head;
    for( i = 0; i < m; i++ ) {
        if( current->next ){
            current = current->next;
        } else {
            return NULL;
        }
    }

    /* Start mBehind at beginning and advance pointers
     * together until current hits last element
     */
    mBehind = head;
    while( current->next ){
        current = current->next;
        mBehind = mBehind->next;
    }

    /* mBehind now points to the element we were
     * searching for, so return it
     */
    return mBehind;
}
```

List Flattening

PROBLEM *Start with a standard doubly linked list. Now imagine that in addition to the next and previous pointers, each element has a child pointer, which may or may not point to a separate doubly linked list. These child lists may have one or more children of their own, and so on, to produce a multilevel data structure, as shown in Figure 4-3.*

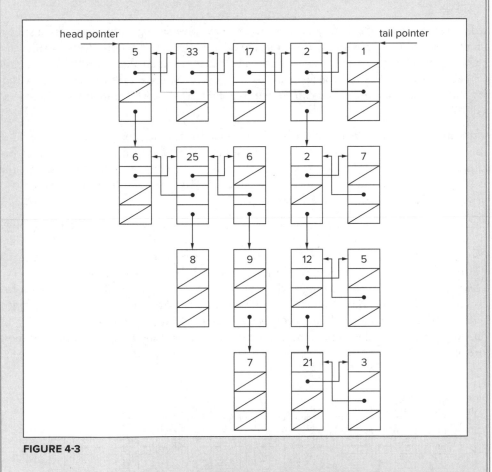

FIGURE 4-3

Flatten the list so that all the nodes appear in a single-level, doubly linked list. You are given the head and tail of the first level of the list. Each node is a C struct *with the following definition:*

```
typedef struct Node {
    struct Node *next;
    struct Node *prev;
    struct Node *child;
    int         value;
} Node;
```

This list-flattening problem gives you plenty of freedom. You have simply been asked to flatten the list. There are many ways to accomplish this task. Each way results in a one-level list with a different node ordering. Start by considering several options for algorithms and the node orders they would yield. Then implement the algorithm that looks easiest and most efficient.

Begin by looking at the data structure. This data structure is a little unusual for a list. It has levels and children — somewhat like a tree. A tree also has levels and children, as you'll see in the next chapter, but trees don't have links between nodes on the same level. You might try to use a common tree traversal algorithm and copy each node into a new list as you visit it as a simple way to flatten the structure.

The data structure is not exactly a normal tree, so any traversal algorithm you use must be modified. From the perspective of a tree, each separate child list in the data structure forms a single extended tree node. This may not seem too bad: Where a standard traversal algorithm checks the child pointers of each tree node directly, you just need to do a linked list traversal to check all the child pointers. Every time you check a node, you can copy it to a duplicate list. This duplicate list will be your flattened list.

Before you work out the details of this solution, consider its efficiency. Every node is examined once, so this is an $O(n)$ solution. There is likely to be some overhead for the recursion or data structure required for the traversal. In addition, you make a duplicate copy of each node to create the new list. This copying is inefficient, especially if the structure is large. See if you can identify a more efficient solution that doesn't require so much copying.

So far, the proposed solution has concentrated on an algorithm, letting the ordering follow. Instead, try focusing on an ordering and then try to deduce an algorithm. You can focus on the data structure's levels as a source of ordering. It helps to define the parts of a level as *child lists*. Just as rooms in a hotel are ordered by level, you can order nodes by the level in which they occur. Every node is in a level and appears in an ordering within that level (arranging the child lists from left to right). Therefore, you have a logical ordering just like hotel rooms. You can order by starting with all the first-level nodes, followed by all the second-level nodes, followed by all the third-level nodes, and so on. Applying these rules to the example data structure, you should get the ordering shown in Figure 4-4.

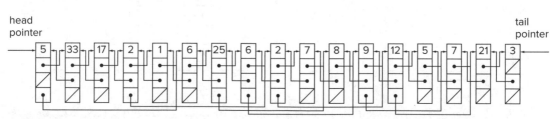

FIGURE 4-4

Now try to discover an algorithm that yields this ordering. One property of this ordering is that you never rearrange the order of the nodes in their respective levels, so you could connect all the nodes on each level into a list and then join all the connected levels. However, to find all the nodes on a given level so that you can join them, you would need to do a breadth-first search of that level. Breadth-first searching is inefficient, so you should continue to look for a better solution.

In Figure 4-3, the second level is composed of two child lists. Each child list starts with a different child of a first-level node. You could try to append the child lists one at a time to the end of the first level instead of combining the child lists.

To append the child lists one at a time, traverse the first level from the start, following the next pointers. Every time you encounter a node with a child, append the child (and thus the child list) to the end of the first level and update the tail pointer. Eventually, you append the entire second level to the end of the first level. You can continue traversing the first level and arrive at the start of the old second level. If you continue this process of appending children to the end of the first level, you eventually append every child list to the end and have a flattened list in the required order. More formally, this algorithm is as follows:

```
Start at the beginning of the first level
While you are not at the end of the first level
    If the current node has a child
        Append the child to the end of the first level
        Update the tail pointer
    Advance to next node
```

This algorithm is easy to implement because it's so simple. In terms of efficiency, every node after the first level is examined twice. Each node is examined once when you update the tail pointer for each child list and once when you examine the node to see if it has a child. The nodes in the first level are examined only once when you examine them for children because you had a first-level tail pointer when you began. Therefore, there are no more than $2n$ comparisons in this algorithm, and it is an $O(n)$ solution. This is the best time order you can achieve because every node must be examined. Although this solution has the same time order as the tree traversal approach considered earlier, it is more efficient because it requires no recursion or additional memory. (There are other equally efficient solutions to this problem. One such solution involves inserting child lists after their parents, rather than at the end of the list.)

The code for this algorithm is as follows. Note that the function takes a pointer to the tail pointer so that changes to the tail pointer are retained when the function returns:

```
void flattenList( Node *head, Node **tail ){
    Node *curNode = head;
    while( curNode ){
        /* The current node has a child */
        if( curNode->child ){
            append( curNode->child, tail );
        }
        curNode = curNode->next;
    }
}

/* Appends the child list to the end of the tail and updates  ;
 * the tail.
 */
```

```
void append( Node *child, Node **tail ){
    Node *curNode;

    /* Append the child child list to the end */
    (*tail)->next = child;
    child->prev = *tail;

    /* Find the new tail, which is the end of the child list. */
    for( curNode = child; curNode->next;  curNode = curNode->next )
        ; /* Body intentionally empty */

    /* Update the tail pointer now that curNode is the new tail. */
    *tail = curNode;
}
```

List Unflattening

> **PROBLEM** *Unflatten the list created by the previous problem and restore the data structure to its original condition.*

This problem is the reverse of the previous problem, so you already know a lot about this data structure. One important insight is that you created the flattened list by combining all the child lists into one long level. To get back the original list, you must separate the long flattened list back into its original child lists.

Try doing the exact opposite of what you did to create the list. When flattening the list, you traversed down the list from the start and added child lists to the end. To reverse this, you go backward from the tail and break off parts of the first level. You could break off a part when you encounter a node that was the beginning of a child list in the unflattened list. Unfortunately, this is more difficult than it might seem because you can't easily determine whether a particular node is a child (indicating that it started a child list) in the original data structure. The only way to determine whether a node is a child is to scan through the child pointers of all the previous nodes. All this scanning would be inefficient, so you should examine some additional possibilities to find a better solution.

One way to get around the child node problem is to go through the list from start to end, storing pointers to all the child nodes in a separate data structure. Then you could go backward through the list and separate every child node. Looking up nodes in this way frees you from repeated scans to determine whether a node is a child. This is a good solution, but it still requires an extra data structure. Try looking for a solution without an extra data structure.

It seems you have exhausted all the possibilities for going backward through the list, so try an algorithm that traverses the list from the start to the end. You still can't immediately determine whether a node is a child. One advantage of going forward, however, is that you can find all the child nodes in the same order that you appended them to the first level. You also know that every child node began a child list in the original list. If you separate each child node from the node before it, you get the unflattened list back.

You can't simply traverse the list from the start, find each node with a child, and separate the child from its previous node. You would get to the end of your list at the break between the first and second level, leaving the rest of the data structure untraversed. This approach seems promising, though. You can traverse every child list, starting with the first level (which is a child list itself). When you find a child, continue traversing the original child list and also traverse the newly found child list. You can't traverse both at the same time, however. You could save one of these locations in a data structure and traverse it later. However, rather than design and implement this data structure, you can use recursion. Specifically, every time you find a node with a child, separate the child from its previous node, start traversing the new child list, and then continue traversing the original child list.

This is an efficient algorithm because each node is checked at most twice, resulting in an $O(n)$ running time. Again, an $O(n)$ running time is the best you can do because you must check each node at least once to see if it is a child. In the average case, the number of function calls is small in relation to the number of nodes, so the recursive overhead is not too bad. In the worst case, the number of function calls is no more than the number of nodes. This solution is approximately as efficient as the earlier proposal that required an extra data structure, but somewhat simpler and easier to code. Therefore, this recursive solution would probably be the best choice in an interview. In outline form, the algorithm looks like the following:

```
Explore path:
    While not at the end
        If current node has a child
            Separate the child from its previous node
            Explore path beginning with the child
        Go onto the next node
```

It can be implemented in C as:

```
/* unflattenList wraps the recursive function and updates the tail pointer. */
void unflattenList( Node *start, Node **tail ){
    Node *curNode;

    exploreAndSeparate( start );

    /* Update the tail pointer */
    for( curNode = start; curNode->next; curNode = curNode->next )
        ; /* Body intentionally empty */

    *tail = curNode;
}

/* exploreAndSeparate actually does the recursion and separation */
void exploreAndSeparate( Node *childListStart ){
    Node *curNode = childListStart;

    while( curNode ){
        if( curNode->child->prev){
            /* terminates the child list before the child */
            curNode->child->prev->next = NULL;
            /* starts the child list beginning with the child */
            curNode->child->prev = NULL;
```

```
        exploreAndSeparate( curNode->child );
    }
    curNode = curNode->next;
    }
}
```

Null or Cycle

PROBLEM *You are given a linked list with at least one node that is either null-terminated (acyclic), as shown in Figure 4-5, or ends in a cycle (cyclic), as shown in Figure 4-6.*

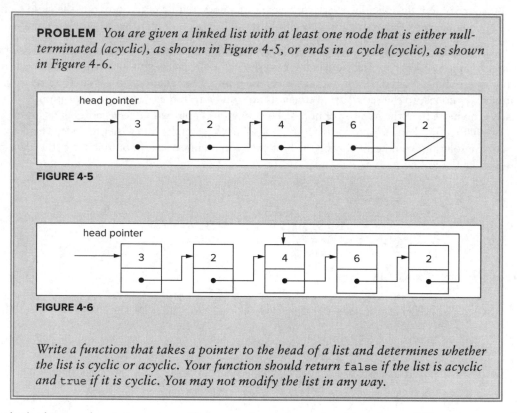

FIGURE 4-5

FIGURE 4-6

Write a function that takes a pointer to the head of a list and determines whether the list is cyclic or acyclic. Your function should return `false` *if the list is acyclic and* `true` *if it is cyclic. You may not modify the list in any way.*

Start by looking at the pictures to see if you can determine an intuitive way to differentiate a cyclic list from an acyclic list.

The difference between the two lists appears at their ends. In the cyclic list, there is an end node that points back to one of the earlier nodes. In the acyclic list, there is an end node that is null terminated. Thus, if you can find this end node, you can test whether the list is cyclic or acyclic.

In the acyclic list, it is easy to find the end node. You traverse the list until you reach a null terminated node.

In the cyclic list, though, it is more difficult. If you just traverse the list, you go in a circle and won't know whether you're in a cyclic list or just a long acyclic list. You need a more sophisticated approach.

Try looking at the end node a bit more. The end node points to a node that has another node pointing at it. This means that there are two pointers pointing at the same node. This node is the only node with two elements pointing at it. You can design an algorithm around this property. You can traverse the list and check every node to determine whether two other nodes are pointing at it. If you find such a node, the list must be cyclic. Otherwise, the list is acyclic, and you will eventually encounter a null pointer.

Unfortunately, it is difficult to check the number of nodes pointing at each element. See if you can find another special property of the end node in a cyclic list. When you traverse the list, the end node's next node is a node that you have previously encountered. Instead of checking for a node with two pointers pointing at it, you can check whether you have already encountered a node. If you find a previously encountered node, you have a cyclic list. If you encounter a null pointer, you have an acyclic list. This is only part of the algorithm. You still need to figure out how to determine whether you have previously encountered a node.

The easiest way to do this would be to mark each element as you visit it, but you've been told you're not allowed to modify the list. You could keep track of the nodes you've encountered by putting them in a separate list. Then you would compare the current node to all the nodes in the already-encountered list. If the current node ever points to a node in the already-encountered list, you have a cycle. Otherwise, you'll get to the end of the list and see that it's null terminated and thus acyclic. This would work, but in the worst case the already-encountered list would require as much memory as the original list. See if you can reduce this memory requirement.

What are you storing in the already-encountered list? The already-encountered list's first node points to the original list's first node, its second node points to the original list's second node, its third node points to the original list's third node, and so on. You're creating a list that mirrors the original list. This is unnecessary — you can just use the original list.

Try this approach: Because you know your current node in the list and the start of the list, you can compare your current node's next pointer to all its previous nodes directly. For the ith node, compare its next pointer to see if it points to any of nodes 1 to $i - 1$. If any are equal, you have a cycle.

What's the time order of this algorithm? For the first node, 0 previous nodes are examined; for the second node, one previous node is examined; for the third node, two previous nodes are examined, and so on. Thus, the algorithm examines $0 + 1 + 2 + 3 + ... + n$ nodes. As discussed in Chapter 3, such an algorithm is $O(n^2)$.

That's about as far as you can go with this approach. Although it's difficult to discover without some sort of hint, there is a better solution involving two pointers. What can you do with two pointers that you couldn't do with one? You can advance them on top of each other, but then you might as well have one pointer. You could advance them with a fixed interval between them, but this doesn't seem to gain anything. What happens if you advance the pointers at different speeds?

In the acyclic list, the faster pointer reaches the end. In the cyclic list, they both loop endlessly. The faster pointer eventually catches up with and passes the slower pointer. If the fast pointer is ever behind or equal to the slower pointer, you have a cyclic list. If it encounters a null pointer, you have an acyclic list. You'll need to start the fast pointer one node ahead of the slow pointer so they're not equal to begin with. In outline form, this algorithm looks like this:

```
Start slow pointer at the head of the list
Start fast pointer at second node
Loop infinitely
```

```
        If the fast pointer reaches a null pointer
            Return that the list is null terminated
        If the fast pointer moves onto or over the slow pointer
            Return that there is a cycle
        Advance the slow pointer one node
        Advance the fast pointer two nodes
```

You can now implement this solution:

```
/* Takes a pointer to the head of a linked list and determines if
 * the list ends in a cycle or is NULL terminated
 */
bool determineTermination( Node *head ){
    Node *fast, *slow;
    slow = head;
    fast = head->next;
    while( true ){
        if( !fast || !fast->next )
            return false;
        else if( fast == slow || fast->next == slow )
            return true;
        else {
            slow = slow->next;
            fast = fast->next->next;
        }
    }
}
```

Is this algorithm faster than the earlier solution? If this list is acyclic, the faster pointer comes to the end after examining n nodes, while the slower pointer traverses $1/2$ n nodes. Thus, you examine $3/2n$ nodes, which is an $O(n)$ algorithm.

What about a cyclic list? The slower pointer never goes around any loop more than once. When the slower pointer has examined n nodes, the faster pointer will have examined $2n$ nodes and have "passed" the slower pointer, regardless of the loop's size. Therefore, in the worst case you examine $3n$ nodes, which is still $O(n)$. Regardless of whether the list is cyclic or acyclic, this two-pointer approach is much better than the single-pointer approach to the problem.

SUMMARY

Although they are simple data structures, problems with linked lists often arise in interviews focusing on C or C++ experience as a way to determine whether a candidate understands basic pointer manipulation. Each element in a singly linked list contains a pointer to the next element in the list, whereas each element in a doubly linked list points to both the previous and the next elements. The first element in both list types is referred to as the *head,* whereas the last element is referred to as the *tail.* Circular linked lists have no head or tail; instead, the elements are linked together to form a cycle.

List operations are much simpler to perform on doubly linked lists, so most interview problems use singly linked lists. Typical operations include updating the head of the list, traversing the list to find a specific element from the end of the list, and inserting or removing list elements.

5

Trees and Graphs

Trees and graphs are common data structures, so both are fair game in a programming interview. Tree problems are more common, however, because they are simple enough to implement within the time constraints of an interview and enable an interviewer to test your understanding of recursion and runtime analysis. Graph problems are interesting but often more complicated, so you won't see them as frequently.

Unlike the previous chapter's focus on implementations in C, this and subsequent chapters focus on implementations in more modern object-oriented languages.

TREES

A tree is made up of *nodes* (data elements) with zero, one, or several references (or *pointers*) to other nodes. Each node has only one other node referencing it. The result is a data structure that looks like Figure 5-1.

As in a linked list, a node is represented by a structure or class, and trees can be implemented in any language that includes pointers or references. In object-oriented languages you usually define a class for the common parts of a node and one or more subclasses for the data held by a node. For example, the following are the C# classes you might use for a tree of integers:

```csharp
public class Node {
    public Node[] children;
}

public class IntNode : Node {
    public int value;
}
```

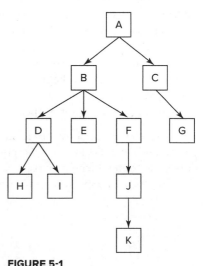

FIGURE 5-1

In this definition, `children` is an array that keeps track of all the nodes that this node references. For simplicity, these classes expose the children as public data members, but this isn't good coding practice. A proper class definition would make them private and instead expose public methods to manipulate them. A somewhat more complete Java equivalent (with methods and constructors) to the preceding classes is:

```java
public abstract class Node {
    private Node[] children;

    public Node( Node[] children ){
        this.children = children;
    }

    public int getNumChildren(){
        return children.length;
    }

    public Node getChild( int index ){
        return children[ index ];
    }
}

public class IntNode extends Node {
    private int value;

    public IntNode( Node[] children, int value ){
        super( children );
        this.value = value;
    }

    public int getValue(){
        return value;
    }
}
```

This example still lacks error handling and methods to add or remove nodes from a tree. During an interview you may want to save time and keep things simple by using public data members, folding classes together, and sketching out the methods needed to manage the tree rather than fully implementing them. Ask the interviewer how much detail she wants and write your code accordingly. Any time you take shortcuts that violate good object-oriented design principles, be sure to mention the more correct design to the interviewer and be prepared to implement it that way if asked. This way you avoid getting bogged down in implementation details, but don't give the impression that you're a sloppy coder who can't properly design classes.

Referring to the tree shown in Figure 5-1, you can see there is only one top-level node. From this node, you can follow links and reach every other node. This top-level node is called the root. The *root* is the only node from which you have a path to every other node. The root node is inherently the start of any tree. Therefore, people often say "tree" when talking about the root node of the tree.

Some additional tree-related terms to know are:

➤ **Parent** — A node that points to other nodes is the *parent* of those nodes. Every node except the root has one parent. In Figure 5-1, B is the parent of D, E, and F.

➤ **Child** — A node is the *child* of any node that points to it. In Figure 5-1, each of the nodes D, E, and F is a child of B.

➤ **Descendant** — All the nodes that can be reached by following a path of child nodes from a particular node are the *descendants* of that node. In Figure 5-1, D, E, F, H, I, J, and K are the descendants of B.

➤ **Ancestor** — An *ancestor* of a node is any other node for which the node is a descendant. For example, A, B, and D are the ancestors of I.

➤ **Leaves** — The *leaves* are nodes that do not have any children. G, H, I, and K are leaves.

Binary Trees

So far, we've used the most general definition of a tree. Most tree problems involve a special type of tree called a *binary tree*. In a binary tree, each node has no more than two children, referred to as *left* and *right*. Figure 5-2 shows an example of a binary tree.

The following is an implementation of a binary tree. For simplicity, everything is combined into a single class:

```
public class Node {
    private Node left;
    private Node right;
    private int  value;

    public Node( Node left, Node right, int value ){
        this.left = left;
        this.right = right;
        this.value = value;
    }

    public Node getLeft() { return left; }
    public Node getRight() { return right; }
    public int getValue() { return value; }
}
```

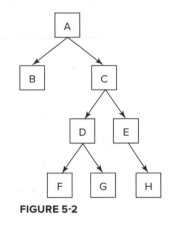

FIGURE 5-2

When an element has no left or right child, the corresponding reference is null.

Binary tree problems can often be solved more quickly than equivalent generic tree problems, but they are no less challenging. Because time is at a premium in an interview, most tree problems will be binary tree problems. If an interviewer says "tree," it's a good idea to clarify whether she is referring to a generic tree or a binary tree.

> **NOTE** *When interviewers say "tree," they often mean a* binary tree.

Binary Search Trees

Trees are often used to store sorted or ordered data. The most common way to store ordered data in a tree is to use a special tree called a *binary search tree (BST)*. In a BST, the value held by a node's left child is less than or equal to its own value, and the value held by a node's right child is greater than or equal to its value. In effect, the data in a BST is sorted by value: All the descendants to the left of a node are less than or equal to the node, and all the descendants to the right of the node are greater than or equal to the node. Figure 5-3 shows an example of a BST.

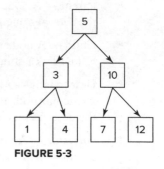

FIGURE 5-3

BSTs are so common that many people mean a BST when they say "tree." Again, ask for clarification before proceeding.

> **NOTE** *When interviewers say "tree," they often mean a* binary search tree.

One advantage of a binary search tree is that the lookup operation (locating a particular node in the tree) is fast and simple. This is particularly useful for data storage. In outline form, the algorithm to perform a lookup in a BST is as follows:

```
Start at the root node
Loop while current node is non-null
    If the current node's value is equal to the search value
        Return the current node
    If the current node's value is less than the search value
        Make the right node the current node
    If the current node's value is greater than the search value
        Make the left node the current node
End loop
```

If you fall out of the loop, the node wasn't in the tree.

Here's an implementation of the search in C# or Java:

```
Node findNode( Node root, int value ){
    while( root != null ){
        int currval = root.getValue();
        if( currval == value ) break;
        if( currval < value ){
            root = root.getRight();
        } else { // currval > value
            root = root.getLeft();
        }
    }

    return root;
}
```

This lookup is fast because you eliminate half the remaining nodes from your search on each iteration by choosing to follow the left subtree or the right subtree. In the worst case, you will know whether the lookup was successful by the time there is only one node left to search. Therefore, the running time of the lookup is equal to the number of times that you can halve n nodes before you get to 1.

This number, x, is the same as the number of times you can double 1 before reaching n, and it can be expressed as $2^x = n$. You can find x using a logarithm.

For example, $\log_2 8 = 3$ because $2^3 = 8$, so the running time of the lookup operation is $O(\log_2(n))$. Because logarithms with different bases differ only by a constant factor, it's common to omit the base 2 and call this $O(\log(n))$. $\log(n)$ is very fast. For an example, $\log_2(1,000,000,000) \approx 30$.

> **NOTE** *Lookup is an O(log(n)) operation in a balanced binary search tree.*

One important caveat exists in saying that lookup is $O(\log(n))$ in a BST: Lookup is only $O(\log(n))$ if you can guarantee that the number of nodes remaining to be searched will be halved or nearly halved on each iteration. Why? Because in the worst case, each node has only one child, in which case you end up with a linked list and lookup becomes an $O(n)$ operation. This worst case may be encountered more commonly than you might expect, such as when a tree is created by adding data already in sorted order.

> **NOTE** *Deletion and insertion are O(log(n)) operations in binary search trees.*

Binary search trees have other important properties. For example, you can obtain the smallest element by following all the left children and the largest element by following all the right children. The nodes can also be printed out, in order, in $O(n)$ time. Given a node, you can even find the next highest node in $O(\log(n))$ time.

Tree problems are often designed to test your ability to think recursively. Each node in a tree is the root of a subtree beginning at that node. This subtree property is conducive to recursion because recursion generally involves solving a problem in terms of similar subproblems and a base case. In tree recursion you start with a root, perform an action, and then move to the left or right subtree (or both, one after the other). This process continues until you reach a null reference, which is the end of a tree (and a good base case). For example, the preceding lookup operation can be reimplemented recursively as follows:

```
Node findNode( Node root, int value ){
    if( root == null ) return null;
    int currval = root.getValue();
    if( currval == value ) return root;
    if( currval < value ){
        return findNode( root.getRight(), value );
    } else { // currval > value
        return findNode( root.getLeft(), value );
    }
}
```

Most problems with trees have this recursive form. A good way to start thinking about any problem involving a tree is to start thinking recursively.

> **NOTE** *Many tree operations can be implemented recursively. The recursive implementation may not be the most efficient, but it's usually the best place to start.*

Heaps

Another common tree is a *heap*. Heaps are trees (usually binary trees) where (in a *max-heap*) each child of a node has a value less than or equal to the node's own value. (In a *min-heap*, each child is greater than or equal to its parent.) Consequently, the root node always has the largest value in the tree, which means that you can find the maximum value in constant time: Simply return the root value. Insertion and deletion are still $O(\log(n))$, but lookup becomes $O(n)$. You cannot find the next higher node to a given node in $O(\log(n))$ time or print out the nodes in sorted order in $O(n)$ time as in a BST. Although conceptually heaps are trees, the underlying data implementation of a heap often differs from the trees in the preceding discussion.

You could model the patients waiting in a hospital emergency room with a heap. As patients enter, they are assigned a priority and put into the heap. A heart attack patient would get a higher priority than a patient with a stubbed toe. When a doctor becomes available, the doctor would want to examine the patient with the highest priority. The doctor can determine the patient with the highest priority by extracting the max value from the heap, which is a constant time operation.

> **NOTE** *If extracting the max value needs to be fast, use a heap.*

Common Searches

It's convenient when you have a tree with ordering properties such as a BST or a heap. Often you're given a tree that isn't a BST or a heap. For example, you may have a tree that is a representation of a family tree or a company organization chart. You must use different techniques to retrieve data from this kind of tree. One common class of problems involves searching for a particular node. When you search a tree without the benefit of ordering, the time to find a node is $O(n)$, so this type of search is best avoided for large trees. You can use two common search algorithms to accomplish this task.

Breadth-First Search

One way to search a tree is to do a *breadth-first search (BFS)*. In a BFS you start with the root, move left to right across the second level, then move left to right across the third level, and so forth. You continue the search until either you have examined all the nodes or you find the node you are searching for. A BFS uses additional memory because it is necessary to track the child nodes for all nodes on a given level while searching that level.

Depth-First Search

Another common way to search for a node is by using a *depth-first search (DFS)*. A depth-first search follows one branch of the tree down as many levels as possible until the target node is found or the end is reached. When the search can't go down any farther, it is continued at the nearest ancestor with unexplored children.

DFS has much lower memory requirements than BFS because it is not necessary to store all the child pointers at each level. If you have additional information on the likely location of your target node, one or the other of these algorithms may be more efficient. For instance, if your node is likely to be in the upper levels of the tree, BFS is most efficient. If the target node is likely to be in the lower levels of the tree, DFS has the advantage that it doesn't examine any single level last. (BFS always examines the lowest level last.)

For example, if you were searching a job hierarchy tree looking for an employee who started less than 3 months ago, you would suspect that lower-level employees are more likely to have started recently. In this case, if the assumption were true, a DFS would usually find the target node more quickly than a BFS.

There are other types of searches, but these are the two most common that you will encounter in an interview.

Traversals

Another common type of tree problem is called a *traversal*. A traversal is just like a search, except that instead of stopping when you find a particular target node, you visit every node in the tree. Often this is used to perform some operation on each node in the tree. There are many types of traversals, each of which visits nodes in a different order, but you're most likely to be asked about the three most common types of depth-first traversals for binary trees:

- ➤ **Preorder** — Performs the operation first on the node itself, then on its left descendants, and finally on its right descendants. In other words, a node is always visited *before* any of its children.

- ➤ **Inorder** — Performs the operation first on the node's left descendants, then on the node itself, and finally on its right descendants. In other words, the left subtree is visited first, then the node itself, and then the node's right subtree.

- ➤ **Postorder** — Performs the operation first on the node's left descendants, then on the node's right descendants, and finally on the node itself. In other words, a node is always visited *after* all its children.

These classes of traversals can also apply to nonbinary trees as long as you have a way to classify whether a child is "less than" (on the left of) or "greater than" (on the right of) its parent node.

Recursion is usually the simplest way to implement a depth-first traversal.

> **NOTE** *If you're asked to implement a traversal, recursion is a good way to start thinking about the problem.*

GRAPHS

Graphs are more general and more complex than trees. Like trees, they consist of nodes with children — a tree is actually a special case of a graph. But unlike tree nodes, graph nodes (or *vertices*) can have multiple "parents," possibly creating a loop (a *cycle*). In addition, the links between nodes, as well as the nodes themselves, may have values or weights. These links are called *edges* because they may contain more information than just a pointer. In a graph, edges can be one-way or two-way. A graph with one-way edges is called a *directed graph*. A graph with only two-way pointers is called an *undirected graph*. Figure 5-4 shows a directed graph, and Figure 5-5 shows an undirected graph.

Graphs are commonly used to model real-world problems that are difficult to model with other data structures. For example, a directed graph could represent the aqueducts connecting cities because water flows only one way. You might use such a graph to help you find the fastest way to get water from city A to city D. An undirected graph can represent something such as a series of relays in signal transmission.

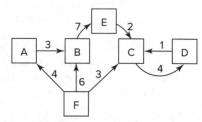

FIGURE 5-4

There are several common ways to represent graph data structures. The best representation is often determined by the algorithm being implemented. One common representation has the data structure for each node include an *adjacency list*: a list of references to other nodes with which the node shares edges. This list is analogous to the child references of the tree node data structure, but the adjacency list is usually a dynamic data structure since the number of edges at each node can vary over a wide range. Another graph representation is an *adjacency matrix*, which is a square matrix with dimension equal to the number of nodes. The matrix element at position i,j represents the number of edges extending from node i to node j.

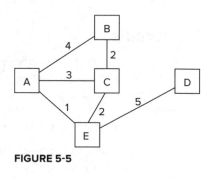

FIGURE 5-5

All the types of searches possible in trees have analogs in graphs. The graph equivalents are usually slightly more complex due to the possibility of cycles.

Graphs are often used in real-world programming, but they are less frequently encountered in interviews, in part because graph problems can be difficult to solve in the time allotted for an interview.

TREE AND GRAPH PROBLEMS

Most tree problems involve binary trees. You may occasionally encounter a graph problem, especially if the interviewer thinks you're doing particularly well with easier problems.

Height of a Tree

> **PROBLEM** *The height of a tree (binary or not) is defined to be the maximum distance from the root node to any leaf node. The tree in Figure 5-2, for example, has a height of 4 because the path from A to F, G, or H involves four nodes. Write a function to calculate the height of an arbitrary binary tree.*

Start by looking at some simple trees to see if there's a way to think recursively about the problem. Each node in the tree corresponds to another subtree rooted at that node. For the tree in Figure 5-2, the heights of each subtree are:

➤ A: height 4

➤ B: height 1

➤ C: height 3

➤ D: height 2

➤ E: height 2

➤ F: height 1

➤ G: height 1

➤ H: height 1

Your initial guess might be that the height of a node is the sum of the height of its children because height A = 4 = height B + height C, but a quick test shows that this assumption is incorrect because height C = 3, but the heights of D and E add up to 4, not 3.

Look at the two subtrees on either side of a node. If you remove one of the subtrees, does the height of the tree change? Yes, but only if you remove the taller subtree. This is the key insight you need: *The height of a tree equals the height of its tallest subtree plus one.* This is a recursive definition that is easy to translate to code:

```
public static int treeHeight( Node n ){
    if( n == null ) return 0;
    return 1 + Math.max( treeHeight( n.getLeft() ),
                         treeHeight( n.getRight() ) );
}
```

What's the running time for this function? The function is recursively called for each child of each node, so the function will be called once for each node in the tree. Since the operations on each node are constant time, the overall running time is $O(n)$.

Preorder Traversal

> **PROBLEM** *Informally, a preorder traversal involves walking around the tree in a counter-clockwise manner starting at the root, sticking close to the edges, and printing out the nodes as you encounter them. For the tree shown in Figure 5-6, the result is 100, 50, 25, 75, 150, 125, 110, and 175. Perform a preorder traversal of a binary search tree, printing the value of each node.*

To design an algorithm for printing out the nodes in the correct order, you should examine what happens as you print out the nodes. Go to the left as far as possible, come up the tree, go one node to the right, and then go to the left as far as possible, come up the tree again, and so on. The key is to think in terms of subtrees.

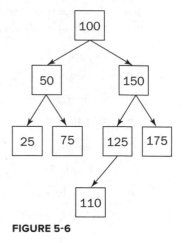

The two largest subtrees are rooted at 50 and 150. All the nodes in the subtree rooted at 50 are printed out before any of the nodes in the subtree rooted at 150. In addition, the root node for each subtree is printed out before the rest of the subtree.

Generally, for any node in a preorder traversal, you would print the node itself, followed by the left subtree and then the right subtree. If you begin the printing process at the root node, you would have a recursive definition as follows:

FIGURE 5-6

1. Print out the root (or the subtree's root) value.

2. Do a preorder traversal on the left subtree.

3. Do a preorder traversal on the right subtree.

Assume you have a binary tree Node class with a printValue method. (Your interviewer probably wouldn't ask you to write out the definition for this class, but if she did, an appropriate definition would be the same as the Node class in the introduction to this chapter, with the addition of a printValue method.) The preceding pseudocode algorithm is easily coded using recursion:

```
void preorderTraversal( Node root ){
    if( root == null ) return;
    root.printValue();
    preorderTraversal( root.getLeft() );
    preorderTraversal( root.getRight() );
}
```

What's the running time on this algorithm? Every node is examined once, so it's $O(n)$.

The inorder and postorder traversals are almost identical; all you vary is the order in which the node and subtrees are visited:

```
void inorderTraversal( Node root ){
    if( root == null ) return;
```

```
        inorderTraversal( root.getLeft() );
        root.printValue();
        inorderTraversal( root.getRight() );
    }

    void postorderTraversal( Node root ){
        if( root == null ) return;
        postorderTraversal( root.getLeft() );
        postorderTraversal( root.getRight() );
        root.printValue();
    }
```

Just as with the preorder traversal, these traversals examine each node once, so the running time is always $O(n)$.

Preorder Traversal, No Recursion

> **PROBLEM** *Perform a preorder traversal of a binary search tree, printing the value of each node, but this time you may not use recursion.*

Sometimes recursive algorithms can be replaced with iterative algorithms that accomplish the same task in a fundamentally different manner using different data structures. Consider the data structures you know and think about how they could be helpful. For example, you might try using a list, an array, or another binary tree.

Because recursion is so intrinsic to the definition of a preorder traversal, you may have trouble finding an entirely different iterative algorithm to use in place of the recursive algorithm. In such a case, the best course of action is to understand what is happening in the recursion and try to emulate the process iteratively.

Recursion implicitly uses a stack data structure by placing data on the call stack. That means there should be an equivalent solution that avoids recursion by explicitly using a stack.

Assume you have a stack class that can store nodes. (Implementing the stack is a separate problem.) The following is a skeleton class definition for the stack. (If you're not sure what these methods do, revisit the stack implementation problem in Chapter 4.)

```
public class NodeStack {
    public void push( Node n ){ .... }
    public Node pop() { .... }
}
```

Now consider the recursive preorder algorithm, paying close attention to the data that are implicitly stored on the call stack so you can explicitly store the same data on a stack in your iterative implementation:

```
Print out the root (or subtree's root) value.
Do a preorder traversal on the left subtree.
Do a preorder traversal on the right subtree.
```

When you first enter the procedure, you print the root node's value. Next, you recursively call the procedure to traverse the left subtree. When you make this recursive call, the calling procedure's state is saved on the stack. When the recursive call returns, the calling procedure can pick up where it left off.

What's happening here? Effectively, the recursive call serves to implicitly store the address of the right subtree on the stack, so it can be traversed after the left subtree traversal is complete. Each time you print a node and move to its left child, the right child is first stored on an implicit stack. Whenever there is no child, you return from a recursive call, effectively popping a right child node off the implicit stack, so you can continue traversing.

To summarize, the algorithm prints the value of the current node, pushes the right child onto an implicit stack, and moves to the left child. The algorithm pops the stack to obtain a new current node when there are no more children (when it reaches a leaf). This continues until the entire tree has been traversed and the stack is empty.

Before implementing this algorithm, first remove any unnecessary special cases that would make the algorithm more difficult to implement. Instead of coding separate cases for the left and right children, why not push pointers to both nodes onto the stack? Then all that matters is the order in which the nodes are pushed onto the stack: You need to find an order that enables you to push both nodes onto the stack so that the left node is always popped before the right node.

Because a stack is a last-in-first-out data structure, push the right node onto the stack first, followed by the left node. Instead of examining the left child explicitly, simply pop the first node from the stack, print its value, and push both of its children onto the stack in the correct order. If you start the procedure by pushing the root node onto the stack and then pop, print, and push as described, you can emulate the recursive preorder traversal. To summarize:

```
Create the stack
Push the root node on the stack
While the stack is not empty
    Pop a node
    Print its value
    If right child exists, push the node's right child
    If left child exists, push the node's left child
```

The code (with no error checking) for this algorithm is as follows:

```
void preorderTraversal( Node root ){
    NodeStack stack = new NodeStack();
    stack.push( root );
    while( stack.size() > 0 ){
        Node curr = stack.pop();
        curr.printValue();
        Node n = curr.getRight();
        if( n != null ) stack.push( n );
        n = curr.getLeft();
        if( n != null ) stack.push( n );
    }
}
```

What's the running time for this algorithm? Each node is examined only once and pushed on the stack only once. Therefore, this is still an $O(n)$ algorithm. You don't have the overhead of many recursive function calls in this implementation. On the other hand, the stack used in this implementation probably requires dynamic memory allocation, so it's unclear whether the iterative implementation would be more or less efficient than the recursive solution. The point of the problem, however, is to demonstrate your understanding of recursion.

Lowest Common Ancestor

> **PROBLEM** *Given the value of two nodes in a binary search tree, find the lowest (nearest) common ancestor. You may assume that both values already exist in the tree.*
>
> *For example, using the tree shown in Figure 5-7, assume 4 and 14 are the two given nodes. The lowest common ancestor would be 8 because it's an ancestor to both 4 and 14, and there is no node lower on the tree that is an ancestor to both 4 and 14.*

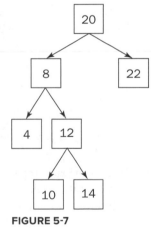

Figure 5-7 suggests an intuitive algorithm: Follow the lines up from each of the nodes until they converge. To implement this algorithm, make lists of all the ancestors of both nodes, and then search through these two lists to find the first node where they differ. The node immediately above this divergence is the lowest common ancestor. This is a good solution, but there is a more efficient one.

The first algorithm works for any type of tree but doesn't use any of the special properties of a binary search tree. Try to use some of those special properties to help you find the lowest common ancestor more efficiently.

Consider the two special properties of binary search trees. The first property is that every node has zero, one, or two children. This fact doesn't seem to help find a new algorithm.

FIGURE 5-7

The second property is that the left child's value is less than or equal to the value of the current node, and the right child's value is greater than or equal to the value of the current node. This property looks more promising.

Looking at the example tree, the lowest common ancestor to 4 and 14, the node with value 8, is different from the other ancestors to 4 and 14 in an important way. All the other ancestors are either greater than both 4 and 14 or less than both 4 and 14. Only 8 is between 4 and 14. You can use this insight to design a better algorithm.

The root node is an ancestor to all nodes because there is a path from it to all other nodes. Therefore, you can start at the root node and follow a path through the common ancestors of both nodes. When your target values are both less than the current node, you go left. When they are both greater, you go right. The first node you encounter that is between your target values is the lowest common ancestor.

Based on this description, and referring to the values of the two nodes as `value1` and `value2`, you can derive the following algorithm:

```
Examine the current node
If value1 and value2 are both less than the current node's value
    Examine the left child
If value1 and value2 are both greater than the current node's value
    Examine the right child
Otherwise
    The current node is the lowest common ancestor
```

This solution may seem to suggest using recursion because it is a tree and the algorithm has a recursive structure to it, but recursion is not necessary here. Recursion is most useful when moving through multiple branches of a tree or examining some special pattern of nodes. Here you are only traveling down the tree. It's easy to implement this kind of search iteratively:

```
Node findLowestCommonAncestor( Node root, int value1, int value2 ){
    while( root != null ){
        int value = root.getValue();

        if( value > value1 && value > value2 ){
            root = root.getLeft();
        } else if( value < value1 && value < value2 ){
            root = root.getRight();
        } else {
            return root;
        }
    }

    return null; // only if empty tree
}
```

What's the running time of this algorithm? You travel down a path to the lowest common ancestor. Recall that traveling a path to any one node takes $O(\log(n))$. Therefore, this is an $O(\log(n))$ algorithm. In addition, this is slightly more efficient than a similar recursive solution because you don't have the overhead of repeated function calls.

The problem states that you'll be given the value of two nodes in the tree, but it's trivial to write an overloaded wrapper for the function you just implemented that would cover the case where you're given references to the two nodes:

```
Node findLowestCommonAncestor( Node root, Node child1, Node child2 ){
    if( root == null || child1 == null || child2 == null ){
        return null;
    }

    return findLowestCommonAncestor( root, child1.getValue(),
                                     child2.getValue() );
}
```

Binary Tree to Heap

> **PROBLEM** *You are given a set of integers in an unordered binary tree. Use an array sorting routine to transform the tree into a heap that uses a balanced binary tree as its underlying data structure.*

To use an array sorting routine, as the problem requires, you must convert the tree you start with into an array. Because you both start and end with binary tree data structures, transforming into an array probably isn't the most efficient way to accomplish the end goal. You might comment to your interviewer that if not for the requirement to use an array sorting routine, it would be more efficient to simply *heapify* the nodes of the starting tree: that is, reorder them such that they meet the criteria of a heap. You can heapify the tree in $O(n)$ time, while just the array sort is at least $O(n \log(n))$. But, as is often the case, this problem includes an arbitrary restriction to force you to demonstrate certain skills — here, it's the ability to transform between tree and array data structures.

Your first task is to convert the tree into an array. You need to visit each node to insert its associated value into your array. You can accomplish this with a tree traversal. One wrinkle (assuming you're working with static arrays) is that you have to allocate the array before you can put anything in it, but you don't know how many values there are in the tree before you traverse it, so you don't know how big to make the array. This is solved by traversing the tree twice: once to count the nodes and a second time to insert the values in the array. After the array has been filled, a simple call to the sorting routine yields a sorted array. The major challenge of this problem is to construct the heap from the sorted array.

The essential property of a heap is the relationship between the value of each node and the values of its children: less than or equal to the children for a min-heap and greater than or equal for a max-heap. The problem doesn't specify a min-heap or max-heap; we'll arbitrarily choose to construct a min-heap. Because each value in the sorted array is less than or equal to all the values that follow it, you need to construct a tree where the children of each node come from further down the array (closer to the end) than their parent.

If you made each node the parent of the node to the right of it in the array, you would satisfy the heap property, but your tree would be completely unbalanced. (It would effectively be a linked list.) You need a better way to select children for each node that leaves you with a balanced tree. If you don't immediately see a way to do this, you might try working in reverse: Draw a balanced binary tree, and then put the nodes into a linear ordering (as in an array) such that parents always come before children. If you can reverse this process, you'll have the procedure you're looking for.

One simple way to linearly arrange the nodes while keeping parents ahead of children is by level: first the root (the first level of the tree), then both of its children (the second level), then all *their* children (the third level), and so on. This is the same order in which you would encounter the nodes in a breadth-first traversal. Think about how you can use the relationship you've established between this array and the balanced tree that it came from.

The key to constructing the balanced heap from the array is identifying the location of a node's children relative to the node itself. If you arrange the nodes of a binary tree in an array by level, the root node (at index 0) has children at indexes 1 and 2. The node at index 1 has children at 3 and 4, and the node at 2 has children at 5 and 6. Expand this as far as you need to identify the pattern: It looks like each node's children have indexes just past two times the parent's index. Specifically, the children of the node at index i are located at $2i + 1$ and $2i + 2$. Verify that this works with an example you can draw out, and then consider whether this makes sense. In a complete binary tree, there are 2^n nodes at each level of the tree, where n is the level. Therefore, each level has one more node than the sum of the nodes in all the preceding levels. So, it makes sense that the indexes of the children of the first node in a level would be $2i + 1$ and $2i + 2$. As you move further along the level, since there are two children for each parent, the index of the child must increase by two for every increase in the index of the parent, so the formula you've derived continues to make sense.

At this point, it's worth stopping to consider where you are with this solution. You've ordered the elements in an array such that they satisfy the heap property. (Beyond just satisfying the heap property, they are fully ordered because you were required to perform a full sort: This additional degree of ordering is why this step was $O(n \log(n))$ instead of just the $O(n)$ that it would have been to merely satisfy the heap property.) You've also determined how to find the children of each node (and by extension, the parent of each node) within this array without needing the overhead of explicit references or pointers between them. Although a binary heap is conceptually a tree data structure, there's no reason why you can't represent it using an array. In fact, arrays using implicit links based on position are the most common underlying data representation used for binary heaps. They are more compact than explicit trees, and the operations used to maintain ordering within the heap involve exchanging the locations of parents and children, which is easily accomplished with an array representation.

Although the array representation of your heap is probably a more useful data structure, this problem explicitly requires that you unpack your array into a tree data structure. Now that you know how to calculate the position of the children of each node, that's a fairly trivial process.

Because you're both starting and ending with a binary tree data structure, you can take a shortcut in implementation by creating an array of node objects and sorting that, rather than extracting the integer from each node into an array. Then you can simply adjust the child references on these nodes instead of having to build the tree from scratch. A Java implementation looks like:

```java
public static Node heapifyBinaryTree( Node root ){

    int size = traverse( root, 0, null ); // Count nodes
    Node[] nodeArray = new Node[size];
    traverse( root, 0, nodeArray );        // Load nodes into array

    // Sort array of nodes based on their values, using Comparator object
    Arrays.sort( nodeArray, new Comparator<Node>(){
            @Override public int compare(Node m, Node n){
                int mv = m.getValue(), nv = n.getValue();
                return ( mv < nv ? -1 : ( mv == nv ? 0 : 1));
            }
        });

    // Reassign children for each node
    for( int i = 0; i < size; i++ ){
        int left = 2*i + 1;
```

```
            int right = left + 1;
            nodeArray[i].setLeft( left >= size ? null : nodeArray[left] );
            nodeArray[i].setRight( right >= size ? null : nodeArray[right] );
        }
        return nodeArray[0]; // Return new root node
    }

    public static int traverse( Node node, int count, Node[] arr ){
        if( node == null )
            return count;
        if( arr != null )
            arr[count] = node;
        count++;
        count = traverse( node.getLeft(), count, arr );
        count = traverse( node.getRight(), count, arr );
        return count;
    }
```

Unbalanced Binary Search Tree

> **PROBLEM** *Given an unbalanced binary search tree with more nodes in the left subtree than the right, reorganize the tree to improve its balance while maintaining the properties of a binary search tree*

This would be a trivial problem with a binary tree, but the requirement to maintain the ordering of a BST makes it more complex. If you start by thinking of a large BST and all the possible ways it could be arranged, it's easy to get overwhelmed by the problem. Instead, it may be helpful to start by drawing a simple example of an unbalanced binary search tree, such as the one in Figure 5-8.

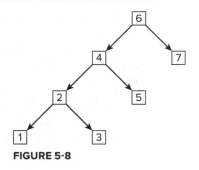

What are your options for rearranging this tree? Since there are too many nodes on the left and not enough on the right, you need to move some nodes from the left subtree of the root to the right subtree. For the tree to remain a BST, all of the nodes in the left

FIGURE 5-8

subtree of the root must be less than or equal to the root, and all the nodes in the right subtree greater than or equal to the root. There's only one node (7) that is greater than the root, so you won't be able to move any nodes to the right subtree if 6 remains the root. Clearly, a different node will have to become the root in the rearranged BST.

In a balanced BST, half of the nodes are less than or equal to the root and half are greater or equal. This suggests that 4 would be a good choice for the new root. Try drawing a BST with the same set of nodes, but with 4 as the root, as seen in Figure 5-9. Much better! For this example, the tree ends up perfectly balanced. Now look at how you need to change the child links on the first tree to get to the second one.

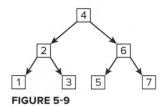

FIGURE 5-9

The new root is 4 and 6 becomes its right child, so you need to set the right child of the new root to be the original root. You've changed the right child of the new root, so you need to reattach its original right child (5) to the tree. Based on the second diagram, it becomes the left child of the old root. Comparing the previous two figures, the left subtree of 4 and the right subtree of 6 remain unchanged, so these two modifications, illustrated in Figure 5-10, are all you need to do.

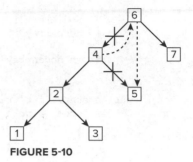

FIGURE 5-10

Will this approach work for larger, more complex trees, or is it limited to this simple example? There are two cases to consider: first where the "root" in this example is actually a child of a larger tree and second where the "leaves" in this example are actually parents and have additional nodes beneath them.

In the first case, the larger tree was a BST to begin with, so we won't violate the BST properties of the larger tree by rearranging the nodes in a subtree — just remember to update the parent node with the new root of the subtree.

In the second case, consider the properties of the subtrees rooted at the two nodes that get new parents. We must make sure that the properties of a BST won't be violated. The new root was the old root's left child, so the new root and all of its original children are less than or equal to the old root. Therefore there's no problem with one of the new root's child subtrees becoming the left subtree of the old root. Conversely, the old root and its right subtree are all greater than or equal to the new root, so there's no problem with these nodes being in the right subtree of the new root.

Since there's no case in which the properties of a BST will be violated by the transformation you've devised, this algorithm can be applied to any BST. Moreover, it can be applied to any subtree within a BST. You can imagine that a badly unbalanced tree could be balanced by applying this procedure repeatedly; a tree unbalanced to the right could be improved by applying the procedure with the sides reversed.

At some point during this problem, you may recognize that the algorithm you're deriving is a *tree rotation* (specifically, a *right rotation*). Tree rotations are the basic operations of many self-balancing trees, including AVL trees and red-black trees.

Right rotation can be implemented as:

```
public static Node rotateRight( Node oldRoot ){
    Node newRoot = oldRoot.getLeft();
    oldRoot.setLeft( newRoot.getRight() );
    newRoot.setRight( oldRoot );
    return newRoot;
}
```

An equivalent implementation as a non-static method of the Node class is better object-oriented design:

```
public Node rotateRight() {
    Node newRoot = left;
    left = newRoot.right;
    newRoot.right = this;
    return newRoot;
}
```

`rotateRight` performs a fixed number of operations regardless of the size of the tree, so its run time is O(1).

Six Degrees of Kevin Bacon

> **PROBLEM** *The game "Six Degrees of Kevin Bacon" involves trying to find the shortest connection between an arbitrarily selected actor and Kevin Bacon. Two actors are linked if they appeared in the same movie. The goal of the game is to connect the given actor to Kevin Bacon using the fewest possible links.*
>
> *Given a list of all major movies in history and their casts (assume that the names of movies and actors are unique identifiers), describe a data structure that could be constructed to efficiently solve Kevin Bacon problems. Write a routine that uses your data structure to determine the Bacon number (the minimum number of links needed to connect to Kevin Bacon) for any actor.*

The data structure you need to devise seems to involve nodes (actors) and links (movies), but it's a little more complicated than the tree structures you've been working with up to this point. For one thing, each node may be linked to an arbitrarily large number of other nodes. There's no restriction on which nodes may have links to each other, so it's expected that some sets of links will form cycles (circular connections). Finally, there's no hierarchical relationship between the nodes on either side of a link. (At least in your data structure; how the politics play out in Hollywood is a different matter.) These requirements point toward using a very general data structure: an undirected graph.

Your graph needs a node for each actor. Representing movies is trickier: Each movie has a cast of many actors. You might consider also creating nodes for each movie, but this makes the data structure considerably more complicated: There would be two classes of nodes, with edges allowed only between nodes of different classes. Because you only care about movies for their ability to link two actors, you can represent the movies with edges. An edge connects only two nodes, so each single movie will be represented by enough edges to connect all pairs of actor nodes in the cast. This has the disadvantage of substantially increasing the total number of edges in the graph and making it difficult to extract information about movies from the graph, but it simplifies the graph and the algorithms that operate on it.

One logical approach is to use an object to represent each node. Again, because you only care about movies for establishing links, if two actors have appeared in more than one movie together, you need to maintain only a single edge between them. Edges are often implemented using references (or pointers), which are inherently unidirectional: There's generally no way for an object to determine what is referencing it. The simplest way to implement the undirected edges you need here is to have each node object reference the other. An implementation of the node class in Java might look like:

```java
public class ActorGraphNode{
    private String name;
    private Set<ActorGraphNode> linkedActors;
    public ActorGraphNode( String name ){
        this.name = name;
        linkedActors = new HashSet<ActorGraphNode>();
    }
```

```
public void linkCostar( ActorGraphNode costar ){
    linkedActors.add( costar );
    costar.linkedActors.add( this );
}
}
```

The use of a Set to hold the references to other nodes allows for an unlimited number of edges and prevents duplicates. The graph is constructed by creating an ActorGraphNode object for each actor and calling linkCostar for each pair of actors in each movie.

Using a graph constructed from these objects, the process to determine the Bacon number for any actor is reduced to finding the length of the shortest path between the given node and the "Kevin Bacon" node. Finding this path involves searching across the graph. Consider how you might do this.

Depth-first searches have simple recursive implementations — would that approach work here? In a depth-first search, you repeatedly follow the first edge of each node you encounter until you can go no further, then backtrack until you find a node with an untraversed second edge, follow that path as far as you can, and so on. One challenge you face immediately is that unlike in a tree, where every path eventually terminates in a leaf node, forming an obvious base case for recursion, in a graph there may be cycles, so you need to be careful to avoid endless recursion. (In this graph, where edges are implemented with pairs of references, each edge effectively forms a cycle between the two nodes it connects, so there are a large number of cycles.)

How can you avoid endlessly circling through cycles? If a node has already been visited, you shouldn't visit it again. One way to keep track of whether a node has been visited is to change a variable on the node object to mark it as visited; another is to use a separate data structure to track all the nodes that have been visited. Then the recursive base case is a node with no adjacent (directly connected by an edge) unvisited nodes. This provides a means to search through all the (connected) nodes of the graph, but does it help solve the problem?

It's not difficult to track the number of edges traversed from the starting node — this is just the recursion level. When you find the target node (the node for the actor whose Bacon number you're determining), your current recursion level gives you the number of edges traversed along the path you traveled to this node. But you need the number of edges (links) along the *shortest* path, not just any path. Will this approach find the shortest path? Depth-first search goes as far into the network as possible before backtracking. This means that if you have a network where a node could be reached by either a longer path passing through the starting node's first edge, or a shorter path passing through the second edge, you will encounter it by the longer path rather than the shorter. So there are at least some cases where this approach will fail to find the shortest path; in fact, if you try a few more examples, you'll find that in most cases the path you traverse is not the shortest. You might consider trying to fix this by revisiting previously visited nodes if you encounter them by a shorter path, but this seems overly complicated. Put this idea on hold and see if you can come up with a better algorithm.

Ideally, you want a search algorithm that encounters each node along the shortest path from the starting node. If you extend your search outward from the starting node in all directions, extending each search path one edge at a time, then each time you encounter a node, it will be via the shortest path to that node. This is a description of a breadth-first search. You can prove that this search will always find nodes along the shortest path: When you encounter an unvisited node while you are searching at n edges from the start node, all the nodes that are $n - 1$ or fewer edges from the start have already been visited, so the shortest path to this node must involve n edges. (If you're thinking that this seems simpler than what you remember for the algorithm for finding the shortest path between two nodes in a graph, you may be thinking of Dijkstra's algorithm. *Dijkstra's algorithm*, which is somewhat more complex, finds the shortest path when each edge is assigned a weight, or length, so the shortest path is not necessarily the path with the fewest edges. Breadth-first search is sufficient for finding the shortest path when the edges have no [or equal] weights, such as in this problem.)

You may remember how to implement a breadth-first search for a graph, but we'll assume you don't and work through the details of the implementation. Just as with the depth-first search, you have to make sure you don't follow cycles endlessly. You can use the same strategy you developed for the depth-first search to address this problem.

Your search starts by visiting each of the nodes adjacent to the starting node. You need to visit all the unvisited nodes adjacent to each of these nodes as well, but not until after you visit all the nodes adjacent to the start node. You need some kind of data structure to keep track of unvisited nodes as you discover them so that you can come back to them when it is their turn. Each unvisited node that you discover should be visited, but only after you've already visited all the previously discovered unvisited nodes. A queue is a data structure that organizes tasks to be completed in the order that they're discovered or added: You can add unvisited nodes to the end of the queue as you discover them and remove them from the front of the queue when you're ready to visit them.

A recursive implementation is natural for a depth-first search where you want to immediately visit each unvisited node as soon as you discover it and then return to where you left off, but an iterative approach is simpler here because the nodes you need to visit are queued. Prepare the queue by adding the start node. On each iterative cycle, remove a node from the front of the queue, and add each unvisited adjacent node to the end of the queue. You're done when you find your target node or the queue is empty (meaning you've searched all the graph reachable from the start node).

The final remaining piece of the puzzle is determining the length of the path after you find the target node. You could try to determine what the path that you followed was and measure its length, but with this algorithm there's no easy way to identify that path. One way around this is to constantly keep track of how many edges you are away from the start; that way when you find the target, you know the length of the path. The easiest way to do this is to mark each node with its Bacon number as you discover it. The Bacon number of a newly discovered unvisited node is the Bacon number of the current node plus one. This also provides a convenient means for distinguishing visited from unvisited nodes: If you initialize each node with an invalid Bacon number (for example, –1), then any node with a non-negative Bacon number has been visited and any node with a Bacon number of –1 has not.

In pseudo-code, your current algorithm is:

```
Create a queue and initialize it with the start node
While the queue is not empty
    Remove the first node from the queue
    If it is the target node, return its Bacon number
    For each node adjacent to the current node
```

```
            If the node is unvisited (Bacon number is -1)
                Set the Bacon number to current node's Bacon number + 1
                Add the adjacent node to the end of the queue
    Return failure because the loop terminated without finding the target
```

Before you code this, consider whether you can optimize it for the likely case where you need to determine the Bacon number for several actors. The search is the same each time you run it; the only difference is the target node at which you terminate. So you're recomputing the Bacon numbers for many of the actors each time you run the search, even though these numbers never change. What if instead of terminating the search at a target node, you use this routine once to do a breadth-first traversal of the entire graph (or at least the entire graph reachable from Kevin Bacon) to precompute the Bacon numbers for all of the actors? Then finding the Bacon number for an individual actor is reduced to returning a single precomputed value. Adding to the preceding class definition for `ActorGraphNode`, the code for this is:

```java
private int baconNumber = -1;

public int getBaconNumber() { return baconNumber; }

// To be called only on the Kevin Bacon node
public void setBaconNumbers(){
    baconNumber = 0;
    Queue<ActorGraphNode> queue = new LinkedList<ActorGraphNode>();
    queue.add( this );
    ActorGraphNode current;
    while( (current = queue.poll()) != null ){
        for( ActorGraphNode n : current.linkedActors ){
            if( -1 == n.baconNumber ){  //if node is unvisited
                n.baconNumber = current.baconNumber + 1;
                queue.add( n );
            }
        }
    }
}
```

What's the run time of this algorithm? The function to compute the Bacon numbers evaluates every (reachable) node once and every edge twice, so in a graph with m nodes and n edges, it is $O(m + n)$. In this graph, you would expect that $n \gg m$, so this reduces to $O(n)$. This is the same run time you would have to determine the Bacon number for an individual actor if you did not precompute them. With precomputation, the Bacon number for an individual actor is just a single look up, which is $O(1)$. Of course, this assumes that you have a reference to the relevant actor node. If all you have is the actor's name, a graph traversal to find the node would be $O(m + n)$, so to maintain $O(1)$ performance you need a constant time means of finding the node representing that actor, such as a hash table mapping names to nodes.

For additional practice with graphs, try extending this algorithm to print out the names of the actors forming the connection between the target actor and Kevin Bacon. Alternatively, write a method that adds edges to an existing graph when a new movie is released, and efficiently updates only the Bacon numbers that have changed.

SUMMARY

Trees and graphs are common data structures, and trees are common in interview questions. Both data structures consist of nodes that reference other nodes in the structure. A tree is a special case of a graph where each node (except the root) has exactly one parent and there are no cycles.

Three important kinds of trees are binary trees, binary search trees, and heaps. A binary tree has two children, called *left* and *right*. A binary search tree is an ordered binary tree where all the nodes to the left of a node have values less than or equal to the node's own value and all nodes to the right of a node have values greater than or equal to the node's value. A heap is a tree in which each node is less than or equal to its children (in a min-heap) or greater than or equal to its children (in a max heap) which means the maximum (max-heap) or minimum (min-heap) value is the root and can be accessed in constant time. Many tree problems can be solved with recursive algorithms.

Both tree and graph problems often involve traversals, which progress through each node of the data structure, or searches, which are traversals that terminate when a target node is found. Two fundamental orderings for these are depth-first and breadth-first. Graphs may have cycles, so when these algorithms are applied to graphs, some mechanism is needed to avoid retraversing parts of the graph that have already been visited.

6

Arrays and Strings

Arrays and strings are closely related. In the abstract sense, a string is just a (possibly read-only) array of characters. Most of the string-manipulation problems you encounter are based on your understanding of array data types, particularly in C where strings and character arrays are essentially identical. Other languages consider strings and character arrays as distinct data types, but there's always a way to convert a string to an array and vice versa. When the two are different, it's important to understand how and why they diverge. In addition, not all array problems involve strings, so understanding how arrays work in the abstract and how they're implemented by the language you use is crucial to answering array-focused problems.

ARRAYS

An *array* is a sequence of variables of the same type arranged contiguously in a block of memory. Because arrays play an important role in every major language used in commercial development, we assume you're at least somewhat familiar with their syntax and usage. With that in mind, this discussion focuses on the theory and application of arrays.

Like a linked list, an array provides an essentially linear form of storage, but its properties are significantly different. (Multidimensional arrays are not exactly linear, but they are implemented as linear arrays of linear arrays.) In a linked list, lookup is always an $O(n)$ operation, but array lookup is $O(1)$ as long as you know the index of the element you want. The provision regarding the index is important — if you know only the value, lookup is still $O(n)$ in the average case. For example, suppose you have an array of characters. Locating the sixth character is $O(1)$, but locating the character with value `'w'` is $O(n)$.

The price for this improved lookup is significantly decreased efficiency for insertion and deletion of data in the middle of the array. Because an array is essentially a block of contiguous memory, it's not possible to create or eliminate storage between any two elements as it is with a linked list. Instead, you must physically *move* data within the array to make room for an insertion or to close the gap left by a deletion; this is an $O(n)$ operation.

Arrays are not dynamic data structures: They have a finite, fixed number of elements. Memory must be allocated for every element in an array, even if only part of the array is used. Arrays are best used when you know how many elements you need to store before the program executes. When the program needs a variable amount of storage, the size of the array imposes an arbitrary limit on the amount of data that can be stored. Making the array large enough so that the program always operates below the limit doesn't solve the problem: Either you waste memory or you won't have enough memory to handle the largest data sizes possible.

Most modern languages also have library support for *dynamic arrays*: arrays that can change size to store as much or as little data as necessary. (Some languages, typically scripting languages, use dynamic arrays as their fundamental array type and have no static array type.) This discussion won't go into the details of implementing a dynamic array, but you should know that most dynamic array implementations use static arrays internally. A *static array* cannot be resized, so dynamic arrays are resized by allocating a new array of the appropriate size, copying every element from the old array into the new array, and freeing the old array. This is an expensive operation that should be done as infrequently as possible.

Each language handles arrays somewhat differently, giving each language a different set of array programming pitfalls.

C and C++

Despite the differences between C and C++, they are similar in their treatment of arrays. In most cases, an array name is equivalent to a pointer constant to the first element of the array. This means that you can't initialize the elements of one array with another array using a simple assignment.

> **NOTE** *Pointers and constants can be confusing concepts separately; they are often nearly incomprehensible in combination. When we say* pointer constant *we mean a pointer declared like* `char *const chrPtr` *that cannot be altered to point at a different place in memory, but that can be used to change the contents of the memory it points at. This is not the same as the more commonly seen* constant pointer, *declared like* `const char *chrPtr`, *which can be changed to point at a different memory location but cannot be used to change the contents of a memory location. If you find this confusing, you're certainly not the only one.*

For example,

```
arrayA = arrayB;  /* Compile error: arrayA is not an lvalue */
```

is interpreted as an attempt to make `arrayA` refer to the same area of memory as `arrayB`. If `arrayA` has been declared as an array, this causes a compile error because you can't change the memory location to which `arrayA` refers. To copy `arrayB` into `arrayA`, you must write a loop that does an element-by-element assignment or use a library function such as `memcpy` that does the copying for you (usually much more efficiently).

In C and C++, the compiler tracks only the location of arrays, not their size. The programmer is responsible for tracking array sizes, and there is no bounds checking on array accesses — the language won't complain if you store something in the 20th element of a 10-element array. As you can imagine, writing outside the bounds of an array usually overwrites some other data structure, leading to all manner of curious and difficult-to-find bugs. Development tools are available to help programmers identify out-of-bounds array accesses and other memory-related problems in their C and C++ programs.

Java

Unlike a C array, a Java array is an object in and of itself, separate from the data type it holds. A reference to an array is therefore not interchangeable with a reference to an element of the array. Java arrays are static, and the language tracks the size of each array, which you can access via the implicit `length` data member. As in C, you cannot copy arrays with a simple assignment: If two array references have the same type, assignment of one to the other is allowed, but it results in both symbols referring to the same array, as shown in the following example:

```
byte[] arrayA = new byte[10];
byte[] arrayB = new byte[10];
arrayA = arrayB; // arrayA now refers to the same array as arrayB
```

If you want to copy the contents of one array to another, you must do it element by element in a loop or call a system function:

```
if( arrayA.length <= arrayB.length ){
    System.arraycopy( arrayA, 0, arrayB, 0, array.length );
}
```

Each access to an array index is checked against the current size of the array, and an exception is thrown if the index is out of bounds. This can make array access a relatively expensive operation when compared to C or C++ arrays; although, in cases in which the JVM can prove that the bounds check is unnecessary, it is skipped to improve performance.

When arrays are allocated, the elements are initialized to their default values. Because the default value for object types is `null` for object types, no objects are constructed when you create an array of objects. You must construct the objects and assign them to the elements of the array

```
Button myButtons[] = new Button[3]; // Buttons not yet constructed
for (int i = 0; i < 3; i++) {
    myButtons[i] = new Button();  // Constructing Buttons
}
// All Buttons constructed
```

or use array initialization syntax (which is allowed only where the array is declared):

```
Button myButtons[] = {new Button(), new Button(), new Button()};
```

C#

C# arrays are similar to Java arrays, but there are some differences. The Java concept of a multi-dimensional array — an array of array objects such as `int [2] [3]` — is called a *jagged array* in C#, and multidimensional arrays are specified using comma-separated arguments, as in `int [2,3]`. Arrays can be declared to be read-only. All arrays also derive from the `System.array` abstract base class, which defines a number of useful methods for array manipulation.

JavaScript

Arrays in JavaScript are instances of the `Array` object. JavaScript arrays are dynamic and resize themselves automatically:

```
Array cities = new Array(); // zero length array
cities[0] = "New York";
cities[1] = "Los Angeles"; // now array is length 2
```

You can change the size of an array simply by modifying its `length` property:

```
cities.length = 1; // drop Los Angeles...
cities[ cities.length ] = "San Francisco"; // new cities[1] value
```

You can use methods on the `Array` object to split, combine, and sort arrays.

STRINGS

Strings are sequences of characters. However, what constitutes a *character* depends greatly on the language used and the settings of the operating system on which the application runs. Gone are the days when you could assume each character in a string is represented by a single byte. Multibyte encodings (either fixed length or variable length) of Unicode are needed to accurately store text in today's global economy.

More recently designed languages, such as Java and C#, have a multibyte fundamental character type, whereas a `char` in C and C++ is always a single byte. (Recent versions of C and C++ also define a character type `wchar_t`, which is usually multibyte.) Even with built-in multibyte character types, properly handling all cases of Unicode can be tricky: There are more than 100,000 *code points* (representation-independent character definitions) defined in Unicode, so they can't all be represented with a single, 2-byte Java or C# `char`. This problem is typically solved using variable length encodings, which use sequences of more than one fundamental character type to represent some code points.

One such encoding is UTF-16, used to encode strings in Java and C#. UTF-16 represents most of the commonly used Unicode code points in a single 16-bit `char` and uses two 16-bit `chars` to represent the remainder. UTF-8, another common encoding, is frequently used for text stored in files or transmitted across networks. UTF-8 uses one to four 8-bit `chars` to encode all Unicode code points and has the advantage that all ASCII codes are represented by a single byte, so ASCII encoded text is a subset of UTF-8 encoded text.

Variable length encodings make string manipulation considerably more complicated: There may be fewer characters in a string than the number of `chars` required to store it, and you must take care to avoid interpreting a part of a multi-`char` encoded code point as a complete character. For simplicity, most programming problems involving strings focus on string manipulation algorithms using the language's natural character type and neglect issues of variable length encoding.

If you have specific expertise in internationalization and localization, string problems give you a great opportunity to highlight this valuable experience. Although your interviewer may tell you to assume that your input string has a fixed-length character encoding such as ASCII, you can explain what you would do differently to handle a variable-length character encoding, even as you code the requested fixed-length encoded solution.

No matter how they're encoded, most languages store strings internally as arrays, even if they differ greatly in how they treat arrays and strings. Many string problems involve operations that require accessing the string as an array. In languages where strings and arrays are distinct types, it may be helpful to convert the string to an array and then back to a string after processing.

C

A C string is contained in a `char` array. Because C doesn't track the size of arrays, it can't track the size of strings either. Instead, the end of the string is marked with a null character, represented in the language as `'\0'`. The null character is sometimes referred to as NUL. (Don't confuse NUL, which is a `char` type with value 0 to NULL, which is a pointer to memory address 0.) The character array must have room for the terminator: A 10-character string requires an 11-character array. This scheme makes finding the length of the string an $O(n)$ operation instead of $O(1)$ as you might expect: `strlen()` (the library function that returns the length of a string) must scan through the string until it finds the end.

For the same reason that you can't assign one C array to another, you cannot copy C strings using the = operator. Instead, you generally use the `strlcpy()` function. (Use of the older `strcpy()` is deprecated in most cases because it's a common source of buffer overrun security holes.)

It is often convenient to read or alter a string by addressing individual characters of the array. If you change the length of a string in this manner, make sure you write a null character after the new last character in the string, and that the character array you work in is large enough to accommodate the new string and terminator. It's easy to truncate a C string (although the array that contains the string remains the same size): Just place a null character immediately after the new end of the string.

Modern C compilers also define a wide character type `wchar_t` and extend the standard library functions to operate on strings represented as `wchar_t` arrays. (C doesn't support overloading, so these functions have similar names to their `char` counterparts, replacing `str` with `wcs`.) One caveat to using `wchar_t` is that its size is implementation-dependent and in unusual cases may even be the same as `char`. This makes C code that uses `wchar_t` even less portable than usual.

C++

C-style strings can be used with C++, but the preferred approach is to use the `string` or `wstring` (when you need multibyte characters) class from the Standard Template Library whenever possible. Both of these classes are specializations of the same `basic_string` template class using the `char` and `wchar_t` data types, respectively.

The string classes are well integrated with the C++ Standard Template Library. You can use them with streams and iterators. In addition, C++ strings are not null-terminated, so they can store null bytes, unlike C strings. Multiple copies of the same string share the same underlying buffer whenever possible, but because a string is mutable (the string can be changed), new buffers are created as necessary. For compatibility with older code, it is possible to derive a C-style string from a C++ string, and vice versa.

Java

Java strings are objects of the String class, a special system class. Although strings can be readily converted to and from character and byte arrays — internally, the class holds the string using a char array — they are a distinct type. Java's char type has a size of two bytes. The individual characters of a string cannot be accessed directly but only through methods on the String class. String literals in program source code are automatically converted into String instances by the Java compiler. As in C++, the underlying array is shared between instances whenever possible. The length of a string can be retrieved via the length() method. Various methods are available to search and return substrings, extract individual characters, trim whitespace characters, and so on.

Java strings are immutable: They cannot be changed after the string has been constructed. Methods that appear to modify a string actually return a new string instance. The StringBuffer and StringBuilder classes (the former is in all versions of Java and is thread-safe; the latter is newer and higher performance, but nonthread-safe) create mutable strings that can be converted to a String instance as necessary. The compiler implicitly uses StringBuffer instances when two String instances are concatenated using the + operator, which is convenient but can lead to inefficient code if you're not careful. For example, the code

```
String s = "";
for( int i = 0; i < 10; ++i ){
    s = s + i + " ";
}
```

is equivalent to

```
String s = "";
for( int i = 0; i < 10; ++i ){
    StringBuffer t = new StringBuffer();
    t.append( s );
    t.append( i );
    t.append( " " );
    s = t.toString();
}
```

which would be more efficiently coded as

```
StringBuffer b = new StringBuffer();
for( int i = 0; i < 10; ++i ){
    b.append( i );
    b.append( ' ' );
}
String s = b.toString();
```

Watch for this case whenever you manipulate strings within a loop.

C#

C# strings are almost identical to Java strings. They are instances of the String class (the alternative form string is an alias), which is similar to Java's String class. C# strings are also immutable just like Java strings. You create mutable strings with the StringBuilder class, and similar caveats apply when strings are concatenated.

JavaScript

Although JavaScript defines a `String` object, many developers are unaware of its existence due to JavaScript's implicit typing. However, the usual string operations are there, as well as more advanced capabilities, such as using regular expressions for string matching and replacement.

ARRAY AND STRING PROBLEMS

Many array and string problems require the use of additional temporary data structures to achieve the most efficient solution. In some cases, in languages where strings are objects, it may be more efficient to convert the string to an array than to process it directly as a string.

Find the First Nonrepeated Character

> **PROBLEM** *Write an efficient function to find the first nonrepeated character in a string. For instance, the first nonrepeated character in* "total" *is* 'o' *and the first nonrepeated character in* "teeter" *is* 'r'. *Discuss the efficiency of your algorithm.*

At first, this task seems almost trivial. If a character is repeated, it must appear in at least two places in the string. Therefore, you can determine whether a particular character is repeated by comparing it with all other characters in the string. It's a simple matter to perform this search for each character in the string, starting with the first. When you find a character that has no match elsewhere in the string, you've found the first nonrepeated character.

What's the time order of this solution? If the string is n characters long, then in the worst case, you'll make almost n comparisons for each of the n characters. That gives worst case $O(n^2)$ for this algorithm. [You can improve this algorithm somewhat by comparing each character with only the characters following it, because it has already been compared with the characters preceding it. This is still $O(n^2)$.] You are unlikely to encounter the worst case for single-word strings, but for longer strings, such as a paragraph of text, it's likely that most characters will repeat, and the most common case might be close to the worst case. The ease with which you arrived at this solution suggests that there are better alternatives — if the answer were truly this trivial, the interviewer wouldn't bother you with the problem. There must be an algorithm with a worst case better than $O(n^2)$.

Why was the previous algorithm $O(n^2)$? One factor of n came from checking each character in the string to determine whether it was nonrepeated. Because the nonrepeated character could be anywhere in the string, it seems unlikely that you can improve efficiency here. The other factor of n was due to searching the entire string when trying to look up matches for each character. If you improve the efficiency of this search, you improve the efficiency of the overall algorithm. The easiest way to improve search efficiency on a set of data is to put it in a data structure that allows more efficient searching. What data structures can be searched more efficiently than $O(n)$? Binary trees can be searched in $O(\log(n))$. Arrays and hash tables both have constant time element lookup. [Hash tables have worst-case lookup of $O(n)$ but the average case is $O(1)$.] Begin by trying to take advantage of an array or hash table because these data structures offer the greatest potential for improvement.

You want to quickly determine whether a character is repeated, so you need to be able to search the data structure by character. This means you must use the character as the index (in an array) or key (in a hash table). (You can convert a character to an integer to use it as an index.) What values would you store in these data structures? A nonrepeated character appears only once in the string, so if you store the number of times each character appears, it would help you identify nonrepeating characters. You must scan the entire string before you have the final counts for each character.

When you complete this, you could scan through all the count values in the array or hash table looking for a 1. That would find a nonrepeated character, but it wouldn't necessarily be the first one in the original string.

Therefore, you need to search your count values in the order of the characters in the original string. This isn't difficult — you just look up the count value for each character until you find a 1. When you find a 1, you've located the first nonrepeated character.

Consider whether this new algorithm is actually an improvement. You always have to go through the entire string to build the count data structure. In the worst case, you might have to look up the count value for each character in the string to find the first nonrepeated character. Because the operations on the array or hash you use to hold the counts are constant time, the worst case would be two operations for each character in the string, giving $2n$, which is $O(n)$ — a major improvement over the previous attempt.

Both hash tables and arrays provide constant-time lookup; you need to decide which one to use. On the one hand, hash tables have a higher lookup overhead than arrays. On the other hand, an array would initially contain random values that you would have to take time to set to zero, whereas a hash table initially has no values. Perhaps the greatest difference is in memory requirements. An array would need an element for every possible value of a character. This would amount to a relatively reasonable 128 elements if you process ASCII strings, but if you have to process strings that could potentially contain any Unicode character, you would need more than 100,000 elements. In contrast, a hash table would require storage for only the characters that actually exist in the input string. Therefore, arrays are a better choice for long strings with a limited set of possible character values; hash tables are more efficient for shorter strings or when there are many possible character values.

You could implement the solution either way. We'll assume the code may need to process Unicode strings (a safe bet these days) and choose the hash table implementation. In outline form, the function you write looks like this:

```
First, build the character count hash table:
    For each character
        If no value is stored for the character, store 1
        Otherwise, increment the value
Second, scan the string:
    For each character
        Return character if count in hash table is 1
    If no characters have count 1, return null
```

Now implement the function. You might choose to write the function in Java or C#, both of which have built-in support for both hash tables and Unicode. Because you don't know what class your function would be part of, implement it as a `public static` function:

```java
public static Character firstNonRepeated( String str ){
    HashMap<Character,Integer> charHash =
                new HashMap<Character,Integer>();
```

```
        int i, length;
        Character c;

        length = str.length();
        // Scan str, building hash table
        for (i = 0; i < length; i++) {
            c = str.charAt(i);
            if (charHash.containsKey(c)) {
                // Increment count corresponding to c
                charHash.put(c, charHash.get(c) + 1);
            } else {
                charHash.put(c, 1);
            }
        }
        // Search hash table in order of str
        for (i = 0; i < length; i++) {
            c = str.charAt(i);
            if (charHash.get(c) == 1)
                return c;
        }
        return null;
    }
```

The preceding implementation would probably be sufficient in most interview situations, but it has at least two major flaws. The first is that it assumes that every Unicode character can be represented in a single 16-bit Java char. With the UTF-16 encoding that Java uses internally for strings, only about the first 2^{16} Unicode characters or code points (the Basic Multilingual Plane or BMP) can be represented in a single char; the remaining code points require two chars. Because the preceding implementation iterates through the string one char at a time, it won't interpret anything outside the BMP correctly.

In addition, there's room to improve performance. Although autoboxing makes it less obvious, recall that Java Collections classes work only on reference types. That means that every time you increment the value associated with a key, the Integer object that held the value is thrown away, and a new Integer with the incremented value is constructed. Is there a way you could avoid having to construct so many Integers? Consider what information you actually need about the number of times a character appears in the string. There are only three relevant quantities: You need to know whether it occurs *zero* times, *one* time, or *more than one* time. Instead of storing integers in the hash table, why not just construct two Object values for use as your "one time" and "more than one time" flags (with not present in the hash table meaning "zero times") and store those in the hash table. Here's a reimplementation that addresses these problems:

```
    public static String firstNonRepeated( String str ){
        HashMap<Integer,Object> charHash = new HashMap<Integer,Object>();
        Object seenOnce = new Object(), seenMultiple = new Object();
        Object seen;
        int i;
        final int length = str.length();
        // Scan str, building hash table
        for (i = 0; i < length; ) { //increment intentionally omitted
            final int cp = str.codePointAt(i);
            i += Character.charCount(cp); //increment based on code point
            seen = charHash.get(cp);
            if (seen == null) {  // not present
                charHash.put(cp, seenOnce);
```

```
            } else {
                if (seen == seenOnce) {
                    charHash.put(cp, seenMultiple);
                }
            }
        }
        // Search hash table in order of str
        for (i = 0; i < length; ) {
            final int cp = str.codePointAt(i);
            i += Character.charCount(cp);
            if (charHash.get(cp) == seenOnce) {
                return new String(Character.toChars(cp));
            }
        }
        return null;
    }
```

As this implementation demonstrates, handling Unicode code points encoded as two `chars` requires several changes. The Unicode code points are represented as 32-bit `ints` because they can't always fit in a `char`. Because a code point may take one or two `chars` in the string, you must check the number of `chars` in each code point and advance the string index by this quantity to find the next code point. Finally, the first nonrepeated character could be one that can't be represented in a single `char`, so the function now returns a `String`.

Remove Specified Characters

PROBLEM *Write an efficient function that deletes characters from an ASCII string. Use the prototype*

```
string removeChars( string str, string remove );
```

where any character existing in remove *must be deleted from* str. *For example, given a* str *of* "Battle of the Vowels: Hawaii vs. Grozny" *and a* remove *of* "aeiou", *the function should transform* str *to* "Bttl f th Vwls: Hw vs. Grzny". *Justify any design decisions you make, and discuss the efficiency of your solution.*

This problem breaks down into two separate tasks. For each character in `str`, you must determine whether it should be deleted. Then, if appropriate, you must delete the character. The second task, deletion, is discussed first.

Your initial task is to delete a character from a string, which is algorithmically equivalent to removing an element from an array. An array is a contiguous block of memory, so you can't simply remove an element from the middle as you might with a linked list. Instead, you must rearrange the data in the array so that it remains a contiguous sequence of characters after the deletion. For example, if you want to delete "c" from the string "abcd" you could either shift "a" and "b" forward one position (toward the end) or shift "d" back one position (toward the beginning). Either approach leaves you with the characters "abd" in contiguous elements of the array.

In addition to shifting the data, you need to decrease the size of the string by one character. If you shift characters before the deletion forward, you need to eliminate the first element; if you shift the characters after the deletion backward, you need to eliminate the last element. In most languages, it's easier to shorten strings at the end (by either decrementing the string length or writing a NUL character, depending on the language) than at the beginning, so shifting characters backward is probably the best choice.

How would the proposed algorithm fare in the worst-case scenario in which you need to delete all the characters in str? For each deletion, you would shift all the remaining characters back one position. If str were n characters long, you would move the last character $n - 1$ times, the next to last $n - 2$ times, and so on, giving worst-case $O(n^2)$ for the deletion. [If you start at the end of the string and work back toward the beginning, it's somewhat more efficient but still $O(n^2)$ in the worst case.] Moving the same characters many times seems extremely inefficient. How might you avoid this?

What if you allocated a temporary string buffer and built your modified string there instead of in place? Then you could simply copy the characters you need to keep into the temporary string, skipping the characters you want to delete. When you finish building the modified string, you can copy it from the temporary buffer back into str. This way, you move each character at most twice, yielding $O(n)$ deletion. However, you've incurred the memory overhead of a temporary buffer the same size as the original string, and the time overhead of copying the modified string back over the original string. Is there any way you can avoid these penalties while retaining your $O(n)$ algorithm?

To implement the $O(n)$ algorithm just described, you need to track a source position for the read location in the original string and a destination position for the write position in the temporary buffer. These positions both start at zero. The source position is incremented every time you read, and the destination position is incremented every time you write. In other words, when you copy a character, you increment both positions, but when you delete a character, you increment only the source position. This means the source position is always the same as or ahead of the destination position. After you read a character from the original string (that is, the source position has advanced past it), you no longer need that character — because you're just going to copy the modified string over it. Because the destination position in the original string is always a character you don't need anymore, you can write directly into the original string, eliminating the temporary buffer entirely. This is still an $O(n)$ algorithm but without the memory and time overhead of the earlier version.

Now that you know how to delete characters, consider the task of deciding whether to delete a particular character. The easiest way to do this is to compare the character to each character in remove and delete it if it matches any of them. How efficient is this? If str is n characters long and remove is m characters long, then in the worst case you make m comparisons for each of n characters, so the algorithm is $O(nm)$. You can't avoid checking each of the n characters in str, but perhaps you can make the lookup that determines whether a given character is in remove better than $O(m)$.

If you've already read the solution to "Find the First Nonrepeated Character," this should sound familiar. Just as you did in that problem, you can use remove to build an array or hash table that has constant time lookup, thus giving an $O(n)$ solution. The trade-offs between hash tables and arrays are the same as previously discussed. In this case, an array is most appropriate when str and remove are long and characters have relatively few possible values (for example, ASCII strings). A hash table may be a better choice when str and remove are short or characters have many possible values (for example, Unicode strings). Either choice could be acceptable as long as you justify it appropriately. This time, you're told that the inputs are ASCII strings, so the array wouldn't be too big; because the previous implementation used a hash table, try using an array for this one.

> **NOTE** *Why build an array? Can't you convert* remove *directly to an array? Yes, you can, but it would be an array of characters indexed by an arbitrary (that is, meaningless for this problem) position, requiring you to search through each element. The array referred to here would be an array of* boolean *values indexed by all the possible values for a* char. *This enables you to determine whether a character is in* remove *by checking a single element.*

Your function has three parts:

1. Set all the elements in your lookup array to `false`.

2. Iterate through each character in `remove`, setting the corresponding value in the lookup array to `true`.

3. Iterate through `str` with a source and destination index, copying each character only if its corresponding value in the lookup array is `false`.

Now that you've combined both subtasks into a single algorithm, analyze the overall efficiency for `str` of length n and `remove` of length m. Because the number of characters in the ASCII character set is fixed, zeroing the array is constant time. You perform a constant time assignment for each character in `remove`, so building the lookup array is $O(m)$. Finally, you do at most one constant time lookup and one constant time copy for each character in `str`, giving $O(n)$ for this stage. Summing these parts yields $O(n + m)$, so the algorithm has linear running time.

Having justified and analyzed your solution, you're ready to code it. You can write this function in Java. (The C# implementation would be nearly identical.) Because this problem involves string manipulation and the `String` class is immutable, you need to either convert the string to a `char` array or use a `StringBuilder` for your manipulations. Array access has more compact syntax and typically less overhead than method invocations on a `StringBuilder`, so using an array is probably the better choice.

```java
public static String removeChars( String str, String remove ){
    char[] s = str.toCharArray();
    char[] r = remove.toCharArray();
    int src, dst = 0;

    // flags automatically initialized to false, size of 128 assumes ASCII
    boolean[] flags = new boolean[128];

    // Set flags for characters to be removed
    for( src = 0; src < r.length; ++src ){
        flags[r[src]] = true;
    }

    // Now loop through all the characters,
    // copying only if they aren't flagged
    for( src = 0; src < s.length; ++src ){
        if( !flags[ s[src] ] ){
            s[dst++] = s[src];
        }
    }
    return new String( s, 0, dst );
}
```

Reverse Words

> **PROBLEM** *Write a function that reverses the order of the words in a string. For example, your function should transform the string "Do or do not, there is no try." to "try. no is there not, do or Do". Assume that all words are space delimited and treat punctuation the same as letters.*

You probably already have a good idea how to start this problem. Because you need to operate on words, you must be able to recognize where words start and end. You can do this with a simple token scanner that iterates through each character of the string. Based on the definition given in the problem statement, your scanner can differentiate between *nonword characters* — namely, the space character — and *word characters*, which for this problem are all characters except space. A word begins, not surprisingly, with a word character and ends at the next nonword character or the end of the string.

The most obvious approach is to use your scanner to identify words, write these words into a temporary buffer, and then copy the buffer back over the original string. To reverse the order of the words, you must either scan the string backward to identify the words in reverse order or write the words into the buffer in reverse order (starting at the end of the buffer). It doesn't matter which method you choose; the following discussion identifies the words in reverse order.

As always, consider the mechanics of how this works before you begin coding. First, you need to allocate a temporary buffer of the appropriate size. Next, enter the scanning loop, starting with the last character of the string. When you find a nonword character, you can write it directly to the buffer. When you find a word character, however, you can't write it immediately to the temporary buffer. Because you scan the string in reverse, the first word character you encounter is the last character of the word, so if you were to copy the characters in the order you find them, you'd write the characters within each word backward. Instead, you need to keep scanning until you find the first character of the word and then copy each character of the word in the correct, nonreversed order. (You may think you could avoid this complication by scanning the string forward and writing the words in reverse. However, you then must solve a similar, related problem of calculating the start position of each word when writing to the temporary buffer.) When you copy the characters of a word, you need to identify the end of the word so that you know when to stop. You could do this by checking whether each character is a word character, but because you already know the position of the last character in the word, a better solution is to continue copying until you reach that position.

An example may help to clarify this. Suppose you are given the string `"piglet quantum"`. The first word character you encounter is `'m'`. If you copy the characters as you found them, you end up with the string `"mutnauq telgip"`, which is not nearly as good a name for a techno group as the string you were supposed to produce, `"quantum piglet"`. To get `"quantum piglet"` from `"piglet quantum"` you need to scan until you get to `'q'` and then copy the letters in the word in the forward direction until you get back to `'m'` at position 13. Next, copy the space character immediately because it's a nonword character. Then, just as for `"quantum"`, you would recognize the character `'t'` as a word character, store position 5 as the end of the word, scan backward to `'p'`, and finally write the characters of `"piglet"` until you got to position 5.

After you scan and copy the whole string, copy the buffer back over the original string. Then you can deallocate the temporary buffer and return from the function. This process is illustrated graphically in Figure 6-1.

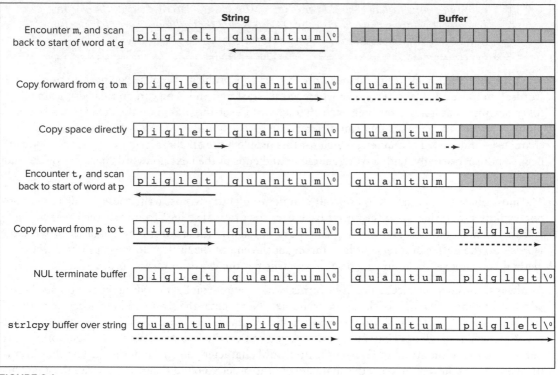

FIGURE 6-1

It's obviously important that your scanner stop when it gets to the first character of the string. Although this sounds simple, it can be easy to forget to check that the read position is still in the string, especially when the read position is changed at more than one place in your code. In this function, you move the read position in the main token scanning loop to get to the next token and in the word scanning loop to get to the next character of the word. Make sure neither loop runs past the beginning of the string.

Just for variety, implement this problem in C, and assume that you're dealing with ASCII characters that can be safely stored in byte arrays.

```c
bool reverseWords( char str[] ){
    char *buffer;
    int slen, tokenReadPos, wordReadPos, wordEnd, writePos = 0;

    slen = strlen(str);
    /* Position of the last character is length - 1 */
    tokenReadPos = slen - 1;
    buffer = (char *) malloc(slen + 1);
```

```
            if( !buffer )
                return false; /* reverseWords failed */
        while( tokenReadPos >= 0 ){
            if( str[tokenReadPos] == ' ' ){ /* Non-word characters */

                /* Write character */
                buffer[writePos++] = str[tokenReadPos--];

            } else {   /* Word characters */

                /* Store position of end of word */
                wordEnd = tokenReadPos;
                /* Scan to next non-word character */
                while( tokenReadPos >= 0 && str[tokenReadPos] != ' ' )
                    tokenReadPos--;
                /* tokenReadPos went past the start of the word */
                wordReadPos = tokenReadPos + 1;
                /* Copy the characters of the word */
                while( wordReadPos <= wordEnd ){
                    buffer[writePos++] = str[wordReadPos++];
                }
            }
        }
        /* null terminate buffer and copy over str */
        buffer[writePos] = '\0';
        strlcpy(str, buffer, slen + 1);
        free(buffer);

        return true; /* ReverseWords successful */
    }
```

The preceding token scanner-based implementation is the general-case solution for this type of problem. It is reasonably efficient, and its functionality could easily be extended. It is important that you are able to implement this type of solution, but the solution is not perfect. All the scanning backward, storing positions, and copying forward is somewhat lacking in algorithmic elegance. The need for a temporary buffer is also less than desirable.

Often, interview problems have obvious general solutions and less-obvious special-case solutions. The special-case solution may be less extensible than a general solution but more efficient or elegant. Reversing the words of a string is such a problem. You have seen the general solution, but a special-case solution also exists. In an interview, you might have been steered away from the general solution before you got to coding it. (The general solution is followed through to code here because token and string scanning are important techniques.)

One way to improve an algorithm is to focus on a particular, concrete deficiency and try to remedy that. Because elegance, or lack thereof, is hard to quantify, you might try to eliminate the need for a temporary buffer from your algorithm. You can probably see that this is going to require a significantly different algorithm. You can't simply alter the preceding approach to write to the same string it reads from — by the time you get halfway through, you will have overwritten the rest of the data you need to read.

Rather than focus on what you can't do without a buffer, you should turn your attention to what you can do. You can reverse an entire string in place by exchanging characters. Try an example to see whether this might be helpful: "in search of algorithmic elegance" would become "ecnagele cimhtiro-gla fo hcraes ni". Look at that! The words are in exactly the order you need them, but the characters in the words are backward. All you have to do is reverse each word in the reversed string. You can do that by locating the beginning and end of each word using a scanner similar to the one used in the preceding implementation and calling a reverse function on each word substring.

Now you just have to design an in-place reverse string function. The only trick is to remember that there's no one-statement method of exchanging two values in C — you have to use a temporary variable and three assignments. Your reverse string function should take a string, a start index, and an end index as arguments. Begin by exchanging the character at the start index with the character at the end index, and then increment the start index and decrement the end index. Continue like this until the start and end index meet in the middle (in a string with odd length) or end is less than start (in a string with even length) — put more succinctly, continue while end is greater than start.

You can continue to implement in C, but to keep things interesting this time, use wide character strings. (Wide character string and character literals are prepended with L to distinguish them from regular byte-sized literals.) These functions look like the following:

```
void wcReverseWords( wchar_t str[] ){
    int start = 0, end = 0, length;
    length = wcslen(str);
    /* Reverse entire string */
    wcReverseString(str, start, length - 1);
    while( end < length ){
        if( str[end] != L' ' ){ /* Skip non-word characters */
            /* Save position of beginning of word */
            start = end;
            /* Scan to next non-word character */
            while( end < length && str[end] != L' ' )
                end++;
            /* Back up to end of word */
            end--;
            /* Reverse word */
            wcReverseString( str, start, end );
        }
        end++; /* Advance to next token */
    }
}

void wcReverseString( wchar_t str[], int start, int end ){
    wchar_t temp;
    while( end > start ){
        /* Exchange characters */
        temp = str[start];
        str[start] = str[end];
        str[end] = temp;
        /* Move indices towards middle */
        start++; end--;
    }
}
```

This solution does not need a temporary buffer and is considerably more elegant than the previous solution. It's also more efficient, mostly because it doesn't suffer from dynamic memory overhead and doesn't need to copy a result back from a temporary buffer.

Integer/String Conversions

> **PROBLEM** *Write two conversion routines. The first routine converts a string to a signed integer. You may assume that the string contains only digits and the minus character ('-'), that it is a properly formatted integer number, and that the number is within the range of an* int *type. The second routine converts a signed integer stored as an* int *back to a string.*

Every language has library routines to do these conversions. For example, in C# the `Convert.ToInt32()` and `Convert.ToString()` methods are available. Java uses the `Integer.parseInt()` and `Integer.toString()` methods. You should mention to the interviewer that under normal circumstances, you know better than to duplicate functionality provided by standard libraries. This doesn't get you off the hook — you still need to implement the functions called for by the problem.

From String to Integer

You can start with the string-to-integer routine, which is passed a valid string representation of an integer. Think about what that gives you to work with. Suppose you were given `"137"`. You would have a three-character string with the character encoding for `'1'` at position 0, `'3'` at position 1, and `'7'` at position 2. Recall from grade school that the 1 represents 100 because it is in the hundred's place, the 3 represents 30 because it is in the ten's place, and the 7 is just 7 because it is in the one's place. Summing these values gives the complete number: 100 + 30 + 7 = 137.

This gives you a framework for dissecting the string representation and building it back into a single integer value. You need to determine the numeric (integer) value of the digit represented by each character, multiply that value by the appropriate place value, and then sum these products.

Consider the character-to-numeric-value conversion first. What do you know about the values of digit characters? In all common character encodings, the values are sequential: `'0'` has a value one less than `'1'`, which in turn is followed by `'2'`, `'3'`, and so on. (Of course, if you didn't know this, you'd have to ask the interviewer.) Therefore, the value of a digit character is equal to the digit plus the value of `'0'`. (The value of `'0'` is the nonzero code number representing the character `'0'`.) This means you subtract the value of `'0'` from a digit character to find the numeric value of the digit. You don't even need to know what the value of `'0'` is; just write `-'0'`, which the compiler interprets as "subtract the value of `'0'`."

Next, you need to know what place value each digit must be multiplied by. Working through the digits left to right seems problematic because you don't know what the place value of the first digit is until you know how long the number is. For example, the first character of `"367"` is identical to that of `"31"`; although it represents 300 in the first case and 30 in the second case. The most obvious solution is to scan the digits from right to left because the rightmost position is always the one's place, the next to rightmost is always the ten's, and so on. This enables you to start at the right end of the string with a place value of 1 and work backward through the string, multiplying the place value by 10 each time you move to a new place. This method, however, requires two multiplications per iteration, one for multiplying the digit by the place value and another for increasing the place value. That seems a little inefficient.

Perhaps the alternative of working through the characters left to right was too hastily dismissed. Is there a way you could get around the problem of not knowing the place value for a digit until you've scanned the whole string? Returning to the example of "367", when you encounter the first character, '3', you register a value of 3. If the next character were the end of the string, the number's value would be 3. However, you encounter '6' as the next character of the string. Now the '3' represents 30 and the 6 represents '6'. On the next iteration, you read the last character, '7', so the '3' represents 300, the '6' represents 60, and the '7' represents 7. In summary, the value of the number you've scanned so far increases by a factor of 10 every time you encounter a new character. It doesn't matter that you don't initially know whether the '3' represents 3, 30, or 30,000 — every time you find a new digit you just multiply the value you've already read by 10 and add the value of the new digit. You're no longer tracking a place value, so this algorithm saves you a multiplication on each iteration. The optimization described in this algorithm is frequently useful in computing checksums and is considered clever enough to merit a name: *Horner's Rule*.

Up to this point, the discussion has touched on only positive numbers. How can you expand your strategy to include negative numbers? A negative number has a '-' character in the first position. You want to skip over the '-' character so that you don't interpret it as a digit. After you scan all the digits and build the number, you need to change the number's sign so that it's negative. You can change the sign with the negation operator: - . You have to check for the '-' character before you scan the digits so that you know whether to skip the first character, but you can't negate the value until after you've scanned the digits. One way around this problem is to set a flag if you find the '-' character and then apply the negation operator only if the flag is set.

In summary, the algorithm is as follows:

```
Start number at 0
If the first character is '-'
    Set the negative flag
    Start scanning with the next character
For each character in the string
    Multiply number by 10
    Add (digit character - '0') to number
If negative flag set
    Negate number
Return number
```

Coding this in Java results in the following:

```java
public static int strToInt( String str ){
    int i = 0, num = 0;
    boolean isNeg = false;
    int len = str.length();

    if( str.charAt(0) == '-' ){
        isNeg = true;
        i = 1;
    }
```

```
        while( i < len ){
            num *= 10;
            num += ( str.charAt(i++) - '0' );
        }
        if( isNeg )
            num = -num;
        return num;
    }
```

Before you declare this function finished, check it for cases that may be problematic. At minimum, you should check –1, 0, and 1, so you've checked a positive value, a negative value, and a value that's neither positive nor negative. You should also check a multidigit value like 324 to ensure that the loop has no problems. The function appears to work properly for these cases, so you can move on to the opposite conversion in intToStr.

From Integer to String

In intToStr, you perform the inverse of the conversion you did in strToInt. Given this, much of what you discovered in writing strToInt should be of use to you here. For example, just as you converted digits to integer values by subtracting '0' from each digit, you can convert integer values back to digits by adding '0' to each digit.

Before you can convert values to characters, you need to know what those values are. Consider how you might do this. Suppose you have the number 732. Looking at this number's decimal representation on paper, it seems a simple matter to identify the digit values 7, 3, and 2. However, you must remember that the computer isn't using a decimal representation, but rather the binary representation 1011011100. Because you can't select decimal digits directly from a binary number, you must calculate the value of each digit. It seems logical to try to find the digit values either left to right or right to left.

Try left to right first. Integer dividing 732 by the place value (100) gives the first digit, 7. However, now if you integer divide by the next place value (10), you get 73, not 3. It looks as if you need to subtract the hundreds value you found before moving on. Starting over with this new process gives you the following:

```
732 ÷ 100 = 7 (first digit); 732 - 7 x 100 = 32
32 ÷ 10 = 3 (second digit); 32 - 3 x 10 = 2
2 ÷ 1 = 2 (third digit)
```

To implement this algorithm, you must find the place value of the first digit and divide the place value by 10 for each new digit. This algorithm seems workable but complicated. What about working right to left?

Starting again with 732, what arithmetic operation can you perform to yield 2, the rightmost digit? Modulo gives the remainder of an integer division. (In languages with C-influenced syntax the modulo operator is %.) 732 modulo 10 gives you 2. Now how can you get the next digit? 732 modulo 100 gives you 32. You could integer divide this by 10 to get the second digit, 3, but now you have to track two separate place values.

What if you did the integer divide before the modulo? Then you'd have 732 integer divide by 10 is 73; 73 modulo 10 is 3. Repeating this for the third digit you have 73 / 10 = 7; 7 % 10 = 7. This seems like an easier solution — you don't even have to track place values; you just divide and modulo until there's nothing left.

The major downside of this approach is that you find the digits in reverse order. Because you don't know how many there will be until you've found them all, you don't know where in the string to begin writing. You could run through the calculations twice — once to find the number of digits so that you know where to start writing them and again to actually write the digits — but this seems wasteful. Perhaps a better solution is to write the digits out backward as you discover them and then reverse them into the proper order when you're done. Because the largest possible value of an integer yields a relatively short string, you could write the digits into a temporary buffer and then reverse them into the final string.

Again, negative numbers have been ignored so far. Unfortunately, the modulo of a negative number is not handled consistently across different languages, so writing code that calculates the modulo of a negative number is likely to be error prone and may confuse others reading your code. One way around this problem is to avoid it entirely. In `strToInt`, you treated the number as if it were positive and then made an adjustment at the end if it were negative. How might you employ this type of strategy here? You could start by negating the number if it were negative. Then it would be positive, so treating it as a positive number wouldn't be a problem. The only wrinkle would be that you'd need to write a `'-'` if the number had originally been negative, but that isn't difficult — just set a flag indicating that the number is negative when you negate it.

You've solved all the important subproblems in `intToStr` — now assemble these solutions into an outline you can use to write your code.

```
If number less than zero:
    Negate the number
    Set negative flag
While number not equal to 0
    Add '0' to number % 10 and write this to temp buffer
    Integer divide number by 10
If negative flag is set
    Write '-' into next position in temp buffer
Write characters in temp buffer into output string in reverse order:
```

Rendering this in Java might give the following:

```java
public static final int MAX_DIGITS = 10;
public static String intToStr( int num ){
    int i = 0;
    boolean isNeg = false;
    /* Buffer big enough for largest int and - sign */
    char[] temp = new char[ MAX_DIGITS + 1 ];
    /* Check to see if the number is negative */
    if( num < 0 ){
        num = -num;
        isNeg = true;
    }

    /* Fill buffer with digit characters in reverse order */
    while( num != 0 ){
        temp[i++] = (char)((num % 10) + '0');
        num /= 10;
```

```
        }
        StringBuilder b = new StringBuilder();
        if( isNeg )
            b.append( '-' );

        while( i > 0 ){
            b.append( temp[--i] );
        }
        return b.toString();
    }
```

Again, check the same potentially problematic cases you tried for strToInt (multidigit, –1, 0, and 1). Multidigit numbers, –1, and 1 cause no problems, but if num is 0 you never go through the body of the while loop. This causes the function to write an empty string instead of "0". How can you fix this bug? You need to go through the body of the while loop at least once so that you write a '0' even if num starts at 0. You can ensure that the body of the loop is executed at least once by changing it from a while loop to a do...while loop. This fix yields the following code, which can handle converting 0 as well as positive and negative values to strings:

```
    public static final int MAX_DIGITS = 10;
    public static String intToStr( int num ){
        int i = 0;
        boolean isNeg = false;
        /* Buffer big enough for largest int and - sign */
        char[] temp = new char[ MAX_DIGITS + 1 ];
        /* Check to see if the number is negative */
        if( num < 0 ){
            num = -num;
            isNeg = true;
        }

        /* Fill buffer with digit characters in reverse order */
        do {
            temp[i++] = (char)((num % 10) + '0');
            num /= 10;
        } while( num != 0 );
        StringBuilder b = new StringBuilder();
        if( isNeg )
            b.append( '-' );

        while( i > 0 ){
            b.append( temp[--i] );
        }
        return b.toString();
    }
```

SUMMARY

Arrays are an essential part of nearly every programming language, so you should expect that they will appear in some of your interview problems. Accessing an array is constant time if you have the index of the element you need, but linear time if you have only the value of the element but not the index. If you insert or delete in the middle of an array, you must move all the elements that follow to open or close the space. Static arrays are created with a fixed size; dynamic arrays grow as needed. Most languages support both types to a greater or lesser extent.

Strings are one of the most common applications of arrays. In C, a string is little more than an array of characters. In object-oriented languages the array is typically hidden within a string object. String objects can be converted to and from character arrays; make sure you know how to do this in the languages you'll be using because the operations required by programming problems are often more convenient with arrays. Basic string objects are immutable (read-only) in C# and Java; other classes provide writeable string functionality. Careless concatenation of immutable strings can lead to inefficient code that creates and throws away many string objects.

Most modern applications support multiple languages using Unicode. There are multiple encodings for representing Unicode, all of which require multiple bytes for at least some characters, and many of which are variable length. (Some characters require more bytes than others.) These encodings can considerably complicate string problems, but most of the time you probably won't need to worry about this for interview problems.

7

Recursion

Recursion is a deceptively simple concept: Any function that calls itself is recursive. Despite this apparent simplicity, understanding and applying recursion can be surprisingly complex. One of the major barriers to understanding recursion is that general descriptions tend to become highly theoretical, abstract, and mathematical. Although there is certainly value in that approach, this chapter instead follows a more pragmatic course, focusing on example, application, and comparison of recursive and iterative (nonrecursive) algorithms.

UNDERSTANDING RECURSION

Recursion is useful for tasks that can be defined in terms of similar subtasks. For example, sort, search, and traversal problems often have simple recursive solutions. A *recursive function* performs a task in part by calling itself to perform the subtasks. At some point, the function encounters a subtask that it can perform without calling itself. This case, in which the function does not recurse, is called the *base case*; the former, in which the function calls itself to perform a subtask, is referred to as the *recursive case*.

> **NOTE** *Recursive algorithms have two cases: recursive cases and base cases.*

These concepts can be illustrated with a simple and commonly used example: the factorial operator. $n!$ (pronounced "n factorial") is the product of all integers between n and 1. For example, $4! = 4 \times 3 \times 2 \times 1 = 24$. $n!$ can be more formally defined as follows:

$$n! = n\,(n-1)!$$

$$0! = 1! = 1$$

This definition leads easily to a recursive implementation of factorial. The task is to determine the value of $n!$, and the subtask is to determine the value of $(n-1)!$. In the recursive case, when n is greater than 1, the function calls itself to determine the value of $(n-1)!$ and multiplies that by *n*. In the base case, when *n* is 0 or 1, the function simply returns 1. Rendered in code, this looks like the following:

```
int factorial( int n ){
    if (n > 1) {       /* Recursive case */
        return factorial(n-1) * n;
    } else {           /* Base case */
        return 1;
    }
}
```

Figure 7-1 illustrates the operation of this function when computing 4!. Notice that n decreases by 1 each time the function recurses. This ensures that the base case will eventually be reached. If a function is written incorrectly such that it does not always reach a base case, it recurses infinitely. In practice, there is usually no such thing as infinite recursion: Eventually a stack overflow occurs and the program crashes — a similarly catastrophic event.

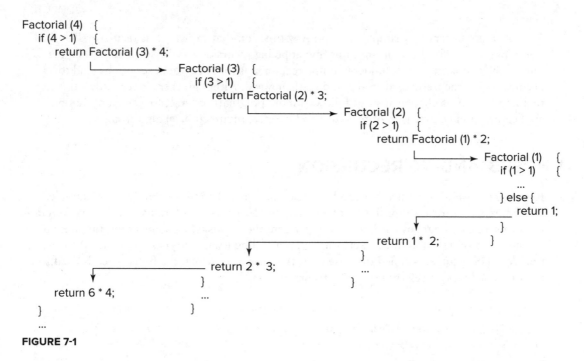

FIGURE 7-1

Note that when the value returned by the recursive call is itself immediately returned, as in the preceding definition for `factorial`, the function is *tail-recursive*. Some compilers can perform *tail call elimination* on tail-recursive functions, an optimization that reuses the same stack frame for each recursive call. An appropriately optimized tail-recursive function could recurse infinitely without overflowing the stack.

> **NOTE** *Every recursive case must eventually lead to a base case.*

This implementation of factorial represents an extremely simple example of a recursive function. In many cases, your recursive functions may need additional data structures or an argument that tracks the recursion level. Often the best solution in such cases is to move the data structure or argument initialization code into a separate function. This wrapper function, which performs initialization and then calls the purely recursive function, provides a clean, simple interface to the rest of the program.

For example, if you need a factorial function that returns all its intermediate results (factorials less than *n*), as well as the final result (*n!*), you most naturally return these results as an integer array, which means the function needs to allocate an array. You also need to know where in the array each result should be written. These tasks are easily accomplished using a wrapper function, as follows:

```
int[] allFactorials( int n ){ /* Wrapper function */
    int[] results = new int[ n == 0 ? 1 : n ];
    doAllFactorials( n, results, 0 );
    return results;
}
int doAllFactorials( int n, int[] results, int level ){
    if( n > 1 ){   /* Recursive case */
        results[level] = n * doAllFactorials( n - 1, results, level + 1 );
        return results[level];
    } else {        /* Base case */
        results[level] = 1;
        return 1;
    }
}
```

You can see that using a wrapper function enables you to hide the array allocation and recursion level tracking to keep the recursive function clean. In this case, you can determine the appropriate array index from n, avoiding the need for the level argument, but in many cases there is no alternative to tracking the recursion level, as shown here.

> **NOTE** *It may be useful to write a separate wrapper function to do initialization for a complex recursive function.*

Although recursion is a powerful technique, it is not always the best approach, and rarely is it the most efficient approach. This is due to the relatively large overhead for function calls on most platforms. For a simple recursive function like factorial, many computer architectures spend more time on call overhead than on the actual calculation. Iterative functions, which use looping constructs instead of recursive function calls, do not suffer from this overhead and are frequently more efficient.

> **NOTE** *Iterative solutions are usually more efficient than recursive solutions.*

Any problem that can be solved recursively can also be solved *iteratively*. Iterative algorithms are often easy to write, even for tasks that might appear to be fundamentally recursive. For example, an iterative implementation of factorial is relatively simple. It may be helpful to reframe the definition of factorial, such that you describe *n*! as the product of every integer between *n* and 1, inclusive. You can use a for loop to iterate through these values and calculate the product:

```
int factorial( int n ){
    int i, val = 1;
    for( i = n; i > 1; i-- )  /* n = 0 or 1 falls through */
        val *= i;
    return val;
}
```

This implementation is significantly more efficient than the previous recursive implementation because it doesn't make any additional function calls. Although it represents a different way of thinking about the problem, it's not any more difficult to write than the recursive implementation.

For some problems, obvious iterative alternatives like the one just shown don't exist, but it's always possible to implement a recursive algorithm without using recursive calls. Recursive calls are generally used to preserve the current values of local variables and restore them when the subtask performed by the recursive call is completed. Because local variables are allocated on the program's stack, each recursive instance of the routine has a separate set of the local variables, so recursive calls implicitly store variable values on the program's stack. You can eliminate the need for recursive calls by allocating your own stack and manually storing and retrieving local variable values from this stack.

Implementing this type of stack-based iterative function tends to be significantly more complicated than implementing an equivalent function using recursive calls. Furthermore, unless the overhead for the stack you use is significantly less than the function call overhead, a function written this way won't be more efficient than a conventional recursive implementation. Therefore you should implement recursive algorithms with recursive calls unless instructed otherwise. An example of a recursive algorithm implemented without recursive calls is given in the solution to the "Preorder Traversal, No Recursion" problem in Chapter 5.

> **NOTE** *A recursive algorithm can be implemented without recursive calls by using a stack, but it's usually more trouble than it's worth.*

In an interview, a working solution is of primary importance; an efficient solution is secondary. Unless you've been told otherwise, go with whatever type of working solution comes to you first. If it's a recursive solution, you might want to mention the inefficiencies inherent in recursive solutions to your interviewer, so it's clear that you know about them. In the rare instance that you see a recursive solution and an iterative solution of roughly equal complexity, you should probably mention them both to the interviewer, indicating that you're going to work out the iterative solution because it's likely to be more efficient.

RECURSION PROBLEMS

Recursive algorithms offer elegant solutions to problems that would be awkward to code nonrecursively. Interviewers like these kinds of problems because many people find recursive thinking difficult.

Binary Search

> **PROBLEM** *Implement a function to perform a binary search on a sorted array of integers to find the index of a given integer. Comment on the efficiency of this search, and compare it with other search methods.*

In a binary search, you compare the central element in your sorted search space (an array, in this case) with the item you're looking for. There are three possibilities. If the central element is less than what you're searching for, you eliminate the first half of the search space. If it's more than the search value, you eliminate the second half of the search space. In the third case, the central element is equal to the search item, and you stop the search. Otherwise, you repeat the process on the remaining portion of the search space. If it's not already familiar to you from computer science courses, this algorithm may remind you of the optimum strategy in the children's number-guessing game in which one child guesses numbers in a given range and a second responds "higher" or "lower" to each incorrect guess.

Because a binary search can be described in terms of binary searches on successively smaller portions of the search space, it lends itself to a recursive implementation. Your method needs to be passed the array it is searching, the limits within which it should search, and the element for which it is searching. You can subtract the lower limit from the upper limit to find the size of the search space, divide this size by two, and add it to the lower limit to find the index of the central element. Next, compare this element to the search element. If they're equal, return the index. Otherwise, if the search element is smaller, the new upper limit becomes the central index – 1; if the search element is larger, the new lower limit is the central index + 1. Recurse until you match the element you're searching for.

Before you code, consider what error conditions you need to handle. One way to think about this is to consider what assumptions you're making about the data you are given and then consider how these assumptions might be violated. One assumption, explicitly stated in the problem, is that only a sorted array can be searched. If the upper limit is ever less than the lower limit, it indicates that the list is unsorted, and you should throw an exception. (Another way to handle this case would be to call a sort routine and then restart the search, but that's more than you need to do in an interview.)

Another assumption implicit in a search may be a little less obvious: The element you're searching for is assumed to exist in the array. If you don't terminate the recursion until you find the element, you'll recurse infinitely when the element is missing from the array. You can avoid this by throwing an exception if the upper and lower limits are equal and the element at that location is not the element you're searching for. Finally, you assume that the lower limit is less than or equal to the upper limit. For simplicity, you can just throw an exception in this case; although in a real program, you'd probably want to define this as an illegal call and use an assertion to check it.

Your recursive function will be easier to use if you write a wrapper that sets the initial values for the limits to the full extent of the array. Now you can translate these algorithms and error checks into Java code:

```java
int binarySearch(int[] array, int target) throws BSException {
    return binarySearch(array, target, 0, array.length-1);
}


int binarySearch( int[] array, int target, int lower,
                  int upper ) throws BSException {
    int center, range;

    range = upper - lower;
    if( range < 0 ){
        throw new BSException("Limits reversed");
    } else if( range == 0 && array[lower] != target ){
        throw new BSException("Element not in array");
    }
    if( array[lower] > array[upper] ){
        throw new BSException("Array not sorted");
    }
    center = ((range)/2) + lower;
    if( target == array[center] ){
        return center;
    } else if( target < array[center] ){
        return binarySearch( array, target, lower, center - 1 );
    } else {
        return binarySearch( array, target, center + 1, upper );
    }
}
```

Although the preceding function completes the given task, it is not as efficient as it could be. As discussed at the beginning of this chapter, recursive implementations are generally less efficient than equivalent iterative implementations.

If you analyze the recursion in the previous solution, you can see that each recursive call serves only to change the search limits. There's no reason why you can't change the limits on each iteration of a loop and avoid the overhead of recursion. (When compiled with tail call elimination, the preceding recursive implementation would likely produce machine code indistinguishable from an iterative implementation.) The method that follows is a more efficient, iterative analog of the recursive binary search:

```java
int iterBinarySearch( int[] array, int target) throws BSException {
    int lower = 0, upper = array.length - 1;
    int center, range;

    if( lower > upper ){
        throw new BSException("Limits reversed");
    }
    while( true ){
        range = upper - lower;
```

```
        if( range == 0 && array[lower] != target ){
            throw new BSException("Element not in array");
        }
        if( array[lower] > array[upper] ){
            throw new BSException("Array not sorted");
        }
        center = ((range)/2) + lower;
        if( target == array[center] ){
            return center;
        } else if( target < array[center] ){
            upper = center - 1;
        } else {
            lower = center + 1;
        }
    }
}
```

A binary search is $O(\log(n))$ because half of the search space is eliminated (in a sense, searched) on each iteration. This is more efficient than a simple search through all the elements, which would be $O(n)$. However, to perform a binary search, the array must be sorted, an operation that is usually $O(n \log(n))$.

Permutations of a String

PROBLEM *Implement a routine that prints all possible orderings of the characters in a string. In other words, print all permutations that use all the characters from the original string. For example, given the string "hat", your function should print the strings "tha", "aht", "tah", "ath", "hta", and "hat". Treat each character in the input string as a distinct character, even if it is repeated. Given the string "aaa", your routine should print "aaa" six times. You may print the permutations in any order you choose.*

Manually permuting a string is a relatively intuitive process, but describing an algorithm for the process can be difficult. In a sense, the problem here is like being asked to describe how you tie your shoes: You know the answer, but you probably still have to go through the process a few times to figure out what steps you're taking.

Try applying that method to this problem: Manually permute a short string and try to reverse-engineer an algorithm out of the process. Take the string "abcd" as an example. Because you're trying to construct an algorithm from an intuitive process, you want to go through the permutations in a systematic order. Exactly which systematic order you use isn't terribly important — different orders are likely to lead to different algorithms, but as long as you're systematic about the process, you should be able to construct an algorithm. You want to choose a simple order that makes it easy to identify any permutations that you might accidentally skip.

You might consider listing all the permutations in alphabetical order. This means the first group of permutations will all start with "a". Within this group, you first have the permutations with a second letter of "b", then "c", and finally "d". Continue in a like fashion for the other first letters.

abcd	bacd	cabd	dabc
abdc	badc	cadb	dacb
acbd	bcad	cbad	dbac
acdb	bcda	cbda	dbca
adbc	bdac	cdab	dcab
adcb	bdca	cdba	dcba

Before you continue, make sure you didn't miss any permutations. Four possible letters can be placed in the first position. For each of these four possibilities, there are three remaining possible letters for the second position. Thus, there are 4 × 3 = 12 different possibilities for the first two letters of the permutations. After you select the first two letters, two different letters remain available for the third position, and the last remaining letter is put in the fourth position. If you multiply 4 × 3 × 2 × 1 you have a total of 24 different permutations; there are 24 permutations in the previous list, so nothing has been missed. This calculation can be expressed more succinctly as 4! — you may recall that n! is the number of possible arrangements of n objects.

Now examine the list of permutations for patterns. The rightmost letters vary faster than the leftmost letters. For each letter that you choose for the first (leftmost) position, you write out all the permutations beginning with that letter before you change the first letter. Likewise, after you pick a letter for the second position, you write out all permutations beginning with this two-letter sequence before changing the letters in either the first or second position. In other words, you can define the permutation process as picking a letter for a given position and performing the permutation process starting at the next position to the right before coming back to change the letter you just picked. This sounds like the basis for a recursive definition of permutation. Try to rephrase it in explicitly recursive terms: To find all permutations starting at position n, successively place all allowable letters in position n, and for each new letter in position n find all permutations starting at position $n + 1$ (the recursive case). When n is greater than the number of characters in the input string, a permutation has been completed; print it and return to changing letters at positions less than n (the base case).

You almost have an algorithm; you just need to define "all allowable letters" a little more rigorously. Because each letter from the input string can appear only once in each permutation, "all allowable letters" can't be defined as every letter in the input string. Think about how you did the permutations manually. For the group of permutations beginning with "b", you never put a "b" anywhere but the first position because when you selected letters for later positions, "b" had already been used. For the group beginning with "bc" you used only "a" and "d" in the third and fourth positions because both "b" and "c" had already been used. Therefore, "all allowable letters" means all letters in the input string that haven't already been chosen for a position to the left of the current position (a position less than n). Algorithmically, you could check each candidate letter for position n against all the letters in positions less than n to determine whether it had been used. You can eliminate these inefficient scans by maintaining an array of boolean values corresponding to the positions of the letters in the input string and using this array to mark letters as used or unused, as appropriate.

In outline form, this algorithm looks like the following:

```
If you're past the last position
    Print the string
    Return
Otherwise
    For each letter in the input string
    If it's marked as used, skip to the next letter
    Else place the letter in the current position
        Mark the letter as used
        Permute remaining letters starting at current position + 1
        Mark the letter as unused
```

Separating the base case from the recursive case as performed here is considered good style and may make the code easier to understand, but it does not provide optimum performance. You can significantly optimize the code by invoking the base case directly without a recursive call if the next recursive call invokes the base case. In this algorithm, that involves checking whether the letter just placed was the last letter — if so, you print the permutation and make no recursive call; otherwise, a recursive call is made. This eliminates $n!$ function calls, reducing the function call overhead by approximately a factor of n (where n is the length of the input string). Short-circuiting the base case in this manner is called arms-length recursion and is considered poor style, especially in academic circles. Whichever way you choose to code the solution, it is worthwhile to mention the advantages of the alternative approach to your interviewer.

Here's a Java implementation of this algorithm:

```java
public class Permutations {
    private boolean[] used;
    private StringBuilder out = new StringBuilder();
    private final String in;

    public Permutations( final String str ){
        in = str;
        used = new boolean[ in.length() ];
    }

    public void permute( ){
        if( out.length() == in.length() ){
            System.out.println( out );
            return;
        }
        for( int i = 0; i < in.length(); ++i ){
            if( used[i] ) continue;
            out.append( in.charAt(i) );
            used[i] = true;
            permute();
            used[i] = false;
            out.setLength( out.length() - 1 );
        }
    }
}
```

This class sets up the array of used flags and the StringBuilder for the output string in the constructor. The recursive function is implemented in permute(), which appends the next available character to out before making the recursive call to permute the remaining characters. After the call returns, the appended character is deleted by decreasing out's length.

Combinations of a String

> **PROBLEM** *Implement a function that prints all possible combinations of the characters in a string. These combinations range in length from one to the length of the string. Two combinations that differ only in ordering of their characters are the same combination. In other words, "12" and "31" are different combinations from the input string "123", but "21" is the same as "12".*

This is a companion problem to finding the permutations of the characters in a string. If you haven't yet worked through that problem, you may want to do so before you tackle this one.

Following the model of the solution to the permutation problem, try working out an example by hand to see where that gets you. Because you are trying to divine an algorithm from the example, you again need to be systematic in your approach. You might try listing combinations in order of length. The input string "wxyz" is used in the example. Because the ordering of letters within each combination is arbitrary, they are kept in the same order as they are in the input string to minimize confusion.

w	wx	wxy	wxyz
x	wy	wxz	
y	wz	wyz	
z	xy	xyz	
	xz		
	yz		

Some interesting patterns seem to be emerging, but there's nothing clear yet, certainly nothing that seems to suggest an algorithm. Listing output in terms of the order of the input string (alphabetical order, for this input string) turned out to be helpful in the permutation problem. Try rearranging the combinations you generated to see if that's useful here:

w	x	y	z
wx	xy	yz	
wxy	xyz		
wxyz	xz		
wxz			
wy			
wyz			
wz			

This looks a little more productive. There is a column for each letter in the input string. The first combination in each column is a single letter from the input string. The remainder of each column's combinations consists of that letter prepended to each of the combinations in the columns to the right. Take, for example, the "x" column. This column has the single letter combination "x". The columns to the right of it have the combinations "y", "yz", and "z", so if you prepend "x" to each of these combinations you find the remaining combinations in the "x" column: "xy", "xyz", and "xz". You could use this rule to generate all the combinations, starting with just "z" in the rightmost column and working your way to the left, each time writing a single letter from the input string at the top of the column and then completing the column with that letter prepended to each of the combinations in columns to the right. This is a recursive method for generating the combinations. It is space inefficient because it requires storage of all previously generated combinations, but it indicates that this problem can be solved recursively. See if you can gain some insight on a more efficient recursive algorithm by examining the combinations you've written a little more closely.

Look at which letters appear in which positions. All four letters appear in the first position, but "w" never appears in the second position. Only "y" and "z" appear in the third position, and "z" is in the fourth position in the only combination that has a fourth position ("wxyz"). Therefore, a potential algorithm might involve iterating through all allowable letters at each position: w–z in the first position, x–z in the second position, and so on. Check this idea against the example to see if it works: It seems to successfully generate all the combinations in the first column. However, when you select "x" for the first position, this candidate algorithm would start with "x" in the second position, generating an illegal combination of "xx". Apparently the algorithm needs some refinement.

To generate the correct combination "xy", you need to begin with "y", not "x", in the second position. When you select "y" for the first position (third column), you need to start with "z" because "yy" is illegal and "yx" and "yw" have already been generated as "xy" and "wy". This suggests that in each output position you need to begin iterating with the letter in the input string following the letter selected for the preceding position in the output string. Call this letter your input start letter.

It may be helpful to summarize this a little more formally. Begin with an empty output string and the first character of the input as the input start position. For a given position, sequentially select all letters from the input start position to the last letter in the input string. For each letter you select, append it to the output string, print the combination, and then generate all other combinations beginning with this sequence by recursively calling the generating function with the input start position set to the next letter after the one you've just selected. After you return from the recursive call, delete the character you appended to make room for the next character you select. You should check this idea against the example to make sure it works. It does — no more problems in the second column. Before you code, it may be helpful to outline the algorithm just to make sure you have it. (For comparison, we've chosen the performance side of the arms-length recursion style/performance trade-off discussed in the permutation problem. The performance and style differences between the two possible approaches are not as dramatic for the combination algorithm as they were for the permutation algorithm.)

```
For each letter from input start position to end of input string
    Append the letter to the output string
    Print letters in output string
```

```
            If the current letter isn't the last in the input string
                Generate remaining combinations starting at next position with
                iteration starting at next letter beyond the letter just selected
            Delete the last character of the output string
```

After all that hard work, the algorithm looks simple! You're ready to code it. In Java, your implementation might look like this:

```java
public class Combinations {
    private StringBuilder out = new StringBuilder();
    private final String in;

    public Combinations( final String str ){ in = str; }

    public void combine() { combine( 0 ); }
    private void combine(int start ){
        for( int i = start; i < in.length(); ++i ){
            out.append( in.charAt(i) );
            System.out.println( out );
            if ( i < in.length() )
                combine( i + 1);
            out.setLength( out.length() - 1 );
        }
    }
}
```

This solution is sufficient in most interviews. Nevertheless, you can make a rather minor optimization to combine that eliminates the if statement. Given that this is a recursive function, the performance increase is probably negligible compared to the function call overhead, but you might want to see if you can figure it out just for practice:

```java
private void combine(int start ){
    for( int i = start; i < in.length() - 1; ++i ){
        out.append( in.charAt(i) );
        System.out.println( out );
        combine( i + 1);
        out.setLength( out.length() - 1 );
    }
    out.append( in.charAt( in.length() - 1 ) );
    System.out.println( out );
    out.setLength( out.length() - 1 );
}
```

The if statement is eliminated by removing the final iteration from the loop and moving the code it would have executed during that iteration outside the loop. The general case of this optimization is referred to as *loop partitioning*, and if statements that can be removed by loop partitioning are called *loop index dependent conditionals*. Again, this optimization doesn't make much difference here, but it can be important inside nested loops.

Telephone Words

PROBLEM *People in the United States often give others their telephone number as a word representing the seven-digit number after the area code. For example, if my telephone number were 866-2665, I could tell people my number is "TOOCOOL," instead of the hard-to-remember seven-digit number. Note that many other possibilities (most of which are nonsensical) can represent 866-2665. You can see how letters correspond to numbers on a telephone keypad in Figure 7-2.*

FIGURE 7-2

Write a function that takes a seven-digit telephone number and prints out all of the possible "words" or combinations of letters that can represent the given number. Because the 0 and 1 keys have no letters on them, you should change only the digits 2–9 to letters. You'll be passed an array of seven integers, with each element being one digit in the number. You may assume that only valid phone numbers will be passed to your function. You can use the helper function

```
char getCharKey( int telephoneKey, int place )
```

which takes a telephone key (0–9) and a place of either 1, 2, 3 and returns the character corresponding to the letter in that position on the specified key. For example, GetCharKey(3,2) will return 'E' because the telephone key 3 has the letters "DEF" on it and 'E' is the second letter.

It's worthwhile to define some terms for this problem. A telephone number consists of digits. Three letters correspond to each digit. (Except for 0 and 1, but when 0 and 1 are used in the context of creating a word, you can call them letters.) The lowest letter, middle letter, and highest letter will be called the digit's low value, middle value, and high value, respectively. You will be creating words, or strings of letters, to represent the given number.

First, impress the interviewer with your math skills by determining how many words can correspond to a seven-digit number. This requires combinatorial mathematics, but if you don't remember this type of math, don't panic. First, try a one-digit phone number. Clearly, this would have three words. Now, try a two-digit phone number — say, 56. There are three possibilities for the first letter, and for each of these there are three possibilities for the second letter. This yields a total of nine words that can correspond to this number. It appears that each additional digit increases the number of words by a factor of 3. Thus, for 7 digits, you have 3^7 words, and for a phone number of length n, you have 3^n words. Because 0 and 1 have no corresponding letters, a phone number with 0s or 1s in it would have fewer words, but 3^7 is the upper bound on the number of words for a seven-digit number.

Now you need to figure out an algorithm for printing these words. Try writing out some words representing one of the author's old college phone numbers, 497-1927, as an example. The most natural manner in which to list the words is alphabetical order. This way, you always know which word comes next, and you are less likely to miss words. You know that there are on the order of 3^7 words that can represent this number, so you won't have time to write them all out. Try writing just the beginning and the end of the alphabetical sequence. You will probably want to start with the word that uses the low letter for each digit of the phone number. This guarantees that your first word is the first word in alphabetical order. Thus, the first word for 497-1927 starts with G for 4 because 4 has "GHI" on it, W for 9, which has "WXY" on it, P for 7, which has "PRS" on it, and so on, resulting in "GWP1WAP".

As you continue to write down words, you ultimately create a list that looks like the following:

GWP1WAP

GWP1WAR

GWP1WAS

GWP1WBP

GWP1WBR

   ...

IYS1YCR

IYS1YCS

It was easy to create this list because the algorithm for generating the words is relatively intuitive. Formalizing this algorithm is more challenging. A good place to start is by examining the process of going from one word to the next word in alphabetical order.

Because you know the first word in alphabetical order, determining how to get to the next word at any point gives you an algorithm for writing all the words. One important part of the process of going from one word to the next seems to be that the last letter always changes. It continually cycles through a pattern of P-R-S. Whenever the last letter goes from S back to P, it causes the next-to-last letter to change. Try investigating this a little more to see if you can come up with specific rules. Again, it's probably best to try an example. You may have to write down more words than in the example list to see a pattern. (A three-digit phone number should be sufficient, or the previous list will work if it's expanded a bit.) It looks as if the following is always true: Whenever a letter changes, its right neighbor goes through all of its values before the original letter changes again. Conversely, whenever a letter resets to its low value, its left neighbor increases to the next value.

From these observations, there are probably two reasonable paths to follow as you search for the solution to this problem. You can start with the first letter and have a letter affect its right neighbor, or you can start with the last letter and have a letter affect its left neighbor. Both of these approaches seem reasonable. For now, try the former and see where that gets you.

You should examine exactly what you're trying to do at this point. You're working with the observation that whenever a letter changes, it causes its right neighbor to cycle through all its values before it changes again. You're using this observation to determine how to get from one word to the next word in alphabetical order. It may help to formalize this observation: Changing the letter in position i causes the letter in position $i + 1$ to cycle through its values. When you can write an algorithm in terms of how elements i and $i + 1$ interact with each other, it often indicates recursion, so try to figure out a recursive algorithm.

You have already discovered most of the algorithm. You know how each letter affects the next; you just need to figure out how to start the process and determine the base case. Looking again at the list to try to figure out the start condition, you'll see that the first letter cycles only once. Therefore, if you start by cycling the first letter, this causes multiple cycles of the second letter, which causes multiple cycles of the third letter — exactly as desired. After you change the last letter, you can't cycle anything else, so this is a good base case to end the recursion. When the base case occurs, you should also print out the word because you've just generated the next word in alphabetical order. The one special case you have to be aware of occurs when there is a 0 or 1 in the given telephone number. You don't want to print out any word three times, so you should check for this case and cycle immediately if you encounter it.

In list form, the steps look like this:

```
If the current digit is past the last digit
    Print the word because you're at the end
Else
    For each of the three digits that can represent the current digit
        Have the letter represent the current digit
        Move to next digit and recurse
        If the current digit is a 0 or a 1, return
```

A Java implementation is:

```java
public class TelephoneNumber {
    private static final int PHONE_NUMBER_LENGTH = 7;
    private final int [] phoneNum;
    private char[] result = new char[ PHONE_NUMBER_LENGTH ];

    public TelephoneNumber ( int[] n ) { phoneNum = n; }

    public void printWords(){ printWords( 0 ); }
```

```
            private void printWords(int curDigit ) {
                if( curDigit == PHONE_NUMBER_LENGTH ) {
                    System.out.println( new String( result ) );
                    return;
                }
                for( int i = 1; i <= 3; ++i ) {
                    result[ curDigit ] = getCharKey( phoneNum[curDigit], i );
                    printWords( curDigit + 1 );
                    if( phoneNum[curDigit] == 0 ||
                        phoneNum[curDigit] == 1) return;
                }
            }
        }
```

What is the running time of this algorithm? Ignoring the operations involved in printing the string, the focus of the function is changing letters. Changing a single letter is a constant time operation. The first letter changes 3 times, the second letter changes 3 times each time the first letter changes for a total of 9 times, and so on for the other digits. For a telephone number of length n, the total number of operations is $3 + 3^2 + 3^3 + ... + 3^{n-1} + 3^n$. Retaining only the highest order term, the running time is $O(3^n)$.

> **PROBLEM** *Reimplement* `PrintTelephoneWords` *without using recursion.*

The recursive algorithm doesn't seem to be helpful in this situation. Recursion was inherent in the way that you wrote out the steps of the algorithm. You could always try emulating recursion using a stack-based data structure, but there may be a better way involving a different algorithm. In the recursive solution, you solved the problem from left to right. You also made an observation that suggested the existence of another algorithm going from right to left: Whenever a letter changes from its high value to its low value, its left neighbor is incremented. Explore this observation to see if you can find a nonrecursive solution to the problem.

Again, you're trying to figure out how to determine the next word in alphabetical order. Because you're working from right to left, you should look for something that always happens on the right side of a word as it changes to the next word in alphabetical order. Looking back at the original observations, you noticed that the last letter always changes. This seems to indicate that a good way to start is to increment the last letter. If the last letter is at its high value and you increment it, you reset the last letter to its low value and increment the second-to-last letter. Suppose, however, that the second-to-last number is already at its high value. Try looking at the list to figure out what you need to do. From the list, it appears that you reset the second-to-last number to its low value and increment the third-to-last number. You continue carrying your increment like this until you don't have to reset a letter to its low value.

This sounds like the algorithm you want, but you still have to work out how to start it and how to know when you're finished. You can start by manually creating the first string as you did when writing out the list. Now you need to determine how to end. Look at the last string and figure out what happens if you try to increment it. Every letter resets to its low value. You could check whether every letter is at its low value, but this seems inefficient. The first letter resets only once, when you've printed out all the words. You can use this to signal that you're done printing out all the words.

Again, you have to consider the cases where there is a 0 or a 1. Because 0 and 1 effectively can't be incremented (they always stay as 0 and 1), you should always treat a 0 or a 1 as if it were at its highest letter value and increment its left neighbor. In outline form, the steps are as follows:

```
Create the first word character by character
Loop infinitely:
     Print out the word
     Increment the last letter and carry the change
     If the first letter has reset, you're done
```

Here is a Java implementation of this iterative algorithm:

```java
public class TelephoneNumber {
    private static final int PHONE_NUMBER_LENGTH = 7;
    private final int [] phoneNum;
    private char[] result = new char[ PHONE_NUMBER_LENGTH ];

    public TelephoneNumber ( int[] n ) { phoneNum = n; }

    public void printWords() {
        // Initialize result with first telephone word
        for( int i = 0; i < PHONE_NUMBER_LENGTH; ++i )
            result[i] = getCharKey( phoneNum[i], 1 );

        for( ; ; ) {  // Infinite loop
            for( int i = 0; i < PHONE_NUMBER_LENGTH; ++i ) {
                System.out.print( result[i] );
            }
            System.out.print( '\n' );

            /* Start at the end and try to increment from right
             * to left.
             */
            for( int i = PHONE_NUMBER_LENGTH - 1; i >= -1; --i ) {
                if( i == -1 ) // if attempted to carry past leftmost digit,
                    return;    // we're done, so return

                /* Start with high value, carry case so 0 and 1
                 * special cases are dealt with right away
                 */
                if( getCharKey( phoneNum[i], 3 ) == result[i] ||
                    phoneNum[i] == 0 || phoneNum[i] == 1 ){
                    result[i] = getCharKey( phoneNum[i], 1 );
                    // No break, so loop continues to next digit
                } else if ( getCharKey( phoneNum[i], 1 ) == result[i] ) {
                    result[i] = getCharKey( phoneNum[i], 2 );
                    break;
                } else if ( getCharKey( phoneNum[i], 2 ) == result[i] ) {
                    result[i] = getCharKey( phoneNum[i], 3 );
                    break;
                }
            }
        }
    }
}
```

You can cut down on the calls to getCharKey by caching each letter's three values in variables, rather than making repeated calls to see whether a value is low, middle, or high. This would make the code a little more complicated and may not make any difference after the code is optimized by the JIT compiler.

What's the running time on this algorithm?

Again, changing a single letter is a constant time operation. The total number of letter changes is the same for this algorithm as for the previous, so the running time remains $O(3^n)$.

SUMMARY

Recursion occurs whenever a function calls itself, directly or indirectly. One or more base cases are needed to end the recursion; otherwise, the algorithm recurses until it overflows the stack.

Algorithms that are intrinsically recursive should be implemented recursively. Some apparently recursive algorithms can also be implemented iteratively; these iterative implementations are generally more efficient than their recursive counterparts.

8

Sorting

Sorting algorithms are useful for two reasons. The first is to order data for presentation to the user, such as sorting a list of employees alphabetically by first or last name. The second is to simplify and optimize other algorithms, either by sorting the input data prior to applying an algorithm or by sorting the intermediate data an algorithm uses as it runs.

You rarely need to code a sorting algorithm. Most languages include at least one sorting algorithm (typically quicksort) in their standard libraries. These built-in algorithms are suitable for general use. In situations in which a general-purpose sorting algorithm doesn't meet your needs, implementations of specialized sorting algorithms can usually be adapted with minimal effort.

Although you're unlikely to implement sorting algorithms, you must understand the differences and trade-offs between them. Each algorithm has benefits and drawbacks, and there's no single best way to sort in all cases. Interviewers like sorting problems because they provide a simple way to address a wide range of issues from algorithmic complexity to memory usage.

SORTING ALGORITHMS

Choosing the right sorting algorithm can have a huge impact on application performance. What's right for one application isn't necessarily right for a different application. Here are some criteria to consider when selecting a sorting algorithm:

> **How much data is to be sorted?** For small data sets it doesn't matter which algorithm you choose because there is little difference in the execution times, but for large data sets, the worst-case bounds become radically different. Beware of data sets that are typically small but may occasionally be much larger — you need to select an algorithm that performs acceptably on the largest data sets your code may encounter.

> **Does the data fit in memory?** Most sorting algorithms are efficient only when the data they operate on resides in memory. If the data set is too large for memory, you may need to split it into smaller chunks for sorting and then combine those sorted chunks to create the final sorted data set.

➤ **Is the data already mostly sorted?** Adding new data to a sorted list can be done efficiently with certain algorithms, but those same algorithms have poor performance on randomly ordered data.

➤ **How much additional memory does the algorithm require?** An *in-place* sorting algorithm sorts the data without using any additional memory, such as by swapping elements in an array. When memory is at a premium, an in-place algorithm may be a better choice than one with otherwise superior efficiency.

➤ **Is relative order preserved?** A *stable* sorting algorithm preserves the relative order of data elements that are otherwise identical for sorting purposes. (In other words, if elements A and B have identical key values and A precedes B in the original data set, A will still precede B after a stable sorting.) Stability is generally a desirable feature, but in many cases it may be worth sacrificing stability for improved performance.

In an interview situation, it's not unusual for the interviewer to vary the criteria as the interview progresses to see how well you understand the differences between sorting algorithms.

For simplicity, the sorting problems used in interviews often deal with simple integer values stored in arrays. In the real world, sorting usually involves more complex data structures with only one or a few of the values in those data structures affecting the sorting order. The value (or values) that determine the sorting order is referred to as the *key*. Most sorting algorithms in standard libraries are *comparison* algorithms, which require only that there is a way to determine whether one key is less than, equal to, or greater than another key. No comparison algorithm can have a more optimal worst-case running time than $O(n \log(n))$.

Selection Sort

Selection sort is one of the simplest sorting algorithms. It starts with the first element in the array (or list) and scans through the array to find the element with the smallest key, which it swaps with the first element. The process is then repeated with each subsequent element until the last element is reached.

The description of this algorithm suggests a recursive approach, as shown here with the selectionSortRecursive method:

```
// Sort an array using a recursive selection sort.
public void selectionSortRecursive( int[] data ){
    selectionSortRecursive( data, 0 );
}

// Sort a subset of the array starting at the given index.
private void selectionSortRecursive( int[] data, int start ) {
    if( start < data.length - 1 ){
        swap( data, start, findMinimumIndex( data, start ) );
        selectionSortRecursive( data, start + 1 );
    }
}
```

This implementation depends on the two helper routines `findMinimumIndex` and `swap`:

```
// Find the position of the minimum value starting at the given index.
private int findMinimumIndex( int[] data, int start ) {
    int minPos = start;

    for( int i = start + 1; i < data.length; ++i ){
        if( data[i] < data[minPos] ){
            minPos = i;
        }
    }

    return minPos;
}

// Swap two elements in an array.
private void swap( int[] data, int index1, int index2 ){
    if( index1 != index2 ){
        int tmp = data[index1];
        data[index1] = data[index2];
        data[index2] = tmp;
    }
}
```

This implementation could be optimized by transforming this tail-recursive procedure into an iterative implementation and inlining the two helper functions.

How efficient is selection sort? The first swap requires $n - 1$ comparisons, the second $n - 2$, the third $n - 3$, and so on. This is the series $(n - 1) + (n - 2) + ... + 1$, which simplifies to $n(n - 1)/2$. This means that the algorithm is $O(n^2)$ in the best, average, *and* worst cases — the initial order of the data has no effect on the number of comparisons. As you'll see later in this chapter, other sorting algorithms have more efficient running times than this.

Selection sort does have the advantage that it requires at most $n - 1$ swaps. In situations in which moving data elements is more expensive than comparing them, selection sort may perform better than other algorithms. The efficiency of an algorithm depends on what you're optimizing for.

Selection sort is an in-place algorithm. Typical implementations of selection sort, such as the one shown here, are not stable.

Insertion Sort

Insertion sort is another simple sorting algorithm. It builds a sorted array (or list) one element at a time by comparing each new element to the already-sorted elements and *inserting* the new element into the correct location, similar to the way you sort a hand of playing cards.

A simple implementation of insertion sort is as follows:

```
// Sort an array using a simple insertion sort.
public void insertionSort( int[] data ){
    for( int which = 1; which < data.length; ++which ){
```

```
            int val = data[which];

            for( int i = 0; i < which; ++i ){
              if( data[i] > val ){
                System.arraycopy( data, i, data, i+1, which - i );
                data[i] = val;
                break;
              }
            }
          }
        }
```

Unlike selection sort, the best-case running time for insertion sort is $O(n)$, which occurs when the list is already sorted. This means insertion sort is an efficient way to add new elements to a presorted list. The average and worst cases are both $O(n^2)$, however, so it's not the best algorithm to use for large amounts of randomly ordered data.

Insertion sort is a stable, in-place sorting algorithm especially suitable for sorting small data sets and is often used as a building block for other, more complicated sorting algorithms.

Quicksort

Quicksort is a divide-and-conquer algorithm that involves choosing a *pivot value* from a data set and splitting the set into two subsets: a set that contains all values less than the pivot and a set that contains all values greater than or equal to the pivot. The pivot/split process is recursively applied to each subset until there are no more subsets to split. The results are combined to form the final sorted set.

A naïve implementation of this algorithm looks like:

```
// Sort an array using a simple but inefficient quicksort.
public int[] quicksortSimple( int[] data ){

  if( data.length < 2 ){
    return data;
  }

  int pivotIndex = data.length / 2;
  int pivotValue = data[ pivotIndex ];

  int leftCount = 0;

  // Count how many are less than the pivot

  for( int i = 0; i < data.length; ++i ){
    if( data[ i ] < pivotValue ) ++leftCount;
  }

  // Allocate the arrays and create the subsets

  int[] left = new int[ leftCount ];
  int[] right = new int[ data.length - leftCount - 1 ];
```

```
        int l = 0;
        int r = 0;

        for( int i = 0; i < data.length; ++i ){
          if( i == pivotIndex ) continue;

          int val = data[ i ];

          if( val < pivotValue ){
            left[ l++ ] = val;
          } else {
            right[ r++ ] = val;
          }
        }

        // Sort the subsets

        left = quicksortSimple( left );
        right = quicksortSimple( right );

        // Combine the sorted arrays and the pivot back into the original array

        System.arraycopy( left, 0, data, 0, left.length );
        data[ left.length ] = pivotValue;
        System.arraycopy( right, 0, data, left.length + 1, right.length );

        return data;
    }
```

The preceding code illustrates the principles of quicksort, but it's not a particularly efficient implementation due to scanning the starting array twice, allocating new arrays, and copying results from the new arrays to the original.

Quicksort's performance is dependent on the choice of pivot value. The ideal pivot value is one that splits the original data set into two subsets of identical (or nearly identical) size. Every time you do a pivot-and-split, you perform constant-time operations on each of the elements involved. How many times do you do this for each element? In the best case, the size of a sublist is halved on each successive recursive call, and the recursion terminates when the sublist size is 1. This means the number of times you operate on an element is equal to the number of times you can divide n by 2 before reaching one: $\log(n)$. Performing $\log(n)$ operations on each of n elements yields a combined *best case* complexity of $O(n \log(n))$.

On the other hand, what if your pivot choice is poor? In the worst case, the pivot is the *minimum* value in the data set, which means that one subset is empty and the other subset contains $n - 1$ items (all the items except for the pivot). The number of recursive calls is then $O(n)$ (analogous to a completely unbalanced tree degrading to a linked list), which gives a combined worst-case complexity of $O(n^2)$. This is the same as selection sort or insertion sort.

On average almost any pivot value will split a data set into two non-empty subsets, making the number of recursive calls fall somewhere between $O(\log(n))$ and $O(n)$. A bit of mathematical work (omitted here) is enough to show that in *most* cases the number of times you operate on an element is still $O(\log(n))$, so the *average case* complexity of quicksort is also $O(n \log(n))$.

For truly randomly ordered data, the value of the pivot is unrelated to its location, so you can choose a pivot from any location because they're all equally likely to be good choices. But if the data is already sorted (or mostly sorted), choosing the value located in the *middle* of the data set ensures that each subset contains approximately half the data, which gives guaranteed $O(n \log(n))$ complexity for sorted data. Because the value in the middle location is the best choice for ordered data and no worse than any other for unordered data, most quicksort implementations use it as the pivot.

Like the preceding implementation, most implementations of quicksort are not stable.

Merge Sort

Merge sort is another divide-and-conquer algorithm that works by splitting a data set into two or more subsets, sorting the subsets, and then merging them together into the final sorted set.

The algorithm can be implemented recursively as follows:

```
// Sort an array using a simple but inefficient merge sort.
public int[] mergeSortSimple( int[] data ){

    if( data.length < 2 ){
        return data;
    }

    // Split the array into two subarrays of approx equal size.

    int   mid = data.length / 2;
    int[] left = new int[ mid ];
    int[] right = new int[ data.length - mid ];

    System.arraycopy( data, 0, left, 0, left.length );
    System.arraycopy( data, mid, right, 0, right.length );

    // Sort each subarray, then merge the result.

    mergeSortSimple( left );
    mergeSortSimple( right );

    return merge( data, left, right );
}

// Merge two smaller arrays into a larger array.
private int[] merge( int[] dest, int[] left, int[] right ){
    int dind = 0;
    int lind = 0;
    int rind = 0;

    // Merge arrays while there are elements in both
    while ( lind < left.length && rind < right.length ){
        if ( left[ lind ] <= right[ rind ] ){
            dest[ dind++ ] = left[ lind++ ];
        } else {
```

```
                dest[ dind++ ] = right[ rind++ ];
            }
        }

        // Copy rest of whichever array remains
        while ( lind < left.length )
            dest[ dind++ ] = left[ lind++ ];

        while ( rind < right.length )
            dest[ dind++ ] = right[ rind++ ];

        return dest;
    }
```

Most of the work is done in the `merge` method, which combines two sorted arrays into a larger sorted array.

A *hybrid* merge sort occurs when a different sorting algorithm is used to sort subsets below a specified minimum size. For example, you can transform the `mergeSortSimple` method into a hybrid algorithm by replacing the termination condition:

```
if( data.length < 2 ){
    return data;
}
```

with an insertion sort:

```
if( data.length < 10 ){ // some small empirically determined value
    insertionSort( data );
    return data;
}
```

This is a common optimization because insertion sort has lower overhead than merge sort and typically has better performance on very small data sets.

Unlike most other sorting algorithms, merge sort is a good choice for data sets that are too large to fit into memory. In a typical scenario, the contents of a large file are split into multiple smaller files. Each of the smaller files is read into memory, sorted using an appropriate algorithm, and written back out. A merge operation is then performed using the sorted files as input and the sorted data is written directly to the final output file.

The best, average, and worst-case running times for merge sort are all $O(n \log(n))$, which is great when you need a guaranteed upper bound on the sorting time. However, merge sort requires $O(n)$ additional memory — substantially more than many other algorithms.

Typical (maximally efficient) merge sort implementations are stable but not in-place.

SORTING PROBLEMS

Sorting problems often involve selecting the most appropriate algorithm for a particular situation, or modifying a standard sorting algorithm to give it a new property.

The Best Sorting Algorithm

> **PROBLEM** *What's the best algorithm to use for sorting?*

This is a bit of a trick question. The key is *not* to just respond with "quicksort" (or any other specific sorting algorithm). If you do, your interviewer will likely describe a scenario in which the algorithm you just named is particularly poorly suited and then ask you if you still think that algorithm is the best choice. Don't get drawn into that trap!

Each sorting algorithm has its strengths and weaknesses, so you need to fully understand the context before you can select the best algorithm for a particular situation. Start by asking the interviewer some questions about the data you are sorting, the requirements for the sort, and the system that will perform the sort. Specifically, you might ask some of these questions:

➤ **What do we know about the data?** Is the data already sorted or mostly sorted? How large are the data sets likely to be? Can there be duplicate key values?

➤ **What are the requirements for the sort?** Do you want to optimize for best-case, worst-case, or average-case performance? Does the sort need to be stable?

➤ **What do we know about the system?** Is the largest data set to be sorted smaller than, the same size as, or larger than available memory?

Sometimes, just asking these questions is enough to illustrate your knowledge of sorting algorithms. (One of the authors started this problem in an interview by asking the question "What can you tell me about the data?" The interviewer responded "Yes, that's the right answer," and moved on to a different problem.) More commonly, the interviewer will answer your questions and describe a scenario that points toward one algorithm as a better choice than the others.

> **PROBLEM** *A master directory server receives a list of accounts, ordered by user ID, from each of several departmental directory servers. What's the best approach for this server to create a master list combining all the accounts ordered by user ID?*

The naïve approach to this is to concatenate all the sublists and apply a general-purpose sorting algorithm such as quicksort to the combined list, yielding $O(n \log(n))$ running time (where n is the combined size of all the departmental lists).

What do you know about the data that might help you find a more efficient solution? In this case, you know that the sublists are sorted. Can you use this to your advantage? You have several sorted sublists and you need to combine them. This sounds very much like part of a merge sort. In fact, the situation here is like the final stage of a merge sort, after the recursive calls have already sorted the sublists. All that's left to do is merge the lists. This is only $O(n)$, so it will outperform the naïve approach. What are the limitations of this strategy? The linear running time is great, but it also requires $O(n)$ auxiliary temporary space (in addition to the space required for storing the records in memory) while performing the merge. If that space is available, then this is an excellent solution.

How would you respond if the interviewer told you that memory on the server is tight and it's not acceptable to use $O(n)$ auxiliary space during the sort? In-place sorting algorithms have minimal requirements for auxiliary storage. If you assume you can get the sublists concatenated without using $O(n)$ auxiliary storage (for example, you might receive them into one large buffer to begin with) then one option is to revert to the naïve method and use an in-place sorting algorithm such as in-place quicksort; you'll sacrifice some performance, but $O(n \log(n))$ is not that much worse than $O(n)$.

Before you settle on this solution, consider why the merge approach requires additional space. You have each of the sublists in memory, requiring n records of storage. Then you need to allocate a temporary buffer of size n to store the merged result. There doesn't seem to be any way around the output buffer requirement, but do you actually need to have each of the sublists in memory? The sublists are already sorted, so at each point in the merge you just need the next item from each sublist. Obviously you still need storage for all n account records, but if you merge the sublists as you receive them, you no longer have a requirement for an additional size n buffer. (You probably need a small constant-size buffer for each of the servers sending information, so if there are m departmental servers, additional memory required is $O(m)$; presumably m is much smaller than n.) This is an example of an *online algorithm*: an algorithm that processes data as it becomes available, rather than requiring all data to be available before starting processing.

The online approach has limitations, too. It requires the merge to be integrated with the communications with the departmental servers, increasing complexity and decreasing modularity. Also, if one of the departmental servers has problems during the process and stops sending data, it stalls the entire operation. Everything has trade-offs, but in an appropriately controlled environment, this could be the best option.

> **PROBLEM** *A system that monitors a manufacturing plant maintains a list of serial numbers of every item that has ever failed quality control. During the day, while the plant is operating, new serial numbers are added to the end of the list. Each night, a batch process runs to resort the list. What's the best sorting algorithm for this?*

Each night, only the newly added serial numbers can be out of order because the rest were sorted the previous night. Even the newly added serial numbers are likely partially sorted because serial numbers are usually assigned in order, and the items are likely tested roughly in order. After the plant has been running for more than a few weeks, the number of items added to the list each day will probably be much smaller than the total size of the list.

To summarize, you have a few unsorted items to add to a large sorted list. This sounds like a job for insertion sort! The situation described is close to that for which insertion sort has its best-case $O(n)$ performance. But stop to consider the other properties of insertion sort to see if there are any problems with this choice. Insertion sort is stable and in-place, so no problems there. Worst and average case performance are $O(n^2)$ — that could be a problem. In this scenario the number of unsorted items is usually small, in which case you can expect nearly $O(n)$ performance, but if the factory has a bad day and a large number of items fail, you may see closer to $O(n^2)$. Ask the interviewer if an occasional sort that runs long can be tolerated in this environment: If so, then insertion sort is your answer; if not, you need to keep looking.

Suppose that worst-case $O(n^2)$ is not acceptable. What other options do you have? Instead of looking at your data as a sorted list and some unsorted items to insert, try thinking of it as two lists: a large sorted list and a (usually) small, possibly partially sorted list. Sorted lists can be efficiently merged, so you just need to sort the small (new serials numbers) list and then merge the two of them. Because you'll do at least some merging, you might choose to sort the small list with a merge sort. What's the worst-case efficiency of this approach? If the length of the old, sorted list is l and the new, unsorted list is m, then the sort of the new list is $O(m \log(m))$ and the merge is $O(l + m)$. Combined, this is $O(l + m \log(m))$. This approach does have the drawback that $O(l + m)$ additional memory is needed for the merge. There's no free lunch.

> **PROBLEM** *You need to sort a variety of different kinds of data about which little is known in advance. Data sets will be small enough to fit in memory, but their size may vary widely. What sorting algorithm would you choose?*

If you immediately jumped to something like quicksort for the first problem in this series, the current problem is probably what you had in mind. This general case of sorting in which you don't know much about what you're sorting is common, so you must be able to solve it efficiently. Just make sure that your problem is actually a general-purpose sorting problem and you're not missing an opportunity to select a more appropriate special-purpose sorting algorithm.

Optimizing sorting performance across a wide range of potential inputs is the problem faced by programmers who write frameworks and standard libraries, so typically these sort routines are appropriate choices, such as `Arrays.sort()` in Java. These routines typically employ merge sort (if stability is important) or quicksort (if it isn't) for most datasets, often switching to insertion sort for very small datasets (typically n less than approximately 10).

For all these problems involving selecting a sorting algorithm, the interviewer's objective is not actually for you to arrive at any particular solution. Instead, the interviewer wants to see that you recognize that there's no single sorting algorithm that's optimal in all situations, that you have some knowledge of what sorting algorithms are available, and that you can apply this knowledge to select appropriate algorithms and intelligently discuss the running time and memory trade-offs between different options.

Stable Selection Sort

> **PROBLEM** *Implement a* stable *version of the selection sort algorithm.*

This problem requires that you know what a selection sort is. If you don't remember, ask the interviewer. Briefly, a selection sort works by repeatedly scanning the not-yet-sorted values to find the lowest key, and then swapping the lowest key into sorted position at the end of the already-sorted values, as described in more detail earlier in this chapter. A typical implementation is:

```
// Sort an array using an iterative selection sort.
public void selectionSort( int[] data ){
    for( int start = 0; start < data.length - 1; ++start ){
```

```
            swap( data, start, findMinimumIndex( data, start ) );
        }
    }
```

You're asked to make this sort stable. Recall the definition of a stable sort: It is a sort that preserves the input ordering of elements with equal keys. If a_1 and a_2 are two elements with equal keys, and a_1 comes before a_2 in the original data set, a_1 will always be ahead of a_2 after a stable sort.

You may remember that the standard implementation of a selection sort is not stable; even if you don't, the wording of the problem strongly implies it. It's easier to create a stable version of the sort if you understand exactly why the preceding implementation is unstable. Try working through a simple example that produces an unstable result: $[5_1, 3, 5_2, 2]$. After the first iteration of the sort, this becomes $[2, 3, 5_2, 5_1]$ — already the original ordering of the two equal keys has been lost. It seems that the sort is unstable because of the swapping of keys: When an unsorted key is swapped into the location that the key being sorted came from, information about the position of that unsorted key relative to the other unsorted keys is lost. The net effect of the swapping is that the unsorted keys are shuffled as the sort progresses. If you can eliminate the swapping, you might make the sort stable.

The standard unstable selection sort swaps keys because it's the easiest, most efficient way to create space for the key being sorted. How might you create space for this key without swapping? If you *insert* the key being sorted, then the ordering of the unsorted keys remains unchanged. You'll also need to delete this key from its original location. Remember that you can't arbitrarily insert or delete elements from an array — you must move the adjacent elements to open or close the space. In this case, you can accomplish the deletion and insertion as part of the same process by moving all the keys between the original location of the key being sorted and its destination one element to the right.

For simplicity, you can continue to implement the algorithm to sort an array of int, understanding (and telling your interviewer) that if you were actually just sorting ints, you couldn't distinguish between the results of a stable and an unstable sort. Stable and unstable sorts produce different results only when the key is part of a larger record or object, so objects with the same key value are not necessarily identical. An implementation of stable selection sort for an array of int might look like:

```
// Sort an array using a stable selection sort.
public void selectionSortStable( int[] data ){
    for( int start = 0; start < data.length - 1; ++start ){
        insert( data, start, findMinimumIndex( data, start ) );
    }
}

// Insert the data into the array, shifting the array as necessary.
private void insert( int[] data, int start, int minIndex ){
    if( minIndex > start ){
        int tmp = data[minIndex];
        System.arraycopy( data, start, data, start +1 , minIndex - start);
        data[start] = tmp;
    }
}
```

This stable version of selection sort replaces a fast $O(1)$ swap operation with a much slower $O(n)$ array insertion/deletion operation implemented by the System.arraycopy call. You were already performing an $O(n)$ operation (findMinimumIndex) for each key, so adding another $O(n)$ operation doesn't change the overall runtime complexity — it's still $O(n^2)$ — but because you've replaced a fast operation with a much slower one, the actual performance will be worse.

Is there any situation in which it makes sense to use this kind of implementation of stable selection sort? There are other stable sort algorithms that are more efficient than $O(n^2)$. One advantage that the original unstable selection sort had over many other sort algorithms is that the total number of moves (swaps) is $O(n)$. In the preceding stable implementation, the array insertion/deletion makes $O(n)$ moves, and this happens once for each of the n keys to be sorted: The total number of moves for this stable selection sort is $O(n^2)$. This implementation gains stability at the price of sacrificing the only significant benefit of selection sort, so it's difficult to imagine a scenario in which it would be useful. How might you maintain $O(n)$ total key moves?

The current implementation executes $O(n^2)$ moves because it uses an array, where insertion and deletion are inefficient operations requiring moving $O(n)$ elements. If you used a different data structure where insertion and deletion affect only $O(1)$ elements, then you would regain $O(n)$ total moves. A linked list meets these requirements. The following is an implementation of a stable selection sort using a linked list with $O(n)$ total moves. This implementation also operates on any object implementing `Comparable` rather than being limited to `int`:

```
public void selectionSortStable( CursorableLinkedList data ){
    CursorableLinkedList.Cursor sortedBoundary = data.cursor(0);
    while( sortedBoundary.hasNext() ){
        sortedBoundary.add(
                getMinimum( data, sortedBoundary.nextIndex() ) );
    }
}


// remove and return the first minimum-value element from data
// with position greater than start
private Comparable getMinimum( CursorableLinkedList data, int start ){
    CursorableLinkedList.Cursor unsorted = data.cursor(start);
    CursorableLinkedList.Cursor minPos = data.cursor(start+1);
    Comparable minValue = (Comparable) minPos.previous();

    while( unsorted.hasNext() ){
        if( ((Comparable)unsorted.next()).compareTo( minValue ) < 0 ){
            // advance minPos to new minimum value location
            while( minPos.nextIndex() < unsorted.nextIndex() )
                minValue = (Comparable) minPos.next();
        }
    }
    minPos.remove();
    minPos.close();
    unsorted.close();
    return minValue;
}
```

This implementation uses the Apache Commons Collections `CursorableLinkedList` class rather than `LinkedList` from the Java Collections Framework because `CurorableLinkedList` can maintain the validity of an iterator (cursor) even as the list is modified through other iterators. This capability enables a more efficient implementation of the sort. The implementation could be further optimized if you implemented a custom linked list class that supported copying iterators and moving (rather than just deleting and inserting) elements.

Multi-Key Sort

PROBLEM *You have an array of objects, each of which represents an employee:*

```
public class Employee {
    public String extension;
    public String givenname;
    public String surname;
}
```

Using a standard library sorting routine, sort the array so it is ordered alphabetically by surname and then by given name as in a company phone book.

To sort the data using a routine from the standard library, you need a *comparator*: a function that compares two objects. A comparator returns a negative value if the first object is "less than" the second object; zero if the two objects have equal keys; or a positive value if the first object is "greater than" the second.

For this problem, there are two components of the key: The surname and the given name, so the comparator needs to use both of these values. You must order first by surname and then by given name, so the comparator should start by comparing the surnames and then resolve ties by comparing the given names.

In Java, comparators implement the `java.util.Comparator` interface:

```java
import java.util.Comparator;

// A comparator for Employee instances.
public class EmployeeNameComparator implements Comparator<Employee> {

    public int compare( Employee e1, Employee e2 ){
        // Compare surnames
        int ret = e1.surname.compareToIgnoreCase( e2.surname );

        if( ret == 0 ){ //Compare givennames if surnames are the same
            ret = e1.givenname.compareToIgnoreCase( e2.givenname );
        }
        return ret;
    }
}
```

Now it's just a matter of invoking the `Arrays.sort` method with the array and the comparator:

```java
public void sortEmployees( Employee[] employees ){
    Arrays.sort( employees, new EmployeeNameComparator() );
}
```

The approach shown here of using a comparator that considers both parts of the key in a single sort is the most efficient approach, but there is another alternative. If the sort routine you use is stable (the modified merge sort used by `Arrays.sort` is), you can achieve the same result by calling the sort routine twice and sorting on one part of the key at a time. For this problem, you would first sort by given name and then make a second call to sort by surname. During the second sort, by the definition of a stable sort, employees with the same surname would retain their relative ordering based on given name, established by the first sort.

Make a Sort Stable

> **PROBLEM** *You are working on a platform that has a very fast, hardware-accelerated sort routine. The routine,* `shakySort()`, *is not stable, but you need to perform a fast, stable sort. Write code that uses* `shakySort()` *to perform a stable sort.*

Stability is all about preserving the relative order of elements with equal keys. When the data set being sorted has keys that are equal, an unstable sort is not guaranteed to yield the same result as a stable sort. But what if there are *no* equal keys? Stability is meaningless in this case, and all sorting algorithms produce the same result. If you can transform the input data to ensure that there are no equal keys in the data set, then it won't matter that `shakySort()` isn't stable.

One approach you might consider is to scan through the data, identify keys with equal values, and then modify the values based on their positions in the input data set so that keys with earlier positions have lower values. Then when you do an unstable sort, the formerly equal keys retain their original relative ordering. Think about how this might be implemented. If the keys have discrete values, then you might have a situation in which there aren't enough intermediate values available to easily modify the keys. For instance, if you had the integer keys [5, 4, 6, 5] you must modify 4 or 6 in addition to at least one of the 5s. Furthermore the keys likely represent data that may be needed for other purposes. This seems like an overly complicated and undesirable approach.

Because modifying the keys seems undesirable, you need another way to represent information about their original order. What if you added another value and used that as part of the key? You could have a field that represented the relative ordering of each otherwise identical key and compare these values when the main part of the key has the same value. After processing this way, the previous example becomes $[5_1, 4, 6, 5_2]$, where subscripts represent the new field. This is a definite improvement, but it's still somewhat complex: You need to scan the data, using some additional data structure to track what the next number in sequence is for each main key value.

Try to simplify this further. Is it necessary for each repeated key to be ordinally numbered (that is: 1, 2, 3…)? No; You just need earlier occurrences of the key to have lower sequence numbers than later ones. Based on this observation, you can just assign the value for the sequence field based on the element's starting position: $[5_1, 4_2, 6_3, 5_4]$. For repeated keys, this meets the requirement of establishing the relative ordering; for nonrepeated keys you can ignore the sequence number.

With the sequence number as a secondary part of the key, each key is now unique, and the result of an unstable sort using the new expanded key is the same as that of a stable sort on the original key.

Implementation is simpler if you have something concrete to sort: Add a `sequence` field to the `Employee` class in the previous problem and sort objects of that class.

You must reinitialize the sequence fields before each sort:

```
public void sortEmployeesStable( Employee[] employees ){
    for( int i = 0; i < employees.length; ++i ){
        employees[i].sequence = i;
    }
    shakySort( employees, new EmployeeSequenceComparator() );
}
```

You also must create a comparator that uses the sequence number as a *tie breaker* for otherwise identical keys. For instance, to perform a stable sort by surname:

```
// A comparator for Employee instances.
public class EmployeeSequenceComparator implements Comparator<Employee> {

    public int compare( Employee e1, Employee e2 ){
        // Compare surname first.
        int ret = e1.surname.compareToIgnoreCase( e2.surname );

        // Ensure stability
        if( ret == 0 ){
            ret = e1.sequence - e2.sequence;
        }

        return ret;
    }
}
```

What's the complexity of making shakySort() stable? Assigning the sequence numbers takes $O(n)$ time, but because no comparison sort can be more efficient than $O(n \log(n))$, the asymptotic running time is not increased ($O(n + n \log(n)) = O(n \log(n))$). There's one sequence number for each element, so this approach requires $O(n)$ additional memory.

Optimized Quicksort

PROBLEM *Implement an efficient, in-place version of the quicksort algorithm.*

Before you can start on any implementation, you must understand the quicksort algorithm. Briefly, quicksort begins by selecting a *pivot value* from the elements to be sorted. The remaining elements are then divided into two new lists: one list L containing all the values less than the pivot and another list G containing all the values greater than or equal to the pivot. Then quicksort is recursively called to sort L and G. After these calls return, L, the pivot, and G are concatenated (in that order) to yield the sorted data set. If you didn't remember at least that much about quicksort, you'd probably have to ask the interviewer to help you get started.

The simplest implementations of quicksort (such as the one earlier in this chapter) allocate new lists (or arrays) for L and G and copy results back from them after the recursive calls return, which is inefficient and requires additional memory. For this problem, you're asked to write an implementation that avoids this.

The memory allocations that you need to eliminate happen during the partitioning step: when the values are rearranged into L and G. Considering the partitioning, there's no change in the number of elements, just their position, so it should be possible to store L, the pivot, and G all in the original array. How might you do this?

You need to move elements to one end of the array or the other depending on the list to which they belong. Assume that L is on the left side of the array and G is on the right side of the array. Initially you don't know what the sizes of L and G are, just that the sum of their sizes is equal to the array. You know the pivot value, so you can determine whether an individual element belongs to L or G.

If you scan through the elements left to right, each time you find a value greater than or equal to the pivot, you need to move it to the right, into G. Because, again, you don't know what the final size of G will be, it makes sense to have G start at the end of the array and grow toward the left. You don't have any extra space available, so when you move an element to the right into G, you also must move an element to the left to open space. The easiest way to do this is to swap the positions of the element going into G with the element at its destination.

After you swap, the element moving to the left as part of the swap hasn't been checked yet, so be sure to check it before advancing. In addition to tracking your position as you scan through the array, you also need to track the location of the leftmost element of G as it grows to the left, so you know where to put elements when you swap them into G. When your scan position reaches the leftmost element of G, all the elements greater than or equal to the pivot have been moved into G, so the remaining elements in the left portion of the array constitute L. The array is now partitioned into L and G without using any additional memory. This algorithm can then be recursively applied to both lists.

In summary, this algorithm is:

```
Select a pivot
Start the current position at the first element
Start the head of G at the last element
While current position < head of G
    If the current element ≤ pivot
        Swap current element with head of G and advance head of G
    Else
        Advance current position
Recursively call the routine on the L and G segments of the array
```

As with any complex procedure that you design, you should test this with a few potentially problematic cases before you code it. Some cases to check include a two-element array and an array with several identical values. When you work through the latter case, you can identify a bug: If all the values in an array are equal, the algorithm never terminates because all the elements are greater than or equal to the pivot, so they all end up in G on each recursive call!

How can you fix this bug? It occurs because G is exactly the same on each successive recursive call. With the current algorithm, G contains all the elements including the pivot (because the pivot is equal to the pivot value). What if you separate the pivot from the rest of G? Then G can never equal the initial array because it's always at least one element smaller. You need somewhere to store the pivot while you do the partition. One convenient location to keep it out of the way is the end of the array. When you start the procedure, swap the pivot element to the end of the array and then partition the remainder of the array. After partitioning, swap the first element of G with the pivot you had previously stored at the end of the array. Now the pivot is in its correct location with all the smaller elements (in L) on its left; G is everything to the right of the pivot. When you make recursive calls on L and G, the pivot is now excluded, so G decreases in size by at least one on each cycle.

An implementation of this algorithm is as follows:

```
public void quicksortSwapping( int[] data ){
    quicksortSwapping( data, 0, data.length );
}
```

```
private void quicksortSwapping( int[] data, int start, int len ){

    if( len < 2 ) return; // Nothing to sort!

    int pivotIndex = start + len / 2;     // Use the middle value.
    int pivotValue = data[ pivotIndex ];
    int end = start + len;
    int curr = start;

    // Swap the pivot to the end.

    swap( data, pivotIndex, --end );

    // Partition the rest of the array.

    while( curr < end ){
        if( data[ curr ] < pivotValue ){
            curr++;
        } else {
            swap( data, curr, --end );
        }
    }

    // Swap the pivot back to its final destination.

    swap( data, end, start + len - 1 );

    // Apply the algorithm recursively to each partition.

    int llen = end - start;
    int rlen = len - llen - 1;

    if( llen > 1 ){
        quicksortSwapping( data, start, llen );
    }

    if( rlen > 1 ){
        quicksortSwapping( data, end + 1, rlen );
    }
}
```

The version of quicksort you just developed keeps track of two indexes, one on the left and one on the right. The partitions are determined by where the indexes meet. But you're only comparing values on the left side of the array. Can you compare values on the right as well? Instead of blindly swapping values between left and right, wouldn't it make sense to swap mismatched pairs of values? In other words, on the left you would swap a value greater than or equal to the pivot for one on the right that is less than or equal to the pivot. This could considerably reduce the total number of swaps.

While you're at it, you can also make the math a bit simpler by using indexes to mark partition boundaries instead of a starting index and a length. The result is this optimized version of quicksort:

```
public void quicksortOptimized( int[] data ){
    quicksortOptimized( data, 0, data.length - 1 );
}
```

```
public void quicksortOptimized( int[] data, int left, int right ){
    int pivotValue = data[ ( left + right ) / 2 ];
    int i = left;
    int j = right;

    while( i <= j ){
        // Find leftmost value greater than or equal to the pivot.
        while( data[i] < pivotValue ) i++;

        // Find rightmost value less than or equal to the pivot.
        while( data[j] > pivotValue ) j--;

        // If the values are in the wrong order, swap them.
        if( i <= j ){
            swap( data, i, j );
            i++;
            j--;
        }
    }

    // Apply the algorithm to the partitions we made, if any.

    if( left < j ){
        quicksortOptimized( data, left, j );
    }

    if( i < right ){
        quicksortOptimized( data, i, right );
    }
}
```

Note that this implementation doesn't need to explicitly move the pivot as the previous implementation did. Since it compares values at both ends, and values equal to the pivot are swapped into the partition at the other end, there is no case in which all the values end up in one partition. This means that values equal to the pivot may end up in either partition, but the sort is still correct.

This is about as good as quicksort can get! The only other optimization that might be worth considering is to replace the recursive call to quicksort with another sorting algorithm like insertion sort after the partition size falls below a certain threshold.

Pancake Sorting

> **PROBLEM** *Imagine you have a stack of* n *pancakes, each with a different diameter. You also have a pancake flipper. You can insert your flipper into the stack at any point, lift up all the pancakes in the substack above the flipper and flip them over as a unit. In the worst case, how many flips will it take you to sort all the pancakes by size (largest at the bottom) using an optimal algorithm?*

At first this seems like a simple sorting problem: You have a set of items to sort and you'd like to optimize the worst-case running time of the sort. A merge sort has worst-case $O(n \log(n))$; this seems like an easy solution.

Any time there's a solution that seems this simple, it probably isn't correct. Compare the situation in this problem to the usual problem of sorting. In most sorting problems, you can arbitrarily rearrange or exchange the items to be sorted; here, you're limited to using flips of a substack.

There's one other important difference: In analysis of the running time of sort algorithms, you must include the time required to examine each item. In this problem you must optimize the number of flips — in a sense you get to examine the pancakes to determine their locations and plan your strategy for free. After you recognize these differences, it becomes clear that this problem involves more than applying a standard sorting algorithm.

It's hard to calculate the worst-case number of flips that a sorting algorithm requires without knowing what the algorithm is, so start by trying to devise an algorithm for sorting pancakes. You're allowed to use only one operation for changing the order of pancakes: the flip. Think about what happens every time you perform a flip. The order of the pancakes above the point you inserted your flipper is reversed, but the order of the pancakes below the flipper remains unchanged. It seems like it may be difficult to maintain pancakes in sorted order near the top of the stack because they keep getting flipped over, so try sorting the stack starting at the bottom.

The largest pancake should end up on the bottom. How can you get it there? Consider three cases for where the largest pancake could start out: on the bottom, somewhere in the middle, or on the top. If the largest pancake starts out on the bottom, then you don't need to move it. If it's in the middle, things seem a little complicated — certainly there's no way to get it to the bottom with a single flip. If you don't see how to deal with this case right away, put it aside, and come back to it later. What if the largest pancake starts out on the top? Then you could flip the entire stack, moving the pancake from the top to where you want it on the bottom. This also gives you a method for solving the middle case: You just need to first move the largest pancake to the top and then flip it to the bottom. It's quite simple to move a pancake from somewhere in the middle to the top: Insert the flipper immediately underneath the pancake and do a flip. Combining all this, you see that in the worst case it takes two flips to move the largest pancake to the bottom of the stack.

Because the pancakes at the bottom of the stack are unaffected by flips above them, you can continue sorting from the bottom up using the same procedure. On each cycle, identify the next largest not-yet-sorted pancake, flip it to the top, and then flip the stack above the largest already-sorted pancake to move the current pancake from the top into its sorted position. This would be a worst case of $2n$ flips.

Can you do better than this? You've already worked through sorting the first few pancakes; now think about what happens when you sort the last pancakes. After you've sorted the next-to-smallest pancake, all the other pancakes larger than it are in sorted order beneath it. There's only one position left that the smallest pancake can be in: its sorted location at the top of the stack. If you apply the sorting procedure to the smallest pancake at this point, you just flip it over twice. This wastes two flips without changing anything, so you can skip these flips. The worst case is no more than $2n - 2$ flips.

There seems to be room for optimization at the end of the sort, so try backing up one more step to see if you can do any better (assuming that $n > 1$). After you've sorted all but the last two pancakes, you've (worst case) performed $2n - 4$ flips. There are only two ways the final two pancakes can be arranged at this point. Either they're already in sorted order and you're done, or the larger one is above the smaller. In the latter case, you just have to flip the two pancakes. This gives a worst-case total of $2n - 4 + 1 = 2n - 3$ flips.

Yet more optimal solutions can be derived, but this is probably as far as anyone would expect you to go in an interview. This problem has an interesting history. Although commonly known as *the pancake problem*, it's more formally classified as *sorting by prefix reversal* and has applications in routing algorithms. Before he disappointed his family and friends by dropping out of Harvard, Bill Gates published a journal article on the problem (Gates, WH and Papadimitriou, CH, "Bounds for Sorting by Prefix Reversal," *Discrete Mathematics*: 27(1) 47-57, 1979). Gates' algorithm, which is substantially more complex than what we've discussed, stood as the most efficient known solution to the problem for almost 30 years.

SUMMARY

Sorting algorithms are selected using criteria such as memory use and stability as well as best, average and worst-case performance. No comparison sort can have better worst-case performance than $O(n \log(n))$.

Selection sort is one of the simplest sorting algorithms, but it is $O(n^2)$ in all cases. It requires only $O(n)$ swaps, however, so it is suitable for data sets where copying is very expensive. Insertion sort is efficient when dealing with mostly sorted data sets, where it can have $O(n)$ performance, but average and worst cases are $O(n^2)$. Quicksort is a divide-and-conquer algorithm that offers $O(n \log(n))$ performance in the best and average cases and $O(n^2)$ in the worst case. Merge sort is another divide-and-conquer algorithm that offers $O(n \log(n))$ performance in all cases. It is especially useful for sorting data sets that cannot fit into memory. You can make any sorting algorithm stable by assigning a sequence number to each element and using the sequence number as the tie-breaker in a multikey sort.

9

Concurrency

Not that long ago, it was common for programs to have a single thread of execution, even if they were running on a multithreading system. Even today, code you write for an application or web server is often single-threaded, even if the server itself is multithreaded. Why? Because multithreaded programming (often referred to as *concurrency*) is hard to do correctly, even when the programming language directly supports it. Incorrect use of threads can easily halt your program's execution or corrupt its data; worse yet, it can lead to intermittent, difficult to reproduce bugs.

However, if you write an application that has a graphical user interface that may perform lengthy operations, you probably need to use threads to maintain a responsive interface. Even non-interactive applications use threads: Increases in processing power these days come mostly in the form of additional cores, which a single-threaded application can't take advantage of. Thread-related issues can appear even in environments that don't explicitly support threads, such as JavaScript programmers doing AJAX-style programming, because the web server responses are processed asynchronously, and hence the JavaScript that runs to process the response may access data used by other parts of the application. That's why good programmers take the time to learn how to write multithreaded programs correctly.

BASIC THREAD CONCEPTS

This chapter starts by reviewing what threads are and how you can control them.

Threads

A *thread* is the fundamental unit of execution within an application: A running application consists of at least one thread. Each thread has its own stack and runs independently from the application's other threads. By default, threads share their resources, such as file handles or memory. Problems can occur when access to shared resources is not properly controlled. Data corruption is a common side effect of having two threads simultaneously write data to the same block of memory, for example.

Threads can be implemented in different ways. On most systems, threads are created and managed by the operating system: These are called *native threads* or *kernel-level threads*. Sometimes the threads are implemented by a software layer above the operating system, such as a virtual machine: These are called *green threads*. Both types of threads have essentially the same behavior. Some thread operations are faster on green threads, but they typically cannot take advantage of multiple processor cores, and implementation of blocking I/O is difficult. As multicore systems have become prevalent, most virtual machines have shifted away from green threads. The remainder of this chapter assumes that the threads are native threads.

Because the number of threads that can be executed at any given instant is limited by the number of cores in the computer, the operating system rapidly switches from thread to thread, giving each thread a small window of time to run. This is known as *preemptive threading,* because the operating system can suspend a thread's execution at any point to let another thread run. (A *cooperative model* requires a thread to explicitly take some action to suspend its own execution and let other threads run.) Suspending one thread so another can start to run is referred to as a *context switch.*

System Threads versus User Threads

A system thread is created and managed by the system. The first (main) thread of an application is a system thread, and the application often exits when the first thread terminates. User threads are explicitly created by the application to do tasks that cannot or should not be done by the main thread.

Applications that display user interfaces must be particularly careful with how they use threads. The main thread in such an application is usually called the *event thread* because it waits for and delivers events (such as mouse clicks and key presses) to the application for processing. Generally speaking, making the event thread unavailable to process events for any length of time (for instance, by performing lengthy processing in this thread or making it wait for something) is considered bad programming practice because it leads to (at best) an unresponsive application or (at worst) a frozen computer. Applications avoid these issues by creating threads to handle potentially time-consuming operations, especially those involving network access. These user threads often communicate data back to the event (main) thread by queueing events for it to process; this allows the event thread to receive data without stopping and waiting or wasting resources by repeatedly polling.

Monitors and Semaphores

Applications must use *thread synchronization* mechanisms to control threads' interactions with shared resources. Two fundamental thread synchronization constructs are monitors and semaphores. Which you use depends on what your system or language supports.

A *monitor* is a set of routines protected by a mutual exclusion lock. A thread cannot execute any of the routines in the monitor until it acquires the lock, which means that only one thread at a time can execute within the monitor; all other threads must wait for the currently executing thread to give up control of the lock. A thread can suspend itself in the monitor and wait for an event to occur, in which case another thread is given the chance to enter the monitor. At some point the suspended thread is notified that the event has occurred, allowing it to awake and reacquire the lock at the earliest possible opportunity.

A *semaphore* is a simpler construct: just a lock that protects a shared resource. Before using a shared resource, the thread is supposed to acquire the lock. Any other thread that tries to acquire the lock to use the resource is blocked until the lock is released by the thread that owns it, at which point one of the waiting threads (if any) acquires the lock and is unblocked. This is the most basic kind of semaphore, a mutual exclusion, or *mutex,* semaphore. Other semaphore types include *counting semaphores* (which let a maximum of *n* threads access a resource at any given time) and *event semaphores* (which notify one or all waiting threads that an event has occurred).

Monitors and semaphores can be used to achieve similar goals, but monitors are simpler to use because they handle all details of lock acquisition and release. When using semaphores, each thread must be careful to release every lock it acquires, including under conditions in which it terminates unexpectedly; otherwise, no other thread that needs the shared resource can proceed. In addition, every routine that accesses the shared resource must explicitly acquire a lock before using the resource, something that can be accidentally omitted when coding. Monitors automatically acquire and release the necessary locks.

Most systems provide a way for the thread to timeout if it can't acquire a resource within a certain amount of time, allowing the thread to report an error and/or try again later.

Thread synchronization doesn't come for free: It takes time to acquire and release locks whenever a shared resource is accessed. This is why some libraries include both thread-safe and non-thread-safe classes, for instance `StringBuffer` and `StringBuilder` in Java.

Deadlocks

Consider the situation in which two threads block each other because each is waiting for a lock that the other holds. This is called a *deadlock*: Each thread is permanently stalled because neither can continue running to the point of releasing the lock that the other needs.

One typical scenario in which this occurs is when two processes each need to acquire two locks (A and B) before proceeding but attempt to acquire them in different orders. If process 1 acquires A, but process 2 acquires B before process 1 does, then process 1 blocks on acquiring B (which process 2 holds) and process 2 blocks on acquiring A (which process 1 holds). There are a variety of complicated mechanisms for detecting and breaking deadlocks, none of which are entirely satisfactory. In theory the best solution is to write code that cannot deadlock — for instance, whenever it's necessary to acquire more than one lock, the locks should always be acquired in the same order and released in reverse order. In practice, it becomes difficult to enforce this across a large application with many locks, each of which may be acquired by code in many different places.

A Threading Example

A banking system provides an illustration of basic threading concepts and the necessity of thread synchronization. The system consists of a program running on a single central computer that controls multiple automated teller machines (ATMs) in different locations. Each ATM has its own thread so that the machines can be used simultaneously and easily share the bank's account data.

The banking system has an `Account` class with a method to deposit and withdraw money from a user's account. The following code is written as a Java class but the code is almost identical to what you'd write in C#:

```java
public class Account {
    int    userNumber;
    String userLastName;
    String userFirstName;
    double userBalance;
    public boolean deposit( double amount ){
        double newBalance;
        if( amount < 0.0 ){
            return false; /* Can't deposit negative amount */
        } else {
            newBalance = userBalance + amount;
            userBalance = newBalance;
            return true;
        }
    }
    public boolean withdraw( double amount ){
        double newBalance;
        if( amount < 0.0 || amount > userBalance ){
            return false; /* Negative withdrawal or insufficient funds */
        } else {
            newBalance = userBalance - amount;
            userBalance = newBalance;
            return true;
        }
    }
}
```

Suppose a husband and wife, Ron and Sue, walk up to different ATMs to withdraw $100 each from their joint account. The thread for the first ATM deducts $100 from the couple's account, but the thread is switched out after executing this line:

```java
newBalance = userBalance - amount;
```

Processor control then switches to the thread for Sue's ATM, which is also deducting $100. When that thread deducts $100, the account balance is still $500 because the variable, `userBalance`, has not yet been updated. Sue's thread executes until completing this function and updates the value of `userBalance` to $400. Then, control switches back to Ron's transaction. Ron's thread has the value $400 in `newBalance`. Therefore, it simply assigns this value to `userBalance` and returns. Thus, Ron and Sue have deducted $200 total from their account, but their balance still indicates $400, or a net $100 withdrawal. This is a great feature for Ron and Sue, but a big problem for the bank.

Fixing this problem is trivial in Java. Just use the `synchronized` keyword to create a monitor:

```java
public class Account {
    int    userNumber;
    String userLastName;
    String userFirstName;
    double userBalance;
    public synchronized boolean deposit( double amount ){
        double newBalance;
```

```
                    if( amount < 0.0 ){
                        return false; /* Can't deposit negative amount */
                    } else {
                        newBalance = userBalance + amount;
                        userBalance = newBalance;
                        return true;
                    }
                }
            public synchronized boolean withdraw( double amount ){
                    double newBalance;
                    if( amount < 0.0 || amount > userBalance ){
                        return false; /* Negative withdrawal or insufficient funds */
                    } else {
                        newBalance = userBalance - amount;
                        userBalance = newBalance;
                        return true;
                    }
                }
            }
```

The first thread that enters either deposit or withdraw blocks all other threads from entering either method. This protects the userBalance class data from being changed simultaneously by different threads. The preceding code can be made marginally more efficient by having the monitor synchronize only the code that uses or alters the value of userBalance instead of the entire method:

```
    public class Account {
        int     userNumber;
        String userLastName;
        String userFirstName;
        double userBalance;
        public boolean deposit( double amount ){
            double newBalance;
            if( amount < 0.0 ){
                return false; /* Can't deposit negative amount */
            } else {
                synchronized( this ){
                    newBalance = userBalance + amount;
                    userBalance = newBalance;
                }
                return true;
            }
        }
        public boolean withdraw( double amount ){
            double newBalance;
            synchronized( this ){
                if( amount < 0.0 || amount > userBalance ){
                    return false;
                } else {
                    newBalance = userBalance - amount;
                    userBalance = newBalance;
                    return true;
                }
            }
        }
    }
```

In fact, in Java a synchronized method such as:

```
synchronized void someMethod(){
    .... // the code to protect
}
```

is exactly equivalent to:

```
void someMethod(){
    synchronized( this ){
        .... // the code to protect
    }
}
```

The `lock` statement in C# can be used in a similar manner, but only within a method:

```
void someMethod(){
    lock( this ){
        .... // the code to protect
    }
}
```

In either case, the parameter passed to `synchronize` or `lock` is the object to use as the lock.

Note that the C# `lock` isn't as flexible as the Java `synchronized` because the latter allows threads to suspend themselves while waiting for another thread to signal them that an event has occurred. In C# this must be done using event semaphores.

CONCURRENCY PROBLEMS

Issues that you encounter with threads in professional development can be Byzantine in their complexity, but concise thread problems appropriate for an interview are difficult to compose. Therefore the questions you get are likely to come from a fairly small set of classic thread problems, several of which are presented here.

Busy Waiting

> **PROBLEM** *Explain the term "busy waiting" and how it can be avoided.*

This is a simple problem, but one with important performance implications for any multithreaded application.

Consider a thread that spawns another thread to complete a task. Assume that the first thread needs to wait for the second thread to finish its work, and that the second thread terminates as soon as its work is done. The simplest approach is to have the first thread keep checking whether the second thread is alive and proceed as soon as it is dead:

```
Thread task = new TheTask();
task.start();
```

```
while( task.isAlive() ){
    ; // do nothing
}
```

This is called *busy waiting* because the waiting thread is still active, but it's not actually accomplishing anything. It's "busy" in the sense that the thread is still executed by the processor, even though the thread is doing nothing but waiting for the second thread to finish. Typically there are more active threads than cores, so this actually "steals" processor cycles away from the second thread (and any other active threads in the system), cycles that could be better spent doing real work.

Busy waiting is avoided by using a monitor or a semaphore, depending on what's available to the programmer. The waiting thread simply sleeps (suspends itself temporarily) until the other thread notifies it that it's done. In Java, any shared object can be used as a notification mechanism:

```
Object theLock = new Object();
synchronized( theLock ){
    Thread task = new TheTask( theLock );
    task.start();
    try {
        theLock.wait();
    }
    catch( InterruptedException e ){
        .... // do something if interrupted
    }
}
.....
class TheTask extends Thread {
    private Object theLock;
    public TheTask( Object theLock ){
        this.theLock = theLock;
    }
    public void run(){
        synchronized( theLock ){
            .... // do the task
            theLock.notify();
        }
    }
}
```

In this case, because TheTask terminates after it completes its task, the first thread could also sleep until it completes using join(), but wait() and notify() provide a more general approach that isn't dependent on thread termination. The preceding code can be simplified somewhat by using the thread object itself for the signaling:

```
Thread task = new TheTask();
synchronized( task ){
    task.start();
    try {
        task.wait();
    }
    catch( InterruptedException e ){
        .... // do something if interrupted
    }
}
```

```
.....
class TheTask extends Thread {
    public void run(){
        synchronized( this ){
            .... // do the task
            this.notify();
        }
    }
}
```

There are a very few circumstances where *spinlocks,* a form of busy waiting, are actually desirable. If you can guarantee that the lock you're waiting for will be released in less time than it would take to acquire a conventional lock (a situation often encountered in kernel programming), it may be more efficient to use a spinlock that busy waits for this short period of time.

Another case where spinlocks are useful is *high-performance computing* (HPC) where the entire system is dedicated to a single application and exactly one compute thread is created per core. In this scenario, if one thread is waiting on data from a second thread running on a different core, there's no useful work that can be performed on the first thread's core until the data arrives, so there's no downside to wasting compute cycles by busy waiting. The time between data arrival and the process proceeding past the lock is often less for a spinlock than a semaphore, so under these specific circumstances an application using spinlocks may have better performance than one using semaphores. In any case, appropriate use of spinlocks requires careful assembly coding (to ensure that the attempts at lock acquisition are atomic); busy waiting should always be avoided in high-level languages.

Producer/Consumer

> **PROBLEM** *Write a Producer thread and a Consumer thread that share a fixed-size buffer and an index to access the buffer. The Producer should place numbers into the buffer, and the Consumer should remove the numbers. The order in which the numbers are added or removed is not important.*

This is one of the canonical concurrency problems. The first step is to answer the problem without using any concurrency control, and then comment on what the problems are. The algorithm isn't difficult when concurrency isn't an issue. The data buffer looks like this:

```
public class IntBuffer {
    private int    index;
    private int[] buffer = new int[8];
    public void add( int num ){
        while( true ){
            if( index < buffer.length ){
                buffer[index++] = num;
                return;
            }
        }
    }
}
```

```
    public int remove(){
        while( true ){
            if( index > 0 ){
                return buffer[--index];
            }
        }
    }
}
```

The producer and consumer are almost trivial:

```
public class Producer extends Thread {
    private IntBuffer buffer;
    public Producer( IntBuffer buffer ){
        this.buffer = buffer;
    }
    public void run(){
        Random r = new Random();
        while( true ){
            int num = r.nextInt();
            buffer.add( num );
            System.out.println( "Produced " + num );
        }
    }
}
public class Consumer extends Thread {
    private IntBuffer buffer;
    public Consumer( IntBuffer buffer ){
        this.buffer = buffer;
    }
    public void run(){
        while( true ){
            int num = buffer.remove();
            System.out.println( "Consumed " + num );
        }
    }
}
```

Then, somewhere in the code you start the threads:

```
IntBuffer b = new IntBuffer();
Producer p = new Producer( b );
Consumer c = new Consumer( b );
p.start();
c.start();
```

There are two problems with this approach, however. First, it uses busy waiting, which wastes a lot of CPU time. Second, there is no access control for the shared resource, the buffer: If a context switch occurs as the index is being updated, the next thread may read from or write to the wrong element of the buffer.

You may think at first that making the add and remove methods synchronized fixes the problem:

```
public class IntBuffer {
    private int    index;
    private int[] buffer = new int[8];
```

```
        public synchronized void add( int num ){
            while( true ){
                if( index < buffer.length ){
                    buffer[index++] = num;
                    return;
                }
            }
        }
        public synchronized int remove(){
            while( true ){
                if( index > 0 ){
                    return buffer[--index];
                }
            }
        }
    }
```

This actually creates an even worse problem. add and remove still busy wait when the buffer is full or empty (respectively). When a thread is busy waiting in add, no thread can enter remove (because the methods are now synchronized), so the buffer remains full forever. A similar problem is encountered if remove is called when the buffer is empty; the first time either of these situations is encountered, the application locks up in an infinite busy wait loop. The code inside the methods needs to be changed so that the producer suspends itself when the buffer is full and waits for a slot to open up, and the consumer suspends itself if the buffer is empty and waits for a new value to arrive:

```
    public class IntBuffer {
        private int    index;
        private int[] buffer = new int[8];
        public synchronized void add( int num ){
            while( index == buffer.length - 1 ){
                try {
                    wait();
                }
                catch( InterruptedException e ){
                }
            }
            buffer[index++] = num;
            notifyAll();
        }
        public synchronized int remove(){
            while( index == 0 ){
                try {
                    wait();
                }
                catch( InterruptedException e ){
                }
            }
            int ret = buffer[--index];
            notifyAll();
            return ret;
        }
    }
```

This code actually allows multiple producers and consumers to use the same buffer simultaneously, so it's even more general-purpose than the two-thread-only solution you'd be expected to come up with.

The Dining Philosophers

> **PROBLEM** *Five introspective and introverted philosophers are sitting at a circular table. In front of each philosopher is a plate of food. A fork (or a chopstick) lies between each philosopher, one by the philosopher's left hand and one by the right hand. A philosopher cannot eat until he or she has forks in both hands. Forks are picked up one at a time. If a fork is unavailable, the philosopher simply waits for the fork to be freed. When a philosopher has two forks, he or she eats a few bites and then returns both forks to the table. If a philosopher cannot obtain both forks for a long time, he or she will starve. Is there an algorithm that will ensure that no philosophers starve?*

This is another concurrency classic, and although it may seem quite contrived — in the real world no one would starve because each philosopher would simply ask the adjacent philosophers for their forks — it accurately reflects real-world concurrency issues involving multiple shared resources. The point of the problem is to see whether you understand the concept of deadlock and know how to avoid it.

A naïve approach would be to have each philosopher wait until the left fork is available, pick it up, wait until the right fork is available, pick that fork up, eat, and then put down both forks. The following code implements this in Java using a separate thread for each philosopher:

```
public class DiningPhilosophers {
    // Each "fork" is just an Object we synchronize on
    private Object[]      forks;
    private Philosopher[] philosophers;
    // Prepare the forks and philosophers
    private DiningPhilosophers( int num ){
        forks = new Object[ num ];
        philosophers = new Philosopher[ num ];
        for ( int i = 0; i < num; ++i ){
            forks[i] = new Object();
            philosophers[i] = new Philosopher( i, i, ( i + 1 ) % num );
        }
    }
    // Start the eating process
    public void startEating() throws InterruptedException {
        for ( int i = 0; i < philosophers.length; ++i ){
            philosophers[i].start();
        }
        // Suspend the main thread until the first philosopher
        // stops eating, which will never happen -- this keeps
        // the simulation running indefinitely
        philosophers[0].join();
    }
```

```
        // Each philosopher runs in its own thread.
        private class Philosopher extends Thread {
            private int id;
            private int fork1;
            private int fork2;
            Philosopher( int id, int fork1, int fork2 ){
                this.id = id;
                this.fork1 = fork1;
                this.fork2 = fork2;
            }
            public void run() {
                status( "Ready to eat using forks " + fork1 +
                        " and " + fork2 );
                while ( true ){
                    status( "Picking up fork " + fork1 );
                    synchronized( forks[ fork1 ] ){
                        status( "Picking up fork " + fork2 );
                        synchronized( forks[ fork2 ] ){
                            status( "Eating" );
                        }
                    }
                }
            }
            private void status( String msg ){
                System.out.println( "Philosopher " + id +
                                    ": " + msg );
            }
        }

        // Entry point for simulation
        public static void main( String[] args ){
            try {
                DiningPhilosophers d = new DiningPhilosophers( 5 );
                d.startEating();
            }
            catch ( InterruptedException e ){
            }
        }
    }
```

What will happen when you run this code? It's not entirely deterministic because you don't know exactly when the scheduler will have each thread running. (This is one of the challenges of debugging multithreaded code.) You do know that each philosopher will try to grab his or her left fork and will always hold it until he or she can pick up the right fork and eat. Any time there's a fork on the table to the right of a philosopher who holds a left fork, you have a *race condition* that determines whether that philosopher gets the fork or the philosopher to his or her right picks it up. In the latter case, you have two philosophers with only left forks, and the first philosopher will have to wait until after the second eats before getting another shot at the fork. This will tend to lead to a lot of philosophers hungrily sitting around the table holding forks in their left hands.

At some point you would expect to reach a situation where four of the philosophers have forks in their left hands and only one fork remains on the table. (In practice, this is reached fairly quickly.) If this last fork is picked up as a right-handed fork, that philosopher eats, puts down both forks, and life goes on. If instead it's picked up as a left-handed fork, then each philosopher has one fork that cannot be released until the philosopher to the right gets a second fork and eats. Because the philosophers are seated around a circular table, this will never happen, so you have five soon-to-be-dead philosophers in a deadlock. (Somewhat more formally: When each philosopher has a left fork, by induction, a given philosopher can't get the right fork until after putting down the left fork but is required to get the right fork before putting down the left fork, so nothing happens.)

How can you avoid this deadlock? One solution is to add a timeout to the waiting: If a philosopher is not able to eat within a predetermined amount of time after acquiring the first fork, then the philosopher drops the fork and tries again. This doesn't actually solve the problem, though: It may get some philosophers eating, but it doesn't stop them from reaching a deadlock. Worse, there's no way to know exactly which philosophers will get to eat — you could have a situation in which the interactions of the timeouts and the scheduler is such that some philosophers starve because they *never* acquire both forks. This is referred to as *livelock*.

Perhaps there's a better solution that can avoid reaching deadlock in the first place. Deadlock occurs when each of the philosophers holds one fork in his or her left hand. What if one of the philosophers went for the right fork first? Then that philosopher would never hold just a left-hand fork (because he or she has to pick up a right fork first), so there's no way to reach the all-left-forks deadlock condition. Another way to look at this is in terms of the order in which the forks are acquired. You know that deadlocks often result from locks (forks) being acquired in different orders. If you number each of the philosophers and forks counterclockwise around the table, then under the left-fork-first strategy, each philosopher tries to pick up first a lower numbered fork and then a higher numbered fork. This is true of every philosopher except for the last, who has fork $n - 1$ on the left and fork 0 on the right. Reversing the left-right order of acquisition for this philosopher means that all the philosophers acquire forks in the same order from a global perspective: lower number first. This can be implemented with a change to the constructor that changes the order in which one of the philosophers picks up forks:

```
// Prepare the forks and philosophers
private DiningPhilosophers( int num ){
    forks = new Object[ num ];
    philosophers = new Philosopher[ num ];
    for ( int i = 0; i < num; ++i ){
        forks[i] = new Object();
        int fork1 = i;
        int fork2 = ( i + 1 ) % num;
        if ( i == 0 ){
            philosophers[i] = new Philosopher( i, fork2, fork1 );
        } else {
            philosophers[i] = new Philosopher( i, fork1, fork2 );
        }
    }
}
```

This solution avoids deadlock and would likely be adequate for most interviews, but it can be improved. Under the current implementation, each philosopher will eat, but will they all get an equal opportunity? Consider the philosopher sitting to the left of the right-hand-first philosopher (number 4, in the preceding implementation). This philosopher is in the unique position that neither neighbor takes one of his forks as a first fork; as a result it's much easier for him to get forks, and he eats like a philosopher king. On the other hand (literally), the right-hand-first philosopher pays the price, frequently waiting for the series of left fork wielding philosophers to the right to eat and put down their forks. The exact ratio of number of times that the lucky philosopher eats to the number of times the unlucky philosopher beside him does will vary by system, but in informal tests of five philosophers on our machines, philosopher 4 eats about a hundred times more frequently than philosopher 0.

How can you make mealtimes more fair for the philosophers? You'll want to preserve an ordering of the forks to avoid deadlocks. Consider whether you need to have all the forks ordered. A philosopher holds at most two forks, so you just need a rule that defines the order for each philosopher for acquisition of a maximum of two forks. One such rule would be that each philosopher must pick up an odd numbered fork before an even numbered fork. (If — as in this problem — there are an odd number of philosophers, then philosopher n sits between two even numbered forks: $n - 1$ and 0. It doesn't matter in which order this philosopher picks up forks because he or she is the only one picking up two even forks.) A constructor that configures the philosophers under this scheme looks like:

```
// Prepare the forks and philosophers
    private DiningPhilosophers( int num ){
        forks = new Object[ num ];
        philosophers = new Philosopher[ num ];
        for ( int i = 0; i < num; ++i ){
            forks[i] = new Object();
            int fork1 = i;
            int fork2 = ( i + 1 ) % num;
            if ( ( i % 2 ) == 0 ){
                philosophers[i] = new Philosopher( i, fork2, fork1 );
            } else {
                philosophers[i] = new Philosopher( i, fork1, fork2 );
            }
        }
    }
```

This approach is completely fair for any even number of philosophers. For an odd number of philosophers, there's still a "lucky" philosopher. Although it's not completely fair in this case, it's a marked improvement for five philosophers: The lucky philosopher eats only about ten times more often than the least lucky one. In addition, as the number of philosophers at the table increases, this approach becomes increasingly fair while the single right-hand-first philosopher algorithm becomes increasingly unfair.

SUMMARY

Using multiple threads of execution within an application can make it more responsive and allow it to take full advantage of a multicore system but also makes programming more complicated. Synchronization is required to avoid data corruption whenever multiple threads access shared resources.

Synchronization is often achieved using monitors or semaphores. These facilities enable applications to control access to shared resources and to signal other threads when the resources are available for processing. Misuse of these constructs can halt threads through deadlock. Writing quality multi-threaded code that avoids both data corruption and deadlock is challenging, requiring care and discipline.

10

Object-Oriented Programming

Most professional development is done using an object-oriented programming (OOP) language such as Java, C#, or C++. Even JavaScript, though not an OOP language, supports some features of OOP through prototype objects and the clever use of function definitions. As such, you need to have a good grasp of fundamental OOP principles.

FUNDAMENTALS

Object-oriented programming's roots date back several decades to languages such as Simula and Smalltalk. OOP has been the subject of much academic research and debate, especially since the widespread adoption of OOP languages by practicing developers.

Classes and Objects

There are many different ways and no clear consensus on how to describe and define object orientation as a programming technique, but all of them revolve around the notions of classes and objects. A *class* is an abstract definition of something that has *attributes* (sometimes called *properties* or *states*) and *actions* (*capabilities* or *methods*). An *object* is a specific instance of a class that has its own state separate from any other object instance. Here's a class definition for Point, which is a pair of integers that represents the *x* and *y* values of a point in a Cartesian coordinate system:

```
public class Point {
    private int x;
    private int y;
    public Point( int x, int y ){
        this.x = x;
        this.y = y;
    }
    public Point( Point other ){
        x = other.getX();
        y = other.getY();
    }
```

```
public int getX(){ return x; }
public int getY(){ return y; }
public Point relativeTo( int dx, int dy ){
    return new Point( x + dx, y + dy );
}
public String toString(){
    StringBuffer b = new StringBuffer();
    b.append( '(' );
    b.append( x );
    b.append( ',' );
    b.append( y );
    b.append( ')' );
    return b.toString();
}
}
```

To represent a specific point, simply create an instance of the `Point` class with the appropriate values:

```
Point p1 = new Point( 5, 10 );
Point p2 = p1.relativeTo( -5, 5 );
System.out.println( p2.toString() ); // prints (0,15)
```

This simple example shows one of the principles of OOP, that of *encapsulation* — the hiding of implementation details.

Inheritance and Polymorphism

Two other important principles are inheritance and polymorphism, which are closely related. *Inheritance* allows a class to be defined as a modified or more specialized version of another class. When class B *inherits* from class A (Java uses the term *extends*), class A is B's *parent* or *base* class, and class B is A's *subclass*. All the behaviors defined by class A are also part of class B, though possibly in a modified form. In fact, an instance of class B can be used wherever an instance of class A is required.

Polymorphism is the capability to provide multiple implementations of an action and to select the correct implementation based on the surrounding context. For example, a class might define two versions of a method with different parameters. Or the same method might be defined both in a parent class and a subclass, the latter *overriding* the former for instances of the subclass. Method selection may occur when the code is compiled or when the application is run.

The classic example of inheritance and polymorphism is a shapes library representing the different shapes in a vector-based drawing application. At the top of the hierarchy is the `Shape` class, which defines the things that all shapes have in common:

```
public abstract class Shape {
    protected Point center;
    protected Shape( Point center ){
        this.center = center;
    }
    public Point getCenter(){
        return center; // because Point is immutable
    }
```

```
    public abstract Rectangle getBounds();
    public abstract void draw( Graphics g );
}
```

You can then specialize the shapes into `Rectangle` and `Ellipse` subclasses:

```
public class Rectangle extends Shape {
    private int h;
    private int w;

    public Rectangle( Point center, int w, int h ){
        super( center );
        this.w = w;
        this.h = h;
    }
    public Rectangle getBounds(){
        return this;
    }
    public int getHeight(){ return h; }
    public int getWidth(){ return w; }
    public void draw( Graphics g ){
        .... // code to paint rectangle
    }
}
public class Ellipse extends Shape {
    private int a;
    private int b;
    public Ellipse( Point center, int a, int b ){
        super( center );
        this.a = a;
        this.b = b;
    }
    public Rectangle getBounds(){
        return new Rectangle( center, a * 2, b * 2 );
    }
    public int getSemiMajorAxis(){ return a; }
    public int getSemiMinorAxis(){ return b; }
    public void draw( Graphics g ){
        .... // code to paint ellipse
    }
}
```

The `Rectangle` and `Ellipse` classes could be further specialized into `Square` and `Circle` subclasses.

Even though many shapes may be defined in the library, the part of the application that draws them on the screen doesn't need to do much work:

```
void paintShapes( Graphics g, List<Shape> shapes ){
    for( Shape s : shapes ){
        s.draw( g );
    }
}
```

Adding a new shape to the library is just a matter of subclassing one of the existing classes and implementing the things that are different.

CONSTRUCTION AND DESTRUCTION

Objects are instances of classes. Creating an object is called *constructing the object*. Part of the process involves invoking a *constructor* method in the class. The constructor initializes the state of the object, which usually involves calling (either explicitly or implicitly) the constructors of its parent classes so that they can initialize their part of the object's state.

Destroying objects is not as straightforward as constructing them. In C++ a method called the *destructor* is invoked to clean up an object's state. Destructors are invoked automatically when an object goes out of scope or when the `delete` operator is used to destroy a dynamically created object — keeping track of objects is important to avoid leaking memory. In languages such as C# and Java, however, the garbage collector is responsible for finding and destroying unused objects, in which case the time and place (it usually happens on a separate, system-defined thread) of the destruction is out of the application's control. An optional *finalizer* method is invoked by the system prior to the object's destruction to give it the opportunity to clean itself up before its "final" destruction. (In C# and Java it's possible for objects to "resurrect" themselves from destruction in their finalizers.)

OBJECT-ORIENTED PROGRAMMING PROBLEMS

Problems you are presented with relating to object-oriented programming are likely to focus on the concepts of object orientation, particularly on issues relevant to the languages the company is using in its coding.

Interfaces and Abstract Classes

> **PROBLEM** *What is the difference between an interface and an abstract class in object-oriented programming?*

The specific answer to this depends on the language, but some general definitions are:

➤ An *interface* declares a set of related methods, outside of any class.

➤ An *abstract class* is an incomplete class definition that declares but does not define all its methods.

Conceptually, then, an interface defines an *application programming interface* (API) that is independent of any class hierarchy. Interfaces are particularly important in languages that support only single inheritance, in which classes can inherit only from one base class. A class that includes all the methods described in an interface is said to *implement* the interface.

Unlike an interface, an abstract class is a proper class: It can have data members and method definitions and can be a subclass of other classes. Unlike a concrete (nonabstract) class, some of its behaviors are deliberately left to be defined by its own subclasses. Abstract classes cannot be instantiated because of this — only instances of concrete subclasses can be created.

An interface is equivalent to an abstract class with no data members and no method definitions. In C++ this is how you define an interface: by declaring a class with no data members and only pure virtual functions. For example:

```
class StatusCallback {
  public:
    virtual void updateStatus( int oState, int nState ) = 0;
}
```

A class implements the interface by deriving from it and providing a definition for the method:

```
class MyClass : SomeOtherClass, StatusCallback {
  public:
    void updateStatus( int oState, int nState ){
        if( nState > oState ){
            ..... // do stuff
        }
    }
    .... // remainder of class
}
```

In Java, an interface is defined using the `interface` keyword:

```
public interface StatusCallback {
    void updateStatus( int oState, int nState );
}
```

The interface is then implemented by a class:

```
public class MyClass implements StatusCallback {
    public void updateStatus( int oState, int nState ){
        if( nState > oState ){
            ..... // do stuff
        }
    }
    .... // remainder of class
}
```

A common pattern you see with languages that support both interfaces and abstract classes is the provision of a *default implementation* of an interface via an abstract class. For example, the following interface:

```
public interface XMLReader {
    public XMLObject fromString( String str );
    public XMLObject fromReader( Reader in );
}
```

might have this default implementation:

```
public abstract class XMLReaderImpl implements XMLReader {
    public XMLObject fromString( String str ){
        return fromReader( new StringReader( str ) );
    }
    public abstract XMLObject fromReader( Reader in );
}
```

A programmer who wants to implement XMLReader would then have the option to create a class that subclasses XMLReaderImpl (likely as a nested class) and implement only one method instead of two.

In general, abstract classes are useful when the classes derived from them are more specific types of the base class (they have an *is-a* relationship), particularly when there's some shared functionality (for example, data members or method definitions) in the abstract base class that derived classes can use. Interfaces are useful when unrelated classes need to provide a common way to invoke conceptually related functionality, but the implementation of this functionality can vary widely from class to class.

Virtual Methods

> **PROBLEM** *What are virtual methods? Why are they useful?*

In OOP, child classes can override (redefine) methods defined by ancestor classes. If the method is virtual, the method definition to invoke is determined at run time based on the actual type (class) of the object on which it is invoked. Nonstatic Java methods are always virtual, but in C# and C++, methods are only virtual when declared with the virtual keyword — nonvirtual methods are the default. If the method is not virtual, then the method definition invoked is determined at compile time based on the type of the reference (or pointer).

Some examples may be helpful to illustrate this. Consider the following three C++ classes:

```
class A {
  public:
    void print() { cout << "A"; }
}
class B : A {
  public:
    void print() { cout << "B"; }
}
class C : B {
  public:
    void print() { cout << "C"; }
}
```

Because print is not virtual, the method invoked depends on the type used at *compile time*:

```
A *a = new A();
B *b = new B();
C *c = new C();
a->print(); // "A"
b->print(); // "B"
c->print(); // "C"
((B *)c)->print(); // "B"
((A *)c)->print(); // "A"
((A *)b)->print(); // "A"
```

If print is declared virtual instead:

```
class A {
  public:
    virtual void print() { cout << "A"; }
}
class B : A {
  public:
    virtual void print() { cout << "B"; }
}
class C : B {
  public:
    virtual void print() { cout << "C"; }
}
```

The *runtime type* of the object determines which method definition is invoked:

```
A *a = new A();
B *b = new B();
C *c = new C();
a->print(); // "A"
b->print(); // "B"
c->print(); // "C"
((B *)c)->print(); // "C"
((A *)c)->print(); // "C"
((A *)b)->print(); // "B"
```

Virtual methods are used for polymorphism: They allow a single method call to invoke different method definitions based on the class of the object. A C++ version of the Shape class defined at the beginning of the chapter would need to declare the draw method as virtual for the paintShapes method — which accesses the objects as Shape references — to work. One special type of virtual method in C++ is a pure virtual method: a method declared but explicitly not defined. (It is actually possible for a C++ class to declare a pure virtual method and also define it, but the definition can be called only from a derived class. When it comes to complexity, C++ never disappoints.) Any class that contains a pure virtual method or inherits one without redefining it is an abstract class. (In Java or C#, the equivalent to a pure virtual method is an abstract method.)

Virtual methods aren't free. It (almost always) takes longer to invoke a virtual method because the address of the appropriate method definition must be looked up in a table before it is invoked. This table also requires a small amount of extra memory. In most applications, the overhead associated with virtual methods is so small as to be negligible.

Multiple Inheritance

PROBLEM *Why do C# and Java disallow the multiple inheritance of classes?*

In C++ a class can inherit (directly or indirectly) from more than one class, which is referred to as *multiple inheritance*. C# and Java, however, limit classes to *single inheritance* — each class inherits from a single parent class.

Multiple inheritance is a useful way to create classes that combine aspects of two disparate class hierarchies, something that often happens when using different class frameworks within a single application. If two frameworks define their own base classes for exceptions, for example, you can use multiple inheritance to create exception classes that can be used with either framework.

The problem with multiple inheritance is that it can lead to ambiguity. The classic example is when a class inherits from two other classes, each of which inherits from the same class:

```
class A {
  protected:
    bool flag;
};
class B : public A {};
class C : public A {};
class D : public B, public C {
  public:
    void setFlag( bool nflag ){
        flag = nflag; // ambiguous
    }
};
```

In this example, the flag data member is defined by class A. But class D descends from class B and class C, which both derive from A, so in essence *two copies* of flag are available because there are two instances of A in D's class hierarchy. Which one do you want to set? The compiler will complain that the reference to flag in D is ambiguous. One fix is to explicitly disambiguate the reference:

```
B::flag = nflag;
```

Another fix is to declare B and C as *virtual base classes*, which means that only one copy of A can exist in the hierarchy, eliminating any ambiguity.

There are other complexities with multiple inheritance, such as the order in which the base classes are initialized when a derived object is constructed, or the way members can be inadvertently hidden from derived classes. To avoid these complexities, some languages restrict themselves to the simpler single inheritance model. Although this does simplify inheritance considerably, it also limits its usefulness because only classes with a common ancestor can share behaviors. Interfaces mitigate this restriction somewhat by allowing classes in different hierarchies to expose common interfaces even if they're not implemented by sharing code.

SUMMARY

Object-oriented programming languages are in widespread use today, so a firm understanding of basic OOP principles is necessary for most jobs. This means understanding the difference between classes and objects as well as concepts such as polymorphism and inheritance.

Be sure you understand how each programming language you use handles the different aspects of OOP.

11

Design Patterns

Although no two programming projects are the same, it's not unusual to feel a sense of déja vu in the middle of a project. The feeling that you've seen a problem before is actually a recognition on your part that you may be able to apply common approaches to solving a wide variety of similar architectural problems. These approaches are called design patterns.

WHAT ARE DESIGN PATTERNS?

Design patterns are guidelines for identifying and solving common design problems in object-oriented programming. Unlike frameworks or class libraries, design patterns are abstract, providing recommendations on how to solve specific kinds of programming problems without providing fully fleshed-out code to implement those recommendations. They distill years of software programming experience into a set of recipes for object-oriented application architecture.

Design patterns were popularized and formalized in the early 90s by the publication of *Design Patterns: Elements of Reusable Object Oriented Software*,[1] but the ideas predate the book. Many of the core design patterns, like Iterator and Singleton, are widely used and familiar to most Java and C++ programmers. Other patterns, like Builder, are less frequently used but are highly useful in the appropriate situation.

Why Use Design Patterns?

Design patterns are useful for two reasons. The obvious reason is that they help to solve common software design problems based on the collected wisdom of many programmers. This makes them invaluable as an educational tool and as a programming resource.

---

[1] *Design Patterns: Elements of Reusable Object-Oriented Software* by Erich Gamma, Richard Helm, Ralph Johnson, and John Vlissides. Addison-Wesley, 1995.

The second — and perhaps more important — reason is that design patterns provide a concise vocabulary for discussing design problems and their solutions. This vocabulary is a valuable aid to communicate design decisions to other programmers in informal discussions, design documents, or program comments.

Despite their general usefulness, design patterns are not a "miracle cure" for programming problems. The wrong design pattern can add unnecessary complexity to an application, and an incorrect or inefficient implementation of a pattern can introduce bugs or compromise performance.

> **NOTE** *Some work has also been done to identify patterns that should not be used. These "antipatterns" are often shortcuts or improper practices that lead to inefficient or ineffective code.*

Some programmers argue that design patterns are only necessary because of the flaws inherent in the structure of popular object-oriented languages like C++ and Java. Whether or not this is true, design patterns remain useful for programmers using these languages on a day-to-day basis.

Design Patterns in Interviews

Direct questions about design patterns aren't that common. It's unlikely that you'll be asked to write code that uses or exemplifies a specific design pattern. Expect to use patterns primarily as a way to communicate design concepts with the interviewer.

If you mention a design pattern, however, the interviewer might ask you questions to see how well you understand the design pattern. Don't use patterns if you can't explain how they work.

COMMON DESIGN PATTERNS

The *Design Patterns* book by Gamma *et al.* (often referred to as "The Gang of Four"), takes a formal and detailed approach to describing 23 fundamental design patterns. It groups these patterns into three basic categories: creational, behavioral, and structural.

> **NOTE** *Other design pattern categories have been developed, including concurrency patterns useful in concurrent programming. These patterns tend to be domain-specific and are not as widely known as the patterns in the three core categories.*

It's well worth reading and studying design patterns as described by The Gang of Four. We can't hope to cover in one chapter everything that others cover in volumes, but the summaries that follow provide a quick review of some common patterns.

Creational Patterns

These patterns manage class selection and object creation. Rather than creating objects directly, it may be advantageous for code to delegate object creation to other parts of an application, or to restrict how object instances can be created and accessed.

Singleton

The Singleton pattern ensures that at most one instance of a class exists at any given time. This instance acts as a gatekeeper to shared resources or as a central communications hub. An application cannot create new instances — all methods are accessed through the singleton. The application obtains the singleton by invoking a static method exposed by the class.

Core system functions are often accessed using singletons. In Java, for example, the `java.lang.Runtime` class is a singleton used to interact with the application's execution environment. Singletons are also sometimes used as a substitute for global variables, but this doesn't avoid any of the global state problems that plague global variables, so many people consider this use an anti-pattern.

Why is a singleton better than a set of static methods?

➤ **Inheritance and interfaces** — Singletons are objects. They can inherit from base classes and implement interfaces.

➤ **Possible multiplicity** — You can change your mind and create multiple objects (for example, one per thread) without changing a lot of code. (Of course, if you do this, it's no longer a singleton.)

➤ **Dynamic binding** — The actual class used to create the singleton can be determined at run time, not at compile time.

Singletons are not without their disadvantages. Methods must be synchronized in multithreaded environments, slowing access to the singleton's state. A singleton may also slow the application's startup time as it initializes, and it may hold onto resources longer than necessary.

Builder

The Builder pattern creates objects in a stepwise manner without knowing or caring how those objects are constructed. Instead of constructing an object directly (or via a factory), you instantiate a Builder and let it create the object on your behalf.

Builders are particularly useful for initializing objects that require multiple constructor parameters, especially parameters of the same or similar types. Here's a simple example:

```
public class Window {
    public Window( boolean visible, boolean modal, boolean dialog ){
        this.visible = visible;
        this.modal = modal;
        this.dialog = dialog;
    }

    private boolean visible;
    private boolean modal;
    private boolean dialog;

    ... // rest of class omitted
}
```

The constructor for `Window` takes three boolean parameters in no obvious order. Rather than always referring to the class documentation to remember which parameter does what, create a builder to encapsulate that knowledge:

```
public class WindowBuilder {
    public WindowBuilder() {}

    public WindowBuilder setDialog( boolean flag ){
        dialog = flag;
        return this;
    }

    public WindowBuilder setModal( boolean flag ){
        modal = flag;
        return this;
    }

    public WindowBuilder setVisible( boolean flag ){
        visible = flag;
        return this;
    }

    public Window build(){
        return new Window( visible, modal, dialog );
    }

    private boolean dialog;
    private boolean modal;
    private boolean visible;
}
```

Instead of directly constructing a `Window` object

```
Window w = new Window( false, true, true ); // ???
```

use a `WindowBuilder` instance to define the new object's initial state:

```
Window w = new WindowBuilder().setVisible( false )
    .setModal( true ).setDialog( true ).build();
```

Not only is the object initialization much clearer and easier to understand, but initialization parameters can be easily added and removed. Certain parameters can be mandatory, and the others can be made optional with default values.

Simpler initialization is one use for builders. Sometimes it's also useful to create a hierarchy of builders. At the top of the hierarchy is an abstract builder class that defines the methods for initializing the different parts of an object. Concrete subclasses override these methods to build the object in different ways. For example, a generic document builder would expose abstract methods like `addHeading` and `addParagraph`, which would be implemented by different subclasses to create HTML documents, PDF documents, and so on.

Use Builder when objects are complex to construct and are constructed in several steps. Otherwise, Abstract Factory may be simpler to use.

Factory Method

The Factory Method pattern applies the concept of a *factory method* — technically, any method whose primary purpose is to create and return a new object — to a class hierarchy. A base class defines a factory method that can be overridden in a subclass, enabling the subclass to determine how a new object is created. The base class may or may not provide a default implementation for the method, but it *always* uses the factory method to create a new object of the required type.

The Factory Method pattern is often used to implement the Abstract Factory pattern.

Abstract Factory

A *factory* is an object that can create other objects. The Abstract Factory pattern separates the factory implementation from the code that uses the factory.

The typical implementation of Abstract Factory has a set of factory classes inheriting from an abstract class. After selecting which factory implementation to use, the application refers to it exclusively via the abstract class, not via its actual (concrete) class. Factory selection can therefore be deferred until run time — perhaps chosen via a configuration file — or even changed midway through a program's execution.

Don't use Abstract Factory if the factories are different from each other or if there will be only one factory class.

Abstract Factory is closely related to the Factory Method pattern. The Singleton pattern is often used to implement Abstract Factory.

Behavioral Patterns

These patterns determine how classes and objects interact and communicate.

Iterator

The Iterator pattern enables you to traverse through all the elements in a data structure without knowing or caring how those elements are stored or represented. Built-in support for iterators is common in many modern languages.

There are many kinds of iterators and different trade-offs to using them. The simplest iterators provide for unidirectional traversal of elements with no changes allowed to the underlying data structure. More complex iterators allow for bidirectional traversal and permit elements to be added to or removed from the underlying data structure.

Observer

The Observer pattern lets objects broadcast changes in state to interested observers without needing to know much about the observers. This loose coupling is also called the *Publish-Subscribe pattern*. Observers register themselves with the subject (the object observed) using a common interface for update notifications. The subject notifies each registered observer whenever its state changes.

The *model-view-controller* (MVC) separation of responsibilities found within many user interface toolkits is a classic example of the Observer pattern in action, where changes to the model (the underlying data) automatically cause the views (the user interface) to redraw themselves.

Note that the Observer pattern does not specify what kind of information is passed to the observers, the order in which they're updated, or how quickly and how often changes are propagated. These implementation details can have quite an impact on the performance and utility of the overall system.

Structural Patterns

These patterns organize relationships between classes and objects, providing guidelines for combining and using related objects together to achieve desired behaviors.

Decorator

The Decorator pattern modifies the behavior of an object by "wrapping" it with another object that implements the same interface as the original object. The Decorator pattern is therefore sometimes referred to as a Wrapper pattern.

There are four kinds of classes in the Decorator pattern: Component, Concrete Component, Decorator and Concrete Decorator. Component is an abstract class or interface that defines the interface shared by Concrete Component and Decorator. Decorator is an abstract class that wraps the Concrete Component (the class you want to be able to modify), and forwards all method calls to the Component. Concrete Decorators, of which there are typically several, modify the behavior of the wrapped Concrete Component by overriding one or more methods of their parent Decorator class. The overridden method typically provides some additional functionality before and/or after calling the corresponding method on the underlying Concrete Component.

Decorators provide an alternative to subclassing. Multiple different Concrete Decorators can be applied to a given instance of Concrete Component, with each successive decoration forming another layer of wrapping around the object. The behavior of the underlying Concrete Component is modified by all of the decorators that wrap it.

DESIGN PATTERN PROBLEMS

Because design patterns are so abstract, you can expect a lot of variation in the types of questions that are asked.

Singleton Implementation

> **PROBLEM** *Your application uses a logging class to write debugging messages to the console. How would you implement this logging facility using the Singleton pattern?*

The Singleton pattern requires that at most one instance of the logging class exists at any given time. The easiest way to do this is to make the constructor private and initialize the single instance within the class. Here's a Java implementation of the logger:

```java
// Implements a simple logging class using a singleton.
public class Logger {

    // Create and store the singleton.
    private static final Logger instance = new Logger();

    // Prevent anyone else from creating this class.
    private Logger(){
    }

    // Return the singleton instance.
    public static Logger getInstance() { return instance; }

    // Log a string to the console.
    //
    //    example: Logger.getInstance().log("this is a test");
    //
    public void log( String msg ){
        System.out.println( System.currentTimeMillis() + ": " + msg );
    }
}
```

If you've claimed deep expertise in Java, an interviewer might ask you how an application could create multiple instances of the Logger class despite the existence of the private constructor and how to prevent that from happening. (Hint: think about cloning and object serialization.)

> **PROBLEM** *Your application uses a singleton, but it's not always necessary, and it's expensive to initialize. How can you improve this situation?*

The Singleton pattern doesn't specify *when* an instance is created, just that there can be *at most* one instance of the class created. It's not necessary for the instance to be created when the class is loaded, it just needs to be created before it's needed. Following this approach, getInstance should initialize the instance before returning it, if it hasn't yet been initialized. This technique is known as *deferred initialization* — also called *lazy initialization* or *lazy loading*.

Deferred initialization has both advantages and disadvantages, and it is not the best choice in every situation.

➤ Deferred initialization yields faster startup times, at the cost of a delay caused by initialization the first time the instance is accessed.

➤ If a deferred initialization singleton is never accessed, it is never initialized, saving the initialization time and resources it would otherwise require if it were initialized by the classloader.

➤ Deferred initialization allows selection of the class of the singleton object to be deferred until run time rather than being specified at compile time. Since the instance is created only once, this selection must be made before the first time the instance is accessed, but there might still be utility in making this selection at run time. For example, this would allow selection of the class based on settings in a configuration file.

➤ In a resource-limited environment, deferred initialization of the instance could fail due to inadequate resources. This could be particularly problematic for something like an error logging class that must be available when needed.

➤ Deferred initialization increases the complexity of the singleton class, especially in a multi-threaded system.

Now modify the `Logger` class you just wrote to use deferred initialization:

```
// Deferred initialization of logger.
public class Logger {

    // Create and store the singleton.
    private static Logger instance = null; // no longer final

    // Prevent anyone else from creating this class.
    private Logger(){
    }

    // Return the singleton instance.
    public static Logger getInstance() {
        if( instance == null ){
            instance = new Logger();
        }

        return instance;
    }

    // Log a string to the console.
    public void log( String msg ){
        System.out.println( System.currentTimeMillis() + ": " + msg );
    }
}
```

This simple change accomplishes deferred initialization, but introduces a new problem — it's no longer thread-safe. In the original version of your class, the instance was initialized when the class was loaded, before any methods could be called. In the revised, deferred initialization version, the instance is created in `getInstance`. What happens if two threads call `getInstance` simultaneously? They might both see `instance` as uninitialized, and both try to create the instance — clearly not what you want for a singleton. You can prevent this from happening by making `getInstance` a synchronized method:

```
// Return the singleton instance.
public synchronized static Logger getInstance() {
    if( instance == null ){
        instance = new Logger();
    }

    return instance;
}
```

There is a significant performance penalty to pay for this change, but if `getInstance` is called infrequently, it may not be important. It is possible to avoid this penalty in cases where the performance of `getInstance` is relevant. Consider that you are synchronizing *every* call to `getInstance` for the lifetime of the program, but once `instance` has been fully initialized, all you're doing is returning `instance`, which doesn't require synchronization to be thread-safe. Ideally, you'd like the method to be synchronized before the instance is initialized, and then stop being synchronized after the deferred initialization to avoid the overhead that synchronization entails.

There are several language-specific idioms that achieve this goal. One such Java idiom combines deferred and static initialization by employing deferred loading of an inner class that performs static initialization of the instance. This is thread-safe because the classloader is guaranteed to be serialized, so the inner class is loaded and initialized only once, no matter how many threads call `getInstance` simultaneously. It also avoids the overhead of synchronization, because serialization is provided by the classloader — after the class has been loaded, the classloader is no longer involved, so there's no residual overhead. This can be implemented for `Logger` by replacing the preceding implementation of `getInstance` with:

```
// Inner class initializes instance on load, won't be loaded
// until referenced by getInstance()
private static class LoggerHolder {
    public static final Logger instance = new Logger();
}

// Return the singleton instance.
public static Logger getInstance() { return LoggerHolder.instance; }
```

Decorator versus Inheritance

> **PROBLEM** *Why would you use the Decorator pattern instead of inheritance?*

Recall that the Decorator pattern *wraps* one object with another object to change the original object's behavior. The wrapper object can take the place of the original object because they share the same abstract base class (or implement the same interface).

Both the Decorator pattern and inheritance provide means of modifying the behavior of an object of the underlying class, but in different ways. Inheritance typically allows modification of the parent class only at compile time, while decorations are applied dynamically at run time.

Suppose you have an object that needs to dynamically change behavior. Accomplishing this with inheritance may be cumbersome and inefficient: Every time you need to change behavior, you'll probably need to construct a new object of a different child class with the desired behavior, copy the state from the existing object to the new one, and throw the old one away. In contrast, modifying the behavior of the existing object using the Decorator pattern is much simpler — just add the appropriate decoration (that is, wrap the existing object with another wrapper that implements the modified behavior).

The dynamic nature of the Decorator pattern has another advantage. Suppose you have several behavior modifications that you'd like to implement for a class. Assume that none of these modifications interfere with any of the others, so you can apply them in any combination. A classic example of this is a GUI toolkit with a `Window` class that may be modified by multiple different behaviors, such as `Bordered`, `Scrollable`, `Disabled`, and so on. You could implement this with inheritance: deriving `BorderedWindow` from `Window`, `ScrollableBorderedWindow` and `DisabledBorderedWindow` from `BorderedWindow`, and so on. This is reasonable for a small number of behaviors, but as the number of behaviors increases, your class hierarchy rapidly gets out of hand. The number of classes doubles each time you add a new behavior. You can avoid this explosion of largely redundant classes with the Decorator pattern. Each behavior is completely described by a single Decorator class, and you can generate whatever combination of behaviors you need by applying the appropriate set of decorations.

The Decorator pattern simplifies object-oriented design when applied correctly, but may have the opposite effect when used indiscriminately. If you *don't* need to dynamically modify the behavior of an object, then it's probably best to use simple inheritance and avoid the complexity of this pattern. Also, Concrete Decorator classes generally shouldn't expose new public methods; so if you need to do this, using Decorators probably isn't the best approach (Concrete Decorator classes shouldn't expose new public methods because they would likely become inaccessible when subsequent decorations are added.) Finally, you should make sure that your Concrete Decorator classes are truly mutually non-interfering. There's no good way to forbid combinations of decorations that are conflicting or don't make sense, so using the Decorator pattern in these circumstances may invite bugs later on.

Efficient Observer Updates

> **PROBLEM** *In the Observer pattern, what strategies can the subject use to efficiently update its observers?*

A naïve implementation of the Observer pattern can yield poor performance if many objects are observing other objects.

The most obvious problem is that a subject updates its state too often, causing it to spend most of its time updating its observers. This can happen when multiple properties are changed many times in rapid succession in a single code sequence. In such situations it may make more sense to briefly turn updates off, make the changes, then turn updates on and send a single update notification to all interested objects.

Another potential problem relates to how observers determine what has changed. In many windowing systems, for example, it's much more efficient to redraw just the part of the screen that has changed, rather than the entire display. To do this properly, the view (the observer) needs to know which part of the model (the subject) has changed. Rather than have the observer query the subject to determine what changed, why not have the subject pass the information along as part of the update notification?

There are also some interesting problems when dealing with updates across multiple threads, such as how to avoid deadlock conditions. We leave these as an exercise for you!

SUMMARY

Design patterns are useful tools for communicating software design concepts to interviewers. Interviewers may use your level of familiarity with design patterns to try to assess how much experience you have with object-oriented design. Make sure you understand and have experience with common design patterns.

12

Databases

With the rise of web-based applications, more programmers use databases for data storage and manipulation, so don't be surprised if you are asked questions about your experience with databases. Although different kinds of databases are available, the *relational database* is the most common.

DATABASE FUNDAMENTALS

There are tools available to help you create and manage databases, many of which hide the complexities of the underlying data structures. Ruby on Rails, for example, abstracts all database access and makes most direct access unnecessary, as do component technologies such as Enterprise JavaBeans and many object-oriented frameworks. Still, you need an understanding of how relational databases work to make good design decisions.

Relational Databases

Relational databases originated in the 1960s from the work of E. F. Codd, a computer scientist who designed a database system based on the concepts of relational algebra. However, you don't need to understand relational algebra or other mathematical concepts to use a relational database.

Data in a relational database is stored in *tables*, which consist of *rows* and *columns* (also known as *tuples* and *attributes*). A set of table definitions is referred to as a *schema*. Each column has a name and data type associated with it. The column data type limits the range of data that can be stored in the column; the column may also have additional constraints beyond those imposed by the type. Typically, the columns of a table are defined when the database is defined and modified infrequently (or never); data is added and removed from a table by inserting and deleting rows. Although the columns are typically ordered, the rows aren't. If ordering of rows is required, it is done when the data is fetched (via a *query*) from the database.

Most tables have keys. A *key* is a column or set of columns that uniquely identifies a particular row in the table. One of the keys is usually designated the *primary key*. For example, in a table of employees, you might use the employee identification number — guaranteed to be unique for each employee — as the primary key.

A table can be linked to another table using a foreign key. A *foreign key* is a key value taken from the other table (usually from a primary key). When every foreign key value in one table exists as a key in the table it references, the database has *referential integrity*. This can be enforced through the use of *foreign key constraints*. Depending on how the constraints are configured, an attempt to delete a row with a key value that exists in another table as a foreign key is either prevented or causes deletion or modification of the rows that reference it.

The most common way to manipulate and query databases is through the use of *Structured Query Language (SQL)*. There are some variations in syntax across different database management systems (DBMS), particularly for advanced features, but basic syntax is standardized.

SQL

SQL is the lingua franca of relational database manipulation. It provides mechanisms for most kinds of database manipulations. Understandably, SQL is a big topic, and numerous books are devoted just to SQL and relational databases. Nevertheless, the basic tasks of storing and retrieving data are fairly simple with SQL.

Most interview database problems involve writing queries for a database with a given schema, so you won't usually need to design a schema. We begin with the following schema:

```
Player (
  name   CHAR(20),
  number INTEGER(4)
);
Stats (
  number      INTEGER(4),
  totalPoints INTEGER(4),
  year        CHAR(20)
);
```

Table 12-1 shows some sample data for `Player`, and Table 12-2 shows sample `Stats` data.

TABLE 12-1: Player Sample Data

name	number
Larry Smith	23
David Gonzalez	12
George Rogers	7
Mike Lee	14
Rajiv Williams	55

TABLE 12-2: Stats Sample Data

number	totalPoints	year
7	59	Freshman
55	90	Senior
23	150	Senior
23	221	Junior
55	84	Junior

In this schema, neither table has a primary key defined. The number column in Player is a good candidate for a primary key because every player has a number, and the player number uniquely identifies each player. The number column in the Stats table is a foreign key — a reference to the number column in the Player table. Explicitly defining these relationships in the schema makes it easier for others to understand — and the database to maintain — the relationship between these tables:

```
Player (
  name    CHAR(20),
  number INTEGER(4) PRIMARY KEY
);
Stats (
  number       INTEGER(4),
  totalPoints INTEGER(4),
  year         CHAR(20),
  FOREIGN KEY (number) REFERENCES Player
);
```

With these changes, the database takes an active role in ensuring the referential integrity of these tables. For example, you can't add a row to the Stats table that references a player not listed in the Player table: The foreign key relationship between Stats.number and Player.number forbids this.

One fundamental SQL statement is INSERT, which is used to add values to a table. For example, to insert a player named Bill Henry with the number 50 into the Player table, you would use the following statement:

```
INSERT INTO Player VALUES('Bill Henry', 50);
```

SELECT is the SQL statement most commonly seen in interviews. A SELECT statement retrieves data from a table. For example, the statement:

```
SELECT * FROM Player;
```

returns all the values in the table Player:

```
+-----------------+--------+
| name            | number |
+-----------------+--------+
| Larry Smith     |     23 |
| David Gonzalez  |     12 |
| George Rogers   |      7 |
| Mike Lee        |     14 |
| Rajiv Williams  |     55 |
| Bill Henry      |     50 |
+-----------------+--------+
```

You can specify which columns you want to return like this:

```
SELECT name FROM Player;
```

which yields:

```
+----------------+
| name           |
+----------------+
| Larry Smith    |
| David Gonzalez |
| George Rogers  |
| Mike Lee       |
| Rajiv Williams |
| Bill Henry     |
+----------------+
```

You may want to be more restrictive about which values you return. For example, if you want to return only the names of the players with numbers less than 10 or greater than 40, you would use the statement:

```
SELECT name FROM Player WHERE number < 10 OR number > 40;
```

which would return:

```
+----------------+
| name           |
+----------------+
| George Rogers  |
| Rajiv Williams |
| Bill Henry     |
+----------------+
```

Much of the power of a relational database comes from the relationships between data in different tables, so you frequently want to use data from more than one table. For example, you may want to print out the names of all players along with the number of points that each player has scored. To do this, you have to *join* the two tables on the `number` field. The `number` field is called a *common key* because it represents the same value in both tables. The query is as follows:

```
SELECT name, totalPoints, year FROM Player, Stats
WHERE Player.number = Stats.number;
```

It returns this:

```
+----------------+-------------+----------+
| name           | totalPoints | year     |
+----------------+-------------+----------+
| George Rogers  |          59 | Freshman |
| Rajiv Williams |          90 | Senior   |
| Rajiv Williams |          84 | Junior   |
| Larry Smith    |         150 | Senior   |
| Larry Smith    |         221 | Junior   |
+----------------+-------------+----------+
```

Some players have played on the team for more than one year, so their names appear multiple times; others have no rows in Stats (apparently they've been warming the bench) so they don't appear at all in the results of this query. Conceptually, when you include two tables in the FROM clause, the query constructs a *Cartesian product* of the tables: a single table containing all possible combinations of rows from the first table with rows from the second table. Then the WHERE limits the results returned by the query to rows where the two keys are equal. This is the most common type of join, called an *inner join*. An alternative syntax that accomplishes exactly the same query is:

```
SELECT name, totalPoints, year FROM Player INNER JOIN Stats
ON Player.number = Stats.number;
```

A less commonly used type of join is the *outer join*. Unlike inner joins, which exclude rows with key values that don't match the corresponding key in the joined table, outer joins include these rows. Because included rows with no match in the other table have no values for the columns from the other table, these values are returned as NULL. There are three kinds of outer joins: left, right and full. A *left outer join* retains all rows from the first table, but only matching rows from the second; a *right outer join* retains all rows from the second table but only matching rows from the first, and a *full outer join* retains all rows from both tables. For this database, a left outer join of the two tables would include the names of the benchwarmers:

```
SELECT name, totalPoints, year FROM Player LEFT OUTER JOIN Stats
ON Player.number = Stats.number;
```

returns:

```
+----------------+-------------+----------+
| name           | totalPoints | year     |
+----------------+-------------+----------+
| George Rogers  |          59 | Freshman |
| David Gonzalez |        NULL | NULL     |
| Mike Lee       |        NULL | NULL     |
| Rajiv Williams |          90 | Senior   |
| Rajiv Williams |          84 | Junior   |
| Larry Smith    |         150 | Senior   |
| Larry Smith    |         221 | Junior   |
| Bill Henry     |        NULL | NULL     |
+----------------+-------------+----------+
```

The *aggregates*, MAX, MIN, SUM, and AVG, are another commonly used SQL feature. These aggregates enable you to retrieve the maximum, minimum, sum, and average, respectively, for a particular column. For example, you may want print the average number of points each player has scored. To do this, use the following query:

```
SELECT AVG(totalPoints) FROM Stats;
```

producing:

```
+------------------+
| AVG(totalPoints) |
+------------------+
|         120.8000 |
+------------------+
```

Other times, you may want to apply aggregates separately over subsets of the data. For example, you may want to calculate each player's average total points per year. This is accomplished with the GROUP BY clause, as in the following query:

```
SELECT name, AVG(totalPoints) FROM Player INNER JOIN Stats
ON Player.number = Stats.number GROUP BY name;
```

which produces

```
+----------------+------------------+
| name           | AVG(totalPoints) |
+----------------+------------------+
| George Rogers  |             59.0 |
| Rajiv Williams |             87.0 |
| Larry Smith    |            185.5 |
+----------------+------------------+
```

Most interview problems focus on using these sorts of INSERT and SELECT statements. You're less likely to encounter SQL problems related to other features, such as UPDATE statements, DELETE statements, permissions, security, or optimization, but you must understand *transactions*.

Database Transactions

The integrity of the data stored in a database is paramount: If the data is corrupted, every application that depends on the database may fail or be in error. Although referential integrity helps keep the data consistent, other forms of inconsistency can occur, even in a database that has referential integrity. An additional mechanism to maintain data integrity is the database transaction.

A *transaction* groups a set of related database manipulations together into a single unit. If any operation within the transaction fails, the entire transaction fails, and any changes made by the transaction are abandoned (*rolled back*). Conversely, if all the operations succeed, then all the changes are *committed* together as a group.

Chapter 8 includes a simple example involving the addition and removal of money from a bank account. If you expand the example to involve the transfer of money between two accounts with account balances maintained in a database, you can see why transactions are so important. A transfer is actually two operations: removing money from the first account and then adding it to the second account. If an error occurs immediately after the money is removed from the first account, you want the system to detect the problem and redeposit the withdrawn money into the original account. As long as both operations are contained in a transaction, there won't be any problems with this: Either both of them are successfully committed and the transfer succeeds, or neither one is committed and the transfer fails. In either case, no money is lost.

The four properties of a transaction are as follows:

➤ **Atomicity** — The database system guarantees that either all operations within the transaction succeed or else they all fail.

> ➤ **Consistency** — The transaction must ensure that the database is in a correct, consistent state at the start and the end of the transaction. No referential integrity constraints can be broken, for example.

> ➤ **Isolation** — All changes to the database within a transaction are isolated from all other queries and transactions until the transaction is committed.

> ➤ **Durability** — When committed, changes made in a transaction are permanent. The database system must have some way to recover from crashes and other problems so that the current state of the database is never lost.

These four properties are generally referred to as *ACID*. As you might imagine, there is a significant performance penalty to be paid if all four properties are to be guaranteed on each transaction. The isolation requirement can be particularly onerous on a system with many simultaneous transactions, so most systems allow the isolation requirements to be relaxed in different ways to provide improved performance.

Note that ACID compliance is *not* a relational database requirement, but most modern databases support it.

DATABASE PROBLEMS

If you indicate on your résumé that you have some database experience or the job you apply for involves working with databases, interviewers will probably ask you database questions to determine the depth of your knowledge.

Simple SQL

> **PROBLEM** *Given a database with the table*
>
> ```
> Olympics(
>     city CHAR(16),
>     year INTEGER(4)
> );
> ```
>
> *write a SQL statement to insert Montreal and 1976 into the database.*

This is an extremely easy problem that an interviewer might use to determine whether you have ever used SQL before or whether you were padding your résumé when you mentioned it. If you know SQL, you're all set. It's a straightforward SQL INSERT statement; no tricks. If you don't know SQL, you're in trouble. The correct answer is

```
INSERT INTO Olympics VALUES( 'Montreal', 1976 );
```

Company and Employee Database

PROBLEM *You are given a database with the following tables:*

```
Company (
    companyName CHAR(30),
    id          INTEGER(4) PRIMARY KEY
);
EmployeesHired (
    id           INTEGER(4),
    numHired     INTEGER(4),
    fiscalQuarter INTEGER(4),
    FOREIGN KEY (id) REFERENCES Company
);
```

You may make the assumption that the only possible fiscal quarters are 1 through 4. Sample data for this schema is presented in Tables 12-3 and 12-4.

TABLE 12-3: Company Sample Data

companyName	id
Hillary Plumbing	6
John Lawn Company	9
Dave Cookie Company	19
Jane Electricity	3

TABLE 12-4: Employees Hired Sample Data

id	numHired	fiscalQuarter
3	3	3
3	2	4
19	4	1
6	2	1

Write a SQL statement that returns the names of all the companies that hired employees in fiscal quarter 4.

This problem involves retrieving data from two tables. You must join the two tables to get all the needed information. `id` is the only key common to both tables, so you want to join on the column id. After you join the two tables, you can select the company name where the fiscal quarter is 4. This SQL statement looks like:

```
SELECT companyName FROM Company, EmployeesHired
WHERE Company.id = EmployeesHired.id AND fiscalQuarter = 4;
```

There is a small problem with this SQL statement. Consider what might happen if a company did not hire anyone in the fourth quarter. There could still be a tuple (a row of data) such as EmployeesHired(6, 0, 4). The company with id 6 would be returned by the preceding query even though it didn't hire anyone during fiscal quarter 4. To fix this bug, you need to ensure that numHired is greater than 0. The revised SQL statement looks like this:

```
SELECT companyName FROM Company, EmployeesHired
WHERE Company.id = EmployeesHired.id AND fiscalQuarter = 4
     AND numHired > 0;
```

> **PROBLEM** *Now, using the same schema, write a SQL statement that returns the names of all companies that did not hire anyone in fiscal quarters 1 through 4.*

The best way to start this problem is by looking at the previous answer. You know how to get the names of all the companies that hired an employee in quarter 4. If you remove the WHERE condition that fiscalQuarter = 4 , you have a query that returns the names of all companies that hired employees during all fiscal quarters. If you use this query as a *subquery* and select all the companies that are not in the result, you get all the companies that did not hire anyone in fiscal quarters 1 through 4. As a slight optimization, you can select just the id from the EmployeesHired table and select the companyName for company id values not in the subquery. The query looks like this:

```
SELECT companyName FROM Company WHERE id NOT IN
(SELECT id from EmployeesHired WHERE numHired > 0);
```

> **PROBLEM** *Finally, return the names of all companies and the total number of employees that each company hired during fiscal quarters 1 through 4.*

You're asked to retrieve the totals of some sets of values, which indicates that you must use the SUM aggregate. In this problem, you don't want the sum of the entire column, you want only a sum of the values that have the same id. To accomplish this task, you need to use the GROUP BY feature. This feature enables you to apply SUM over grouped values of data. Other than the GROUP BY feature, this query is similar to the first query except you omit fiscalQuarter = 4 in the WHERE clause. The query looks like this:

```
SELECT companyName, SUM(numHired)
FROM Company, EmployeesHired
WHERE Company.id = EmployeesHired.id
GROUP BY companyName;
```

This query is almost, but not quite, correct. The problem asks for the names of *all* companies, but the preceding query performs an inner join, so only companies that have rows in EmployeesHired appear in the results. For instance, with the provided sample data, John Lawn Company would not appear in the results. As the query is currently written, you want to retain unmatched rows from the first table, Company, so you must perform a left outer join. (Due to the foreign key constraint, there can't be any unmatched rows in EmployeesHired.) A query performing a left outer join looks like:

```
SELECT companyName, SUM(numHired)
FROM Company LEFT OUTER JOIN EmployeesHired
    ON Company.id = EmployeesHired.id
GROUP BY companyName;
```

There's one final wrinkle: You're instructed to return the total number of employees each company hired, but by the definition of an outer join, numHired will be NULL for companies with no rows in EmployeesHired. SUM(NULL) is NULL, so for these companies the preceding query returns NULL as the number hired instead of 0. You can fix this by applying a SQL function to the result that replaces any NULL values with 0. (If you know the name of this function without having to look it up, you're a real SQL wizard.):

```
SELECT companyName, COALESCE(SUM(numHired), 0)
FROM Company LEFT OUTER JOIN EmployeesHired
    ON Company.id = EmployeesHired.id
GROUP BY companyName;
```

Max, No Aggregates

> **PROBLEM** *Given the following SQL database schema*
>
> ```
> Test (
>     num INTEGER(4)
> );
> ```
>
> *write a SQL statement that returns the maximum value from* num *without using an aggregate (*MAX, MIN, *etc.).*

In this problem, your hands are tied behind your back; you must find a maximum without using the feature designed for finding the maximum. A good way to start is by drawing a table with some sample data, as shown in Table 12-5.

TABLE 12-5: Sample Values for num

num
5
23
-6
7

In this sample data, you want to print out the value 23. 23 has the property that all other numbers are less than it. Though true, this way of looking at things doesn't offer much help with constructing the SQL statement. A similar but more useful way to say the same thing is that 23 is the *only* number that does not have a number that is greater than it. If you could return every value that does not have a number greater than it, you would return only 23, and you would have solved the problem. Try designing a SQL statement to print out every number that does not have a number greater than it.

First, figure out which numbers do have numbers greater than themselves. This is a more manageable query. Begin by joining the table with itself to create all possible pairs for which each value in one column is greater than the corresponding value in the other column, as in the following query (AS gives the table a temporary alias for use within the query, allowing you to use the same table twice in a query):

```
SELECT Lesser.num, Greater.num
FROM Test AS Greater, Test AS Lesser
WHERE Lesser.num < Greater.num;
```

Using the sample data, this yields the results shown in Table 12-6.

TABLE 12-6: Temporary Table Formed after Join

Lesser.num	Greater.num
-6	23
5	23
7	23
-6	7
5	7
-6	5

As desired, every value is in the lesser column except the maximum value of 23. Thus, if you use the previous query as a subquery and select every value not in it, you get the maximum value. This query would look like the following:

```
SELECT num FROM Test WHERE num NOT IN
(SELECT Lesser.num FROM Test AS Greater, Test AS Lesser
WHERE Lesser.num < Greater.num);
```

There is one minor bug in this query. If the maximum value is repeated in the Test table, it will be returned twice. To prevent this, use the DISTINCT keyword. This changes the query to the following:

```
SELECT DISTINCT num FROM Test WHERE num NOT IN
(SELECT Lesser.num FROM Test AS Greater, Test AS Lesser
WHERE Lesser.num < Greater.num);
```

Three-Valued Logic

> **PROBLEM** *Given the following table*
>
> ```
> Address (
>     street CHAR(30) NOT NULL,
>     apartment CHAR(10),
>     city CHAR(40) NOT NULL,
> );
> ```
>
> *write a SQL statement that returns nonapartment addresses only.*

This problem seems simple. The immediately obvious solution is this query:

```
SELECT * FROM Address WHERE apartment = NULL;
```

This won't return any addresses, however, because of SQL's use of *ternary,* or *three-valued,* logic. Unlike the two-value boolean logic used in most programming languages, there are three possible logical values in SQL: TRUE, FALSE and UNKNOWN. As you might expect, UNKNOWN means that the truth is uncertain because it involves a value that is unknown, missing or nonrepresentable.

The familiar AND, OR, and NOT operations, for example, return different values in the presence of an UNKNOWN value, as shown in Tables 12-7, 12-8, and 12-9.

TABLE 12-7: Ternary AND Operations

AND	TRUE	FALSE	UNKNOWN
TRUE	TRUE	FALSE	UNKNOWN
FALSE	FALSE	FALSE	FALSE
UNKNOWN	UNKNOWN	FALSE	UNKNOWN

TABLE 12-8: Ternary OR Operations

OR	TRUE	FALSE	UNKNOWN
TRUE	TRUE	TRUE	TRUE
FALSE	TRUE	FALSE	UNKNOWN
UNKNOWN	TRUE	UNKNOWN	UNKNOWN

TABLE 12-9: Ternary NOT Operations

NOT	
TRUE	FALSE
FALSE	TRUE
UNKNOWN	UNKNOWN

The preceding query fails because it uses the equality operator (=) to test for a NULL column value. In most databases, a comparison to NULL returns UNKNOWN — even when comparing NULL to NULL. The rationale for this is that NULL represents missing or unknown data, so it's unknown whether two NULL values represent the same value or two unequal pieces of missing data. Queries return rows only where the WHERE clause is TRUE; if the WHERE clause contains = NULL, then all the rows have UNKNOWN value and none are returned. The proper way to check for a NULL or non-NULL column is to use the IS NULL or IS NOT NULL syntax. Thus, the original query should be restated as follows:

```
SELECT * FROM Address WHERE apartment IS NULL;
```

Not accounting for UNKNOWN values in WHERE clause conditions is a common error, especially when the appearance of NULL values is less obvious. For instance, the following query doesn't return every row except those where apartment = 1; it returns only rows that have a non-NULL apartment not equal to 1:

```
SELECT * FROM Address WHERE apartment <> 1;
```

SUMMARY

Databases are common building blocks of applications, especially web-based applications. Most database systems are based on the concepts of relational database theory, so you can expect most problems you encounter to involve accessing and manipulating relational data. To do this, you need to understand basic SQL commands such as SELECT and INSERT. Transactions and foreign key constraints are among the mechanisms that databases provide to maintain consistency.

Graphics and Bit Manipulation

Problems involving graphics or bit operators are less common than those we've looked at so far but still appear frequently enough in interviews to merit discussion. Bit manipulation problems in particular often occur early in an interview as a warm-up to more challenging problems.

GRAPHICS

A computer screen consists of pixels arranged in a Cartesian coordinate system. This is commonly called a *raster pixel display*. Computer graphics algorithms change the colors of sets of pixels. Modern computers — even mobile phones — include specialized hardware-based high-performance implementations of graphics algorithms that are orders of magnitude faster than what can be implemented in software on the CPU. The challenge in real-world development is how best to use the graphics hardware; it would be extremely unusual to implement any of the techniques described in the following sections. Nevertheless, you may encounter problems involving the implementation of graphics algorithms both to test your understanding of computer graphics and to examine your ability to translate mathematical concepts into working code.

Often, the algorithm to generate a raster pixel image is based on a geometric equation. Because a computer screen has a finite number of pixels, translating from a geometric equation to a pixel display can be quite complex. Geometric equations usually have real-number (floating-point) solutions, but pixels are found only at fixed, regularly spaced locations. Therefore, every point calculated must be adjusted to pixel coordinates. This requires some kind of rounding, but rounding to the nearest pixel coordinate is not always the correct approach. You often need to round numbers in unusual ways or add error-correcting terms. When rounding is done carelessly, it often leads to gaps in what should be continuous lines. Take care to check your graphics algorithms for distortion or gaps due to poor rounding or error correction.

Consider something as simple as drawing a line segment. Suppose you try to implement a function that takes two endpoints and draws a line between them. After doing a little algebra, you could easily get an equation in the form of $y = mx + b$. Then, you could calculate y for a range of x values and draw the points making up the line. This function seems trivial.

The devil is in the details of this problem. First, you must account for vertical lines. In this case, m is infinity, so the simple procedure can't draw the line. Similarly, imagine that the line is not vertical but close to vertical. For example, suppose that the horizontal distance spanned by the line were 2 pixels, but the vertical distance were 20 pixels. In this case, only 2 pixels would be drawn — not much of a line. To correct for this problem, you must rework your equation to $x = (y - b) / m$. Now, if the line is closer to vertical, you vary y and use this equation; if it is closer to horizontal, you use the original procedure.

Even this won't solve all your problems. Suppose you need to draw a line with a slope of 1, for example, $y = x$. In this case, using either procedure, you would draw the pixels $(0, 0)$, $(1, 1)$, $(2, 2)$…. This is mathematically correct, but the line looks too thin on the screen because the pixels are much more spread out than in other lines. A diagonal line of length 100 has fewer pixels in it than a horizontal line of length 80. An ideal line-drawing algorithm would have some mechanism to guarantee that all lines have nearly equal pixel density.

Another problem involves rounding. If you calculate a point at $(.99, .99)$ and use a type cast to convert this to integers, then the floating-point values will be truncated and the pixel will be drawn at $(0, 0)$. You need to explicitly round the values so that the point is drawn at $(1, 1)$.

If graphics problems seem like never-ending series of special cases, then you understand the issues involved. Even if you were to work out all the problems with the line-drawing algorithm described, it still wouldn't be very good. Although this algorithm effectively illustrates the problems encountered in graphics programming, its reliance on floating-point calculations makes it slow. High-performance algorithms that use only integer math are far more complicated than what is discussed here.

> **NOTE** *Computer graphics involves drawing with pixels. Always check for rounding errors, gaps, and special cases.*

BIT MANIPULATION

Most computer languages have facilities to allow programmers access to the individual bits of a variable. Bit operators may appear more frequently in interviews than in day-to-day programming, so they merit a review.

Binary Two's Complement Notation

To work with bit operators, you need to start thinking on the levels of bits. Numbers are usually internally represented in a computer in *binary two's complement notation*. If you're already familiar with binary numbers, you almost understand binary two's complement notation because binary two's complement notation is very similar to plain binary notation. Actually, it's identical for positive numbers.

The only difference appears with negative numbers. (An integer usually consists of 32 or 64 bits, but to keep things simple, this example uses 8-bit integers.) In binary two's complement notation, a positive integer such as 13 is `00001101`, exactly the same as in regular binary notation. Negative numbers are a little trickier. Two's complement notation makes a number negative by applying the rule "flip each bit and add 1" to the number's positive binary representation. For example, to get the number –1, you start with 1, which is `00000001` in binary. Flipping each bit results in `11111110`. Adding 1 gives you `11111111`, which is the two's complement notation for –1. If you're not familiar with this, it may seem weird, but it makes addition and subtraction simple. For example, you can add `00000001` (1) and `11111111` (–1) simply by adding the binary digits from right to left, carrying values as necessary, to end up with (`00000000`) 0.

The first bit in binary two's complement notation is a sign bit. If the first bit is 0, the number is non-negative; otherwise, it's negative. This has important implications when shifting bits within a number.

Bitwise Operators

Most languages include a series of *bitwise operators*, operators that affect the individual bits of an integer value. C and C++ bitwise operators share the same syntax and behaviors. The bitwise operators in C#, Java, and JavaScript are the same as C and C++ except for the shift operators.

The simplest bit operator is the unary operator (~) called *NOT*. This operator flips or reverses all the bits that it operates on. Thus, every 1 becomes a 0, and every 0 becomes a 1. For example, if ~ is applied to `00001101`, then the result is `11110010`.

Three other bitwise operators are | (*OR*), & (*AND*), and ^ (*XOR*). They are all binary operators applied in a bitwise fashion. This means that the ith bit of one number is combined with the ith bit of the other number to produce the ith bit of the resulting value. The rules for these operators are as follows:

➤ & — If both bits are 1, the result is a 1. Otherwise, the result is 0, for example:

```
  01100110
& 11110100
  01100100
```

➤ | — If any bit is a 1, the result is 1. If both bits are 0, the result is 0, for example:

```
  01100110
| 11110100
  11110110
```

➤ ^ — If the bits are the same, the result is 0. If the bits are different, the result is 1, for example:

```
  01100110
^ 11110100
  10010010
```

Don't confuse the *bitwise* & and | operators with the *logical* && and || operators. The bitwise operators take two integers and return an integer result; the logical operators take two booleans and return a boolean result.

The remaining bit operators are the shift operators: operators that shift the bits within a value to the left or the right. C, C++, and C# have left (<<) and right (>>) shift operators. Java and JavaScript have one left shift (<<) operator but two right shift (>> and >>>) operators.

The value to the right of the operator indicates how many positions to shift the bits. For example, 8 << 2 means shift the bits of the value "8" two positions to the left. Bits that "fall off" either end of a value (the overflow bits) are lost.

The << operator is common to all five languages. It shifts the bits to the left, filling the empty bits on the right with 0. For example, `01100110 << 5` results in `11000000`. Note that the value can change sign depending on the state of the new first bit.

The >> operator is also common to all five languages, but when operating on signed values, its behavior varies depending on the sign. When the sign is positive, 0s are shifted into the empty bits. When the sign is negative, the >> operator performs *sign extension*, filling the empty bits on the left with 1s, so `10100110 >> 5` becomes `11111101`. This way negative values remain negative when they are shifted. (Technically, it is implementation-dependent whether a C or C++ compiler performs sign extension; in practice, almost all of them do.) When an unsigned value is right-shifted, the empty bits are filled with 0s, regardless of whether the first bit was originally a 1 or a 0. Java and JavaScript lack unsigned values, so they accomplish this by defining an additional right shift operator, >>>. This operator does a *logical* shift right, filling the empty spaces with 0 regardless of sign, so `10100110 >>> 5` becomes `00000101`.

Optimizing with Shifts

The shift operators enable you to multiply and divide by powers of 2 quickly. Shifting to the right 1 bit is equivalent to dividing by 2, and shifting to the left 1 bit is equivalent to multiplying by 2. (In the rare case of a C or C++ compiler that does not perform sign extension on right shift of a negative number, this trick would fail for division of negative numbers.)

The equivalence of shifting and multiplying or dividing by a power of the base also occurs in the more familiar base 10 number system. Consider the number 17. In base 10, 17 << 1 results in the value 170, which is exactly the same as multiplying 17 by 10. Similarly, 17 >> 1 produces 1, which is the same as integer dividing 17 by 10.

GRAPHICS PROBLEMS

Graphics problems typically focus on your ability to implement primitive graphics functions rather than using a high-level API as you would in most programming projects.

Eighth of a Circle

PROBLEM *Write a function that draws the upper-eighth of a circle centered at (0, 0) with a given radius, where the upper-eighth is defined as the portion starting at 12 and going to 1:30 on a clock face. Use the following prototype:*

```
void drawEighthOfCircle( int radius );
```

The coordinate system and an example of what you are to draw are shown in Figure 13-1. You can use a function with the following prototype to draw pixels:

```
void setPixel( int xCoord, int yCoord );
```

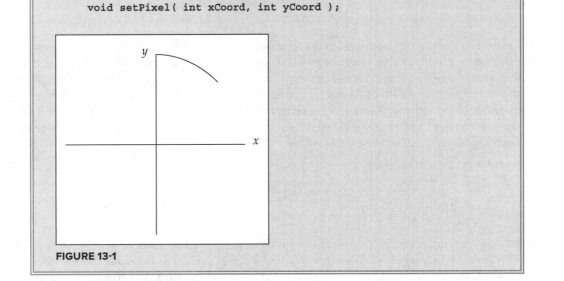

FIGURE 13-1

This problem is not as contrived as it seems. If you were trying to implement a full-circle drawing routine, you would want to do as little calculation as possible to maintain optimum performance. Given the pixels for one-eighth of a circle, you can easily determine the pixels for the remainder of the circle from symmetry.

NOTE *If a point (x, y) is on a circle, so are the points (−x, y), (x, −y), (−x, −y), (y, x), (−y, x), (y, −x), and (−y, −x).*

This problem is an example of a *scan conversion*, converting a geometric drawing to a pixel-based raster image. You need an equation for a circle before you can calculate anything. The common mathematical function that produces a circle is:

$$x^2 + y^2 = r^2$$

This definition is nice because it contains x's, y's, and r's, just like your problem and your coordinate system. You must figure out how to determine pairs of coordinates (x, y) on the circle using the equation, $x^2 + y^2 = r^2$. The easiest way to find a pair of coordinates is to set a value for one and then calculate the other. It's more difficult to set y and calculate x because after the scan conversion there will be several x values for certain y values. Therefore, you should set x and calculate y. Doing some algebra, you can calculate y with the following equation:

$$y = \pm\sqrt{r^2 - x^2}$$

In this problem you deal with only positive values of y, so you can ignore the negative root. This produces the following:

$$y = \sqrt{r^2 - x^2}$$

For example, given an x coordinate of 3 and a radius of 5, $y = \sqrt{5^2 - 3^2} = 4$. You now know how to calculate y, given x. Next, you need to determine the range of x values. x clearly starts at 0, but where does it end? Look again at the figure to try to figure out visually how you know that you are at the end of the one-eighth of the circle. In visual terms, this happens when you are farther out than you are up. In mathematical terms, this means that the x value becomes greater than the y value. Thus, you can use the x range from 0 until $x > y$. If you put these pieces together, you have an algorithm for drawing a circle. In outline form:

```
Start with x = 0 and y = r.
While (y ≤ x)
     Determine the y coordinate using the equation:y=√r²-x²
     Set the pixel (x, y)
     Increment x
```

This algorithm looks correct, but there is a subtle bug in it. The problem arises from treating the y coordinate as an integer, when often y will be a decimal value. For example, if y had the value 9.99, setPixel would truncate it to 9, rather than round to the y pixel of 10 as you probably want. One way to solve this problem is to round all values to the nearest whole integer by adding 0.5 to y before calling setPixel.

This change results in a much better-looking circle. The code for this algorithm is as follows:

```
void drawEighthOfCircle(int radius ){
    int x, y;
    x = 0;
    y = radius;
    while( y <= x ){
        y = Math.sqrt((radius * radius) - (x * x)) + 0.5;
        setPixel( x, y );
        x++;
    }
}
```

What's the efficiency of this algorithm? Its running time is $O(n)$, where n is the number of pixels that you need to set. This is the best possible running time because any algorithm would have to call `setPixel` at least *n* times to draw the circle correctly. The function also uses the `sqrt` function and multiplies during each iteration of the `while` loop. The `sqrt` function and the multiplications are likely to be slow operations. Therefore, this function probably isn't practical for most graphical applications where speed is critical. There are faster circle-drawing algorithms that don't make repeated calls to slow functions like `sqrt` or have repeated multiplications, but you wouldn't be expected to implement them during an interview.

Rectangle Overlap

PROBLEM *You are given two rectangles, each defined by an upper-left (UL) corner and a lower-right (LR) corner. Both rectangles' edges will always be parallel to the x or y axis, as shown in Figure 13-2. Write a function that determines whether the two rectangles overlap. For convenience, you may use the following classes:*

```
class Point {
    public int x;
    public int y;
    public Point( int x, int y ){
        this.x = x;
        this.y = y;
    }
}
class Rect {
    public Point ul;
    public Point lr;
    public Rect( Point ul, Point lr ){
        this.ul = ul;
        this.lr = lr;
    }
}
```

The function should take two `Rect` *objects and return* `true` *if they overlap, and* `false` *if they don't.*

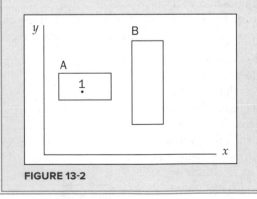

FIGURE 13-2

Before you jump into the problem, it's helpful to work out a few properties about rectangles and their vertices. First, given the upper-left (UL) and lower-right (LR) corners, it is not difficult to get the upper-right (UR) and lower-left (LL) corners. The coordinates of the upper-right corner are the upper left's y and the lower right's x. The lower-left corner is at the upper left's x and the lower right's y.

It is also useful to determine whether a point falls inside a rectangle. A point is inside a rectangle if the point's x is greater than the rectangle's UL corner's x and less than the rectangle's LR corner's x, and the point's y is greater than the rectangle's LR corners's y and less than the rectangle's UL corner's y. You can see this in Figure 13-2, where point 1 is inside rectangle A. Now you can move on to the problem.

This problem seems straightforward. Start by considering the ways in which two rectangles can overlap. Try to divide the different ways into various cases. A good place to begin is by examining where the corners of a rectangle end up when it overlaps another. Perhaps you can enumerate the ways in which two rectangles can overlap by counting the number of corners of one rectangle that are inside the other rectangle. The cases that you must consider are when one of the rectangles has 0, 1, 2, 3, or 4 corners inside the other. Take these cases one at a time. Begin by considering a case in which no corners of either rectangle are inside the other. This is illustrated in Figure 13-3.

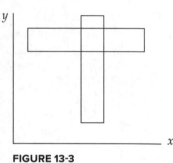

FIGURE 13-3

Consider what conditions must be true for two rectangles to overlap without having any corners inside each other. First, the wider rectangle must be shorter than the narrower rectangle. Next, the two rectangles must be positioned so that the overlap occurs. This means that the narrower rectangle's x coordinates must be between the wider rectangle's x coordinates, and the shorter rectangle's y coordinates must be between the taller rectangle's y coordinates. If all these conditions are true, you have two rectangles that overlap without having any corners inside of each other.

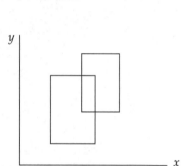

FIGURE 13-4

Now consider the second case, in which rectangles may overlap with one corner inside the other. This is illustrated in Figure 13-4. This case is relatively easy. You can simply check whether any of the four corners of one rectangle are inside the other rectangle.

In the third case, the rectangles may overlap if two points of one rectangle are inside the other. This occurs when one rectangle is half in and half out of the other rectangle, as illustrated in Figure 13-5. Here, one rectangle has no corners inside the other, and one rectangle has two corners inside the other. If you check the corners of the rectangle with no corners inside the other, you will not find overlap. If you check the rectangle with two corners overlapping, you must check at least three corners to determine overlap. However, you can't determine ahead of time which rectangle will have no corners inside the other. Therefore, you must check at least three corners of each rectangle to properly test for overlap.

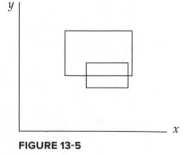

FIGURE 13-5

The three-point case is simple: It's just not possible. No matter how you draw the rectangles, you can't arrange them so that one rectangle has exactly three corners inside the other.

The four-corner case is possible. This happens if one rectangle completely contains the other, as shown in Figure 13-6. If you check one corner of both rectangles, you can correctly determine overlap in this case.

Now, put your tests to determine overlap in the zero-corner, one-corner, two-corner, and four-corner cases together to encompass all these cases. These tests check the widths, heights, and positions of both rectangles, the four corners of one rectangle, the three corners of each rectangle, and the one corner of each rectangle, respectively. You could test each of these cases individually, but that's repetitive. Instead, try to develop a single test that encompasses all these cases. Start by checking the widths, heights, and positions of both rectangles to cover the zero-corner case. Next, check the four corners of one rectangle to cover the one-corner case. Then, to include the two-corner case, check three

FIGURE 13-6

corners of the other rectangle. Luckily, the four-corner case is already covered if you check four corners of one rectangle and three of the other because you're clearly checking one corner of each. The composite test to determine rectangle overlap is to check the following:

➤ The heights, widths, and positions of both rectangles

➤ Whether any of the four corners of one rectangle are inside the other

➤ Whether any of three corners from the second rectangle are inside the first

This solution to test for overlap is correct, but it seems inefficient. It checks the heights, widths, and positions of both rectangles as well as seven of eight possible corners — and each corner check requires four comparisons. This results in 34 comparisons to calculate the answer.

Perhaps there is a better solution. Another way to think about the problem is to consider when the rectangles don't overlap, as opposed to when they do overlap. If you know when the rectangles don't overlap, you know when they do overlap. The conditions for not overlapping are much more straightforward. Call the two rectangles A and B. A and B do not overlap when A is above B, or A is below B, or A is to the left of B, or A is to the right of B. More than one of these conditions can be true at the same time. For example, A could be above and to the right of B. If any one of these conditions is true, the two rectangles do not overlap. The specifics of these conditions can be summarized as follows.

The two rectangles do not overlap when:

➤ A's UL's x value is greater than B's LR's x value or

➤ A's UL's y value is less than B's LR's y value or

➤ A's LR's x value is less than B's UL's x value or

➤ A's LR's y value is greater than B's UL's y value.

This solution is much simpler, requiring only four comparisons and one negation. You can implement the function as follows:

```
boolean overlap( Rect a, Rect b ){
    return !( a.ul.x > b.lr.x ||
              a.ul.y < b.lr.y ||
              a.lr.x < b.ul.x ||
              a.lr.y > b.ul.y );
}
```

This function works, but you can do even better. You can get rid of the logical *NOT*. A bit of logic theory called DeMorgan's Law may be helpful here. This law states the following:

$$¬ (A \text{ OR } B) = ¬A \text{ AND } ¬B$$
$$¬ (A \text{ AND } B) = ¬A \text{ OR } ¬B$$

> **NOTE** *The symbol ¬ means NOT in the logic world.*

In addition, you should recognize that;

➤ $¬(A > B)$ is equivalent to $(A \leq B)$

Working through these rules, you get the following function:

```
boolean overlap( Rect a, Rect b){
    return( a.ul.x <= b.lr.x &&
            a.ul.y >= b.lr.y &&
            a.lr.x >= b.ul.x &&
            a.lr.y <= b.ul.y );
}
```

To ensure that you didn't make a mistake, it's a good idea to verify that these conditions make sense. The preceding function determines that two rectangles overlap if:

➤   A's left edge is to the left of B's right edge and

➤   A's upper edge is above B's bottom edge and

➤   A's right edge is to the right of B's left edge and

➤   A's bottom edge is below B's upper edge.

These conditions mean that rectangle B cannot be outside of rectangle A, so there must be some overlap. This makes sense.

BIT MANIPULATION PROBLEMS

Bit manipulation problems may span the range from dead simple to extremely difficult. In some cases, a single problem covers this whole range with different solutions of increasing efficiency and complexity.

Big-Endian or Little-Endian

> **PROBLEM** *Write a C function that determines whether a computer is big-endian or little-endian.*

This problem tests your knowledge of computer architectures as much as it tests your ability to program. The interviewer wants to know whether you are familiar with the term *endian*. If you are familiar with it, you should define it or at least try to point out the differences between big-endian and little-endian, even if you forget which is which. If you are not familiar with the term, you'll have to ask the interviewer to explain it.

Endianness refers to the order in which a computer stores the bytes of a multibyte value. (Or technically, the units of a multiunit value — for example, the computer may use a 16-bit unit size instead of an 8-bit unit size. We restrict this discussion to 8-bit units for simplicity.) Computers use multibyte sequences to represent certain primitive data types.

The bytes within an integer can be arranged in any order, but they are almost always either least-significant byte (LSB) to most-significant byte (MSB) or MSB to LSB. Significance refers to the place value a byte represents within a multibyte value. If a byte represents the lowest place values, the byte is the LSB. For example, in the number 5A6C, 6C is the LSB. Conversely, if a byte represents the highest place values, it is the MSB. In the 5A6C example, 5A is the MSB.

In a big-endian machine the MSB has the lowest address; in a little-endian machine the LSB has the lowest address. For example, a big-endian machine stores the 2-byte hexadecimal value A45C by placing A4 in the lowest byte and 5C in the next. In contrast, a little-endian machine stores 5C in the lowest byte and A4 in the next.

Endianness is usually transparent to the programmer as long as data remains on systems of the same type. When data exchanges between different systems that have different endianness, problems may arise. Most programming languages default to writing data to files and network devices using the system's native byte ordering (endianness) — however it represents values in memory. This means that data written by an endianness-naïve program running on a little-endian system is likely to be misinterpreted by the same program running on a big-endian system. For the most part endianness is determined by the processor, but the Java virtual machine is big-endian regardless of the underlying processor type.

To answer the problem, you must choose a multibyte data type to work with. It's not important which one you choose, just that the type is more than 1 byte. A 32-bit integer is a good choice. You need to determine how you can test this integer to figure out which byte is the LSB and which is the MSB. If you set the value of the integer to 1, you can distinguish between the MSB and the LSB because in an integer with the value 1, the LSB has the value 1 and the MSB has the value 0.

Unfortunately, it's not immediately clear how to access the bytes of an integer. You might try using the bit operators because they allow access to individual bits in a variable. However, they are not particularly useful because the bit operators act as if the bits are arranged in order from most-significant bit to least-significant bit. For example, if you use the shift left operator to shift the integer 8 bits, the operator works on the integer as if it were 32 consecutive bits regardless of the true byte order in memory. This property prevents you from using the bit operators to determine byte order.

How can you examine the individual bytes of an integer? A C character is a single-byte data type. It could be useful to view an integer as four consecutive characters. To do this, you create a pointer to the integer. Then, you can cast the integer pointer to a character pointer. This enables you to access the integer like an array of 1-byte data types. Using the character pointer, you can examine the bytes and determine the format.

Specifically, to determine the computer's endianness, get a pointer to an integer with the value of 1. Then, cast the pointer to a char *. This changes the size of the data to which the pointer points. When you dereference this pointer, you access a 1-byte character instead of a 4-byte integer. Then you can test the first byte to see if it is 1. If the byte's value is 1, then the machine is little-endian because the LSB is at the lowest memory address. If the byte's value is 0, then the machine is big-endian because the MSB is at the lowest memory address. In outline form, here is the procedure:

```
Set an integer to 1
Cast a pointer to the integer as a char *
If the dereferenced pointer is 1, the machine is little-endian
If the dereferenced pointer is 0, the machine is big-endian
```

The code for this test is as follows:

```
/* Returns true if the machine is little-endian, false if the
 * machine is big-endian
 */
bool isLittleEndian(){
    int    testNum;
    char *ptr;
    testNum = 1;
    ptr = (char *) &testNum;
    return (*ptr); /* Returns the byte at the lowest address */
}
```

This solution is sufficient for an interview. However, because the goal of an interview is not just to solve problems but also to impress your interviewer, you may want to consider a slightly more elegant way to solve this problem. It involves using a feature of C called union types. A *union* is like a struct, except that all the members are allocated starting at the same location in memory. This enables you to access the same data with different variable types. The syntax is almost identical to a struct. Using a union, the code is as follows:

```
/* Returns true if the machine is little-endian, false if the
 * machine is big-endian
 */
bool isLittleEndian(){
    union {
        int theInteger;
        char singleByte;
    } endianTest;
    endianTest.theInteger = 1;
    return endianTest.singleByte;
}
```

Number of Ones

> **PROBLEM** *Write a function that determines the number of 1 bits in the binary representation of a given integer.*

This problem may at first sound like a base conversion problem in which you need to design an algorithm to convert a base 10 number to a two's complement binary number. That approach is circuitous because the computer already stores its numbers in two's complement binary internally. Instead of doing a base conversion, try counting the 1s directly.

You can count the number of 1s by checking the value of each bit. Ideally, you'd like to use an operator that would tell you the value of a specified bit. That way, you could iterate over all the bits and count how many of them were 1s. Unfortunately, this ideal operator doesn't exist.

You can begin by trying to create a procedure that determines the value of each bit using the existing bit operators. Focus on figuring out a way to get the value of the lowest bit. One way to do this is to AND the given integer with the value 1. You can use 8-bit integers to keep the examples manageable, so 1 is stored as 00000001. The result of the AND with 1 would be either 00000000 if the given integer's lowest bit had the value 0, or 00000001 if the given integer's lowest bit had the value 1. In general, you can get the value of any bit if you create the correct *mask*. In this case, the mask is an integer with all the bits set to 0 except the bit you're checking, which is set to 1. When you AND a mask with the value you're checking, the result is either a 0, indicating that the bit you are checking has the value 0, or a nonzero result, indicating that the bit you are checking has the value 1.

You could create a mask for each of the bits and count the number of 1 bits. For example, the first mask would be 00000001, followed by masks of 00000010, 00000100, 00001000, and so on. This would work, but your interviewer probably doesn't want to watch you write out that many masks. Consider the differences between each mask. Each mask is the same as the previous mask, but the 1 bit is moved one place to the left. Instead of predefining your masks, you can construct them using the left shift operator. Simply start with a mask of 00000001 and repeatedly shift the integer 1 bit to the left to generate all the necessary masks. This is a good technique, and if you work it out to its conclusion, it yields an acceptable answer. However, there's a prettier and slightly faster solution that uses only one mask.

Think about what you can do with a single mask. You are trying to examine each bit of the integer, so you need to mask a different bit on each iteration. So far, you've been accomplishing this by shifting the mask and keeping the integer in place, but if you shifted the integer, you could examine all its bits using the same mask. The most natural mask to use is 00000001, which yields the least-significant bit. If you keep shifting the integer right, each bit will eventually become the rightmost bit. Try working through 00000101 as an example. The rightmost bit is 1, so you would add 1 to your count and shift the integer right, yielding 00000010. This time the rightmost bit is 0. Shifting right again produces 00000001. The least significant bit in this integer is 1, so you would increment your count to 2. When you shift right a third time, the integer becomes 00000000. When the integer's value reaches zero, there are no 1 bits remaining, so you can stop counting. As in this example, you may not have to iterate through all the bits to count all the 1s, so in many cases this algorithm is more efficient than the multiple mask algorithm. In outline, the single mask algorithm is as follows:

```
Start with count = 0
While the integer is not 0
    If the integer AND 1 equals 1, increment count
    Shift the integer one bit to the right
Return count
```

Finally, check for any error cases in this code; look for problems with positive numbers, negative numbers, and zero. If the integer has the value of 0, the algorithm immediately and correctly returns that there are zero 1s in the binary representation. Now consider the case in which you are passed a negative number. You will shift the number to the right, but the new bit added on the left becomes a 1 and not a 0 if the right shift operator does sign extension. The solution to this depends on the language you're using. If the language supports unsigned types (for example C, C++, and C#) you can read the value as an unsigned integer. In languages without unsigned types, there's usually a special operator that right-shifts without sign extension (>>> in Java and JavaScript). Using either >>> or an unsigned integer means that the shift operator will not sign extend, and the new bits added during the right shifting will be 0s. The number eventually becomes all 0s. Finally, consider the case in which you are given a positive integer. This is the sample case that you worked with, and the algorithm works correctly here.

The code for this algorithm in Java is as follows:

```
int numOnesInBinary( int number ) {
    int numOnes = 0;
    while( number != 0 ){
        if( ( number & 1 ) == 1 ) {
            numOnes++;
        }
        number = number >>> 1;
    }
    return numOnes;
}
```

What's the running time of this function? The function iterates through the `while` loop until all the 1s have been counted. In the best case, the given integer is 0, and the function never executes the `while` loop. In the worst case, this is $O(n)$, where n is the number of bits in an integer.

Unless you're incredibly good at bitwise operations, this is the best solution you're likely to come up with in an interview. There are better solutions, though. Consider what happens at the bit level when you subtract 1 from a number. Subtracting 1 produces a value that has all the same bits as the original integer except that all the low bits up to and including the lowest 1 are flipped. For example, subtracting 1 from the value 01110000 results in the value 01101111.

If you apply the AND operation to the integer and the result of the subtraction, the result is a new number that is the same as the original integer except that the rightmost 1 is now a 0. For example, 01110000 AND (01110000 − 1) = 01110000 AND 01101111 = 01100000.

You can count the number of times that you can perform this process before the integer's value reaches 0. This is the number of 1s in the computer's representation of the number. In outline form this algorithm is as follows:

```
Start with count = 0
While the integer is not zero
    AND the integer with the integer - 1
    Increment count
Return count
```

Here is the code:

```
int numOnesInBinary( int number ){
    int numOnes = 0;
    while( number != 0 ){
        number = number & (number - 1);
        numOnes++;
    }
    return numOnes;
}
```

This solution has a running time of $O(m)$, where m is the number of 1s in the solution. Even this is not the best solution. One of the best solutions implements a parallel approach that uses bit operations to simultaneously count the number of bits in each adjacent pair of bits and then (in parallel) sums adjacent units of 4 bits, 8 bits, and so on, arriving at a solution in $O(\log n)$ time (where n is the number of bits in the integer). A version of this algorithm appeared in an early programming textbook, *The Preparation of Programs for an Electronic Digital Computer*, Maurice V. Wilkes, David J. Wheeler, Stanley Gill. Addison Wesley (1951).

The operation described by this problem is commonly referred to as a *population count*. Population counts have several applications, notably in cryptography. In fact, they're useful enough that many recent processors implement population count in hardware with a single instruction. C and C++ compilers may allow access to this instruction through extensions, for example `__builtin_popcount()` in the Gnu Compiler Collection and `__popcnt()` in Microsoft Visual C++. When the processor supports it, these are by far the fastest way to perform a population count.

Keep in mind that these additional solutions were presented for interest, and the first solution is likely all that would be expected in an interview.

SUMMARY

Problems involving bit manipulation and computer graphics are common in interviews. Unless you're applying for a graphics-oriented position, the graphics problems you encounter will usually be fairly basic. Carefully enumerate and check all possible special cases and watch for rounding issues when converting between floating point math and fixed pixel positions. Bit manipulation problems are more common than graphics problems. Depending on the type of programming you do, you may not use bit operations often, so refamiliarize yourself with the bit operators and their use before your interview.

14

Counting, Measuring, and Ordering Puzzles

In addition to technical and programming problems, you sometimes encounter brainteasers in your interviews. *Brainteasers* are mathematical and logical puzzles that have indirect relation to computer programming.

Many interviewers feel these problems are silly because they have no direct bearing on the job at hand and so they won't ask any of them. Some interviewers, though, think brainteasers are useful in assessing problem-solving ability — perhaps the most important job skill for a programmer.

Sometimes, performance on brainteasers might say a lot about your puzzle-solving experience and little about whether you're a good coder. Some leading companies, including Google, have asked interviewers to refrain from using brainteasers and to focus exclusively on technical and programming problems.

However, you may encounter brainteasers in your interviews, so this and the next chapter prepare you for them. Because brainteasers share many common themes, the examples in this and the next chapter aim to give you enough experience to solve these kinds of puzzles when they are presented to you during an interview.

TACKLING BRAINTEASERS

You should keep in mind that the solutions to brainteasers are almost never straightforward or obvious. Unlike the programming or technical parts of the interview, where you are sometimes given simple problems just to see whether you know something, brainteasers always require thought and effort. This means that any solution that seems immediately obvious is probably incorrect or not the best solution.

For example, suppose you're asked, "From the time you get on a ski lift to the time you get off, what proportion of the chairs do you pass?" Most people's immediate gut-level response is that you pass half of the chairs. This response is obvious and makes some sense. At any given time, half of the chairs are on each side of the lift, and you pass chairs only on the other side. It's also wrong — because both sides of the lift are moving, you pass all the other chairs. (This answer assumes you get on and off at the extreme ends of the lift. On most real ski lifts, you pass almost all the other chairs.)

This property of brainteasers works most strongly to your advantage when you are faced with a problem that has only two possible answers (for example, any "yes" or "no" question). Whichever answer seems at first to be correct is probably wrong. Of course, it's probably not a good idea to say, "The answer must be 'yes' because if it were 'no' this would be a simple problem, and you wouldn't have bothered to ask it." You can, however, use this knowledge to guide your thinking.

> **NOTE** *Remember that the obvious answer is almost never the right answer.*

Although the correct solutions to brainteasers are usually complex, they rarely require time-consuming computations or mathematics beyond trigonometry. Just as writing pages of code is a warning sign that you're headed in the wrong direction, using calculus or spending a long time crunching numbers is a strong indicator that you're not headed toward the best solution to a puzzle.

Beware of Assumptions

Many of these problems are difficult because they lead you to assume something incorrect. The false assumption then leads to the wrong answer.

You might conclude that the best approach is to avoid making *any* assumptions. Unfortunately, that's not practical — just understanding a problem is difficult without making a whole series of assumptions.

For example, suppose you are given the task to find an arrangement that maximizes the number of oranges you can fit in the bottom of a square box. You would probably automatically assume that the oranges are small spherical fruit, that they are all about the same size, that "in the bottom" means in contact with the bottom surface of the box, and that the oranges must remain intact. (You can't puree them and pour them in.) Calling these statements assumptions may seem ridiculous — they are all rather obvious and are all correct. The point is that assumptions are inherent in all communication or thought; you can't begin to work on a problem without assumptions.

Carrying this example further, you might assume you could model this problem in two dimensions using circles in a square, and that the solution would involve some sort of orderly, repeating pattern. Based on these assumptions and the knowledge that a honeycomb-like hexagonal array provides the tightest pack of circles covering a plane, you might conclude that the best solution is to place the oranges in a regular hexagonal array. Depending on the relative sizes of the oranges and the box, however, this conclusion would be incorrect.

Although you can't eliminate assumptions, it can be useful to try to identify and analyze them. As you identify your assumptions, categorize them as almost certainly correct, probably correct, or possibly incorrect. Starting with the assumption you feel is least likely to be correct, try reworking the problem without each assumption. These puzzles are rarely trick questions, so your definitional assumptions are usually correct.

In the preceding example, for instance, it would be reasonable to classify the assumptions that "oranges are spherical fruit" and that "they must remain intact and in contact with the bottom of the box" as almost certainly correct.

But how would you categorize the assumption that you can reduce this puzzle to a two-dimensional problem of circles in a square? If you think about it, you can see that the oranges make contact with each other in a single plane and that in this plane you're essentially dealing with circles inside a square. This isn't exactly a proof, but it's solid enough to decide that this assumption is probably correct.

On the other hand, you'll find you have more trouble supporting the assumption that the oranges should be in an orderly repeating pattern. It seems reasonable, and it is true for an infinite plane, but it's not clear that the similarities between a plane and the box bottom are sufficient for this assumption to be true. In general, beware of any assumption that you "feel" is true but can't quite explain — this is often the incorrect assumption. You would therefore conclude that the assumption that the oranges must form an ordered array is possibly incorrect.

This assumption *is* incorrect. In many cases the best packing involves putting most of the oranges in an ordered array and the remaining few in unordered positions.

Analyzing your assumptions is a particularly good strategy when you think you've found the only logically possible solution but you're told it's incorrect. It's often the case that your logic was good but based on a flawed assumption.

> **NOTE** *If the solution that seems logical is wrong, you made a false assumption. Categorize your assumptions, and try to identify those that are false.*

Don't Be Intimidated

Some problems are intimidating because they are so complex or difficult that you can't see a path to the solution. You may not even know where to start. Don't let this lock you up. You don't have to devise a plan to get all the way to the solution before you start — things will come to you as you work on the problem:

- ➤ **Break a problem into parts.** If you can identify a subproblem, try solving that, even if you're not sure it's critical to solving the main problem.

- ➤ **Try a simplified problem.** Try solving a simplified version of the problem; you may gain insights that can be useful in solving the full problem.

- ➤ **Try specific examples.** If the problem involves some sort of process, try working through a few specific examples. You may notice a pattern you can generalize to other cases.

Above all, keep talking, keep thinking, and keep working. The pieces of the puzzle are much more likely to fall into place when your mind is in motion than when you sit at the starting line praying for a revelation.

Even if you don't make much progress, it looks much better to the interviewer when you actively attack a problem than when you sit back stumped, looking clueless and overwhelmed. You came to the interview to demonstrate that you will be a valuable employee. Analyzing the problems and patiently trying a variety of approaches shows this almost as well as solving problems.

> **NOTE** *Don't be intimidated by complexity. Try a subproblem, a simplified version, or some examples. Be patient, keep working, and keep talking.*

Beware of Simple Problems

Other problems are tricky for the opposite reason: They are so simple or restricted that it seems that there's no way to solve the problems within the given constraints. In these circumstances, brainstorming can be useful. Try to enumerate all the possible allowed actions within the constraints of the problem, even those that seem counterproductive. If the problem involves physical objects, consider every object, the properties of every object, what you might do to or with each object, and how the objects might interact.

When you're stuck on a problem like this, there may be something allowed by the problem that you're missing. If you make a list of everything allowed by the constraints of the problem, it will include the key to the solution that hasn't occurred to you. It's often easier to enumerate all the possibilities than it is to specifically come up with the one thing you haven't thought of.

When you do this enumeration, don't do it silently; think aloud or write it down. This shows the interviewer what you're doing and helps you be more methodical and thorough.

> **NOTE** *When you're stuck on a simple, restricted problem, brainstorm all the possibilities to identify the one you're missing.*

Estimation Problems

There's one more type of problem worth discussing. This is the estimation problem, where you're asked to use a rational process to estimate the size of some statistic you don't know. These problems are relatively rare in interviews for pure development positions, but they may be more common in interviews for jobs that include a significant management or business aspect. One example is, "How many piano tuners are there in the United States?" It has been so widely reported that this problem was posed by Microsoft that it seems almost certain to be apocryphal; nevertheless, it is a good example.

> **NOTE** *Estimates are used in many real-world scenarios. Perhaps the most famous estimate is the Drake Equation, which estimates the number of detectable extra-terrestrial civilizations in the galaxy.*

These problems are usually not difficult compared with the more common brainteasers. You're not expected to know the actual statistic or fact. Instead, you are expected to do a rough order of magnitude calculation based on facts you do know. Because everything is an estimate anyway, try to adjust or round your figures so that any large numbers you use are powers (or at least multiples) of ten — this can significantly simplify your arithmetic.

BRAINTEASER PROBLEMS

Brainteasers draw from a much broader and more diverse body of knowledge than programming and technical problems, so a comprehensive review is even less possible here. Since any brainteaser you encounter in an interview is likely to be unfamiliar, the problems that follow prepare you by providing opportunities to practice all of the techniques we've described so you can tackle anything that comes your way.

Count Open Lockers

> **PROBLEM** *Suppose you are in a hallway lined with 100 closed lockers. You begin by opening all 100 lockers. Next, you close every second locker. Then you go to every third locker and close it if it is open or open it if it's closed — call this toggling the lockers. You continue toggling every nth locker on pass number n. After your hundredth pass of the hallway, in which you toggle only locker number 100, how many lockers are open?*

This problem is designed to seem overwhelming. You don't have time to draw a diagram of 100 lockers and count 100 passes through them. Even if you did, solving the problem that way won't illustrate any skill or intuition, so there must be some trick that you can use to determine how many doors will be open. You just need to figure out what that trick is.

It's unlikely that you can intuit the solution to this problem by just staring at it. What can you do? Although it's not practical to solve the entire problem by brute force, solving a few lockers in this manner is reasonable. Perhaps you will notice some patterns you can apply to the larger problem.

Start by choosing an arbitrary locker, 12, and determining whether it will end open or closed. On which passes will you toggle locker 12? There are two obvious times: on the first pass, when you toggle every locker, and on the twelfth pass, when you start with locker 12. You don't need to consider any pass after 12 because those will all start farther down the hall than locker 12. This leaves passes 2 through 11. You can count these out: 2, 4, 6, 8, 10, 12 (you toggle on pass 2); 3, 6, 9, 12 (on 3); 4, 8, 12 (on 4); 5, 10, 15 (not on 5); 6, 12 (on 6); 7, 14 (not on 7), and so on. Somewhere in this process, you probably notice that you toggle locker 12 only when the number of the pass you're on is a factor of 12. This is because when counting by n, you hit 12 only when some integer number of n's add to 12, which is another way of saying that n is a factor of 12. The solution seems to have something to do with factors. Though it seems simple in retrospect, this probably wasn't obvious before you worked out an example.

The factors of 12 are 1, 2, 3, 4, 6, and 12. Correspondingly, the operations on the locker door are open, close, open, close, open, close. So locker 12 will end closed.

If factors are involved, perhaps it would be instructive to investigate a prime locker, as primes are numbers with unique factor properties. You might select 17 as a representative prime. The factors are 1 and 17, so the operations are open, close. It ends closed just like 12. Apparently primes are not necessarily different from nonprimes for the purposes of this problem.

What generalizations can you make about whether a locker ends open or closed? All lockers start closed and alternate between being open and closed. So lockers are closed after the second, fourth, sixth, and so on, times they are toggled — in other words, if a locker is toggled an even number of times, then it ends closed; otherwise, it ends open. You know that a locker is toggled once for every factor of the locker number, so you can say that a locker ends open only if it has an odd number of factors.

The task has now been reduced to finding how many numbers between 1 and 100 have an odd number of factors. The two you've examined (and most others, if you try a few more examples) have even numbers of factors.

Why is that? If a number i is a factor of n, what does that mean? It means that i times some other number j is equal to n. Of course, because multiplication is commutative ($i \times j = j \times i$), that means that j is a factor of n, too, so the number of factors is usually even because factors tend to come in pairs. If you can find the numbers that have unpaired factors, you will know which lockers will be open. Multiplication is a binary operation, so two numbers will always be involved, but what if they are both the same number (that is, $i = j$)? In that case, a single number would effectively form both halves of the pair, and there would be an odd number of factors. When this is the case, $i \times i = n$. Therefore, n must be a perfect square. Try a perfect square to check this solution. For example, for 16, the factors are 1, 2, 4, 8, 16; operations are open, close, open, close, open — as expected, it ends open.

Based on this reasoning, you can conclude that only lockers with numbers that are perfect squares end up open. The perfect squares between 1 and 100 (inclusive) are 1, 4, 9, 16, 25, 36, 49, 64, 81, and 100. So 10 lockers would remain open.

> **PROBLEM** *Now generalize the solution: In a hall with* k *lockers, how many lockers remain open after pass* k*?*

Similarly, for the general case of k lockers, the number of open lockers is the number of perfect squares between 1 and k, inclusive. How can you best count these? The perfect squares themselves are inconvenient to count because they're unevenly spaced. However, the square roots of the perfect squares greater than zero are the positive integers. These are easy to count: The last number in the list of square roots gives the number of items in each list. For example, the square roots of 1, 4, 9, 16, and 25 are 1, 2, 3, 4, and 5; the last number in the list of square roots is the square root of the largest perfect square and is equal to the number of perfect squares. You need to find the square root of the largest perfect square less than or equal to k.

This task is trivial when k is a perfect square, but most of the time it won't be. In these cases, the square root of k will be a noninteger. If you round this square root down to the nearest integer, then its square is the largest perfect square less than k — just what you were looking for. The operation of rounding to the largest integer less than or equal to a given number is often called *floor*. Thus, in the general case of k lockers, there will be *floor(sqrt(k))* lockers remaining open.

The key to solving this problem is trying strategies to solve parts of the problem even when it isn't clear how these parts contribute to the overall solution. Although some attempts, such as the investigation of prime numbered lockers, may not be fruitful, others are likely to lead to greater insight about how to attack the problem, such as the strategy of calculating the result for a single locker. Even in the worst case, where none of the things you try lead you closer to the final solution, you show the interviewer that you aren't intimidated by difficult problems with no clear solution and that you are willing to keep trying different approaches until you find one that works.

Three Switches

> **PROBLEM** *You are standing in a hallway next to three light switches, all of which are off. Each switch operates a different incandescent light bulb in the room at the end of the hall. You cannot see the lights from where the switches are. Determine which light corresponds to each switch. You may go into the room with the lights only once.*

The crux of this problem comes quickly to the front: There are only two possible positions for each switch (on or off) but there are three lights to identify. You can easily identify one light, by setting one switch differently than the other two, but this leaves you no way to distinguish the two left in the same position.

When confronted with a seemingly impossible task, you should go back to basics. The two key objects in this problem seem to be the switches and the lights. What do you know about switches and light bulbs? Switches make or break an electrical connection: When a switch is on, current flows through it. An incandescent light bulb consists of a resistive filament inside an evacuated glass bulb. When current flows through the filament, it consumes power, producing light and heat.

How can these properties help you solve the problem? Which of them can you detect or measure? The properties of a switch don't seem too useful. It's much easier to look at the switch to see whether it's off or on than to measure current. The light bulbs sound a little more promising. You can detect light by looking at the bulbs, and you can detect heat by touching them. Whether there is light coming from a bulb is determined entirely by its switch — when the switch is on, there is light; when it's off, there isn't. What about heat? It takes some time for a light to heat up after it's been switched on, and some time for it to cool after it's switched off, so you could use heat to determine whether a bulb had been on, even if it were off when you walked into the room.

You can determine which switch goes with each bulb by turning the first switch on and the second and third off. After 10 minutes, turn the first switch off, leave the second off, and turn the third on. When you go into the room, the hot dark bulb corresponds to the first switch, the cold dark bulb to the second, and the lit bulb to the third.

Although there's nothing truly outlandish about this question — it's not just a stupid play on words, for instance — it is arguably a trick question. The solution involves coming up with something somewhat outside the definition of the problem. Some interviewers believe that questions like this help them identify people who can think outside the box and develop nontraditional, innovative solutions to difficult problems. In the authors' opinion, these problems are cheap shots that don't prove much of anything. Nevertheless, these problems do appear in interviews, and you should be prepared for them.

Bridge Crossing

> **PROBLEM** *A party of four travelers comes to a rickety bridge at night. The bridge can hold the weight of at most two of the travelers at a time, and it cannot be crossed without using a flashlight. The travelers have one flashlight among them. Each traveler walks at a different speed: The first can cross the bridge in 1 minute, the second in 2 minutes, the third in 5 minutes, and the fourth takes 10 minutes to cross the bridge. If two travelers cross together, they walk at the speed of the slower traveler.*
>
> *What is the least amount of time in which all the travelers can cross from one side of the bridge to the other?*

Because there is only one flashlight, each trip to the far side of the bridge (except the last trip) must be followed by a trip coming back. Each of these trips consists of either one or two travelers crossing the bridge. To get a net movement of travelers to the far side of the bridge, you probably want to have two travelers on each outbound trip and one on each inbound trip. This strategy gives you a total of five trips: three outbound and two inbound. Your task is to assign travelers to the trips so that you minimize the total time for the five trips. For clarity, you can refer to each traveler by the number of minutes it takes to cross the bridge.

Number 1 can cross the bridge at least twice as fast as any of the other travelers, so you can minimize the time of the return trips by always having 1 bring the flashlight back. This suggests a strategy whereby 1 escorts each of the other travelers across the bridge one by one.

One possible arrangement of trips using this strategy is illustrated in Figure 14-1. The order in which 1 escorts the other travelers doesn't change the total time: The three outbound trips have times of 2, 5, and 10 minutes, and the two inbound trips are 1 minute each, for a total of 19 minutes.

This solution is logical, obvious, and doesn't take long to discover. In short, it can't possibly be the best solution to an interview problem. Your interviewer would tell you that you can do better than 19 minutes, but even without that hint you should guess you arrived at the preceding solution too easily.

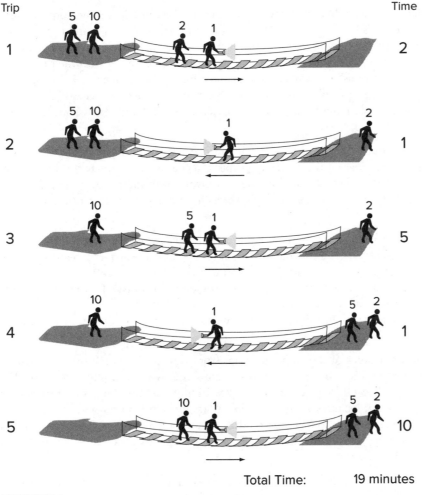

FIGURE 14-1

This puts you in an uncomfortable, but unfortunately not unusual, position. You know your answer is wrong, yet based on the assumptions you made, it's the only reasonable answer. It's easy to get frustrated at this point. You may wonder if this is a trick question: Perhaps you're supposed to throw the flashlight back or have the second pair use a lantern. Such tricks are almost never the right answer, and they are not necessary here. A more efficient arrangement of trips exists. Because the only solution that seems logical is wrong, you must have made a false assumption.

Consider your assumptions, checking each one to see if it might be false. First among your assumptions was that outbound and inbound trips must alternate. This seems correct — there's no way to have an outbound trip followed by another outbound trip because the flashlight would be on the wrong side of the bridge.

Next, you assumed that there would be two travelers on each outbound trip and one on each return trip. This seems logical, but it's harder to prove. Putting two travelers on an inbound trip seems terribly counterproductive; after all, you're trying to get them to the far side of the bridge. An outbound trip with only one traveler is potentially more worthwhile, but coupled with the requisite return trip all it actually accomplishes is exchanging the positions of two travelers. Exchanging two travelers might be useful, but it probably wastes too much time to be worth it. Because this possibility doesn't look promising, try looking for a false assumption elsewhere and reconsider this one if necessary.

You also assumed that 1 should always bring the flashlight back. What basis do you have for this assumption? It minimizes the time for the return trips, but the goal is to minimize total time, not return trip time. Perhaps the best overall solution does not involve minimized return trip times. The assumption that 1 should always return the flashlight seems hard to support, so it probably merits further examination.

If you're not going to have 1 make all the return trips, then how will you arrange the trips? You might try a process of elimination. You obviously can't have 10 make a return trip because then 10 would have at least three trips, which would take 30 minutes. Even without getting the remaining travelers across, this is already worse than your previous solution. Similarly, if 5 makes a return trip, then you have two trips that are at least 5 minutes, plus one that takes 10 minutes (when 10 crosses). Just those three trips total 20 minutes, so you won't find a better solution by having 5 make a return trip.

You might also try analyzing some of the individual trips from your previous solution. Because 1 escorted everyone else, there was a trip with 1 and 10. In a sense, when you send 1 with 10, 1's speed is wasted on that trip because the crossing still takes 10 minutes. Looking at that from a different perspective, any trip that includes 10 always takes 10 minutes, no matter which other traveler goes along. Therefore, if you're going to have to spend 10 minutes on a trip, you might as well take advantage of it and get another slow traveler across. This reasoning indicates that 10 should cross with 5, rather than with 1.

Using this strategy, you might begin by sending 10 and 5 across. However, one of them has to bring the flashlight back, which you already know isn't the right solution. You'll want to already have someone faster than 5 waiting on the far side. Try starting by sending 1 and 2 across. Then have 1 bring the flashlight back. Now that there's someone reasonably fast (2) on the far side, you can send 5 and 10 across together. Then 2 returns the flashlight. Finally, 1 and 2 cross the bridge again. This scheme is illustrated in Figure 14-2.

Trip

Time

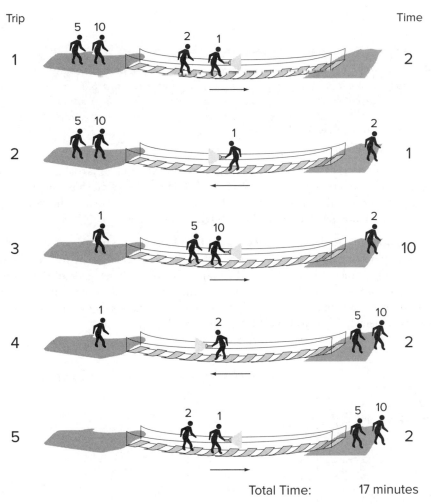

FIGURE 14-2

The times for the respective trips under this strategy are 2, 1, 10, 2, and 2, for a total of 17 minutes. Identifying the false assumption improved your solution by 2 minutes.

This problem is a slightly unusual example of a class of problems involving optimizing the process of moving a group of items a few at a time from one place to another. More commonly, the goal is to minimize the total number of trips, and there are often restrictions on which items can be left together. This particular problem is difficult because it suggests a false assumption (that 1 should escort each of the other travelers) that seems so obvious you may not even realize you're making an assumption.

Heavy Marble

> **PROBLEM** *You have eight marbles and a two-pan scale. All the marbles weigh the same, except for one which is heavier than all the others. The marbles are otherwise indistinguishable. You may make no assumptions about how much heavier the heavy marble is. What is the minimum number of weighings needed to be certain of identifying the heavy marble?*

The first step to solve this problem is to realize that you can put more than one marble in each pan of the scale. If you have equal numbers of marbles in each pan, then the heavy marble must be in the group on the heavy side of the scale. This saves you from having to weigh each marble individually, and it enables you to eliminate many marbles in a single weighing.

When you realize this, you are likely to devise a binary search-based strategy to find the heavy marble. In this method, you begin by putting half the marbles on each side of the scale. Then you eliminate the marbles from the light side of the scale and divide the marbles from the heavy side of the scale between the two pans. As shown in Figure 14-3, you continue this process until each pan holds only one marble, at which point the heavy marble is the only marble on the heavy side of the scale. Using this process you can always identify the heavy marble in three weighings.

Weighing

○ = Normal marble
● = Heavy marble

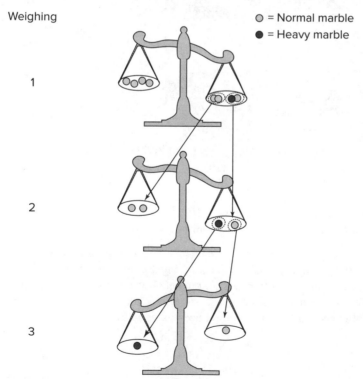

1

2

3

FIGURE 14-3

This may seem to be the correct answer. The solution wasn't completely obvious, and it's an improvement over weighing the marbles one by one. But if you think that this seems too easy, you're right. The method described so far is a good start, but it's not the best you can do.

How can you find the heavy marble in fewer than three weighings? Obviously, you must eliminate more than half the marbles at each weighing, but how can you do that?

Try looking at this problem from an information flow perspective. Information about the marbles comes from the scale, and you use this information to identify the heavy marble. The more information you derive from each weighing, the more efficient your search for the marble can be. Think about how you get information from the scale: You place marbles on it and then look at the result. What are all the possible results? The left pan side could be heavier, the right side could be heavier, or both sides could weigh exactly the same. So there are three possible results, but so far you've been using only two of them. In effect, you're only using two-thirds of the information that each weighing provides. Perhaps if you alter your method so that you use all the information from each weighing you can find the heavy marble in fewer weighings.

Using the binary search strategy, the heavy marble is always in one of the two pans, so there is always a heavy side of the scale. In other words, you can't take advantage of all the information the scale can provide if the heavy marble is always on the scale. What if you divided the marbles into three equal-sized groups, and weighed two of the groups on the scale? Just as before, if either side of the scale is heavier, you know that the heavy marble is in the group on that side. But now it's also possible that the two groups of marbles on the scale weigh the same — in this case, the heavy marble must be in the third group that's not on the scale. Because you divided the marbles into three groups, keeping just the group with the heavy marble eliminates two-thirds of the marbles instead of half of them. This seems promising.

There's still a minor wrinkle to work out before you can apply this process to the problem. Eight isn't evenly divisible by 3, so you can't divide the eight marbles into three equal groups. Why do you need the same number of marbles in each group? You need the same number of marbles so that when you put the groups on the scale the result doesn't have anything to do with differing numbers of marbles on each side. Really, you need only two of the groups to be the same size. You still want all three groups to be approximately the same size so you can eliminate approximately two-thirds of the marbles after each weighing no matter which pile has the heavy marble.

Now you can apply the three-group technique to the problem you were given. Begin by dividing the marbles into two groups of three, which you put on the scale, and one group of two, which you leave off. If the two sides weigh the same, the heavy marble is in the group of two, and you can find it with one more weighing, for a total of two weighings. On the other hand, if either side of the scale is heavier, the heavy marble must be in that group of three. You can eliminate all the other marbles, and place one marble from this group on either side of the scale, leaving the third marble aside. If one side is heavier, it contains the heavy marble; if neither side is heavier, the heavy marble is the one you didn't place on the scale. This is also a total of two weighings, so you can always find the heavy marble in a group of eight using two weighings. Figure 14-4 shows an example of this process.

Weighing

○ Normal marble
● Heavy marble

1

2

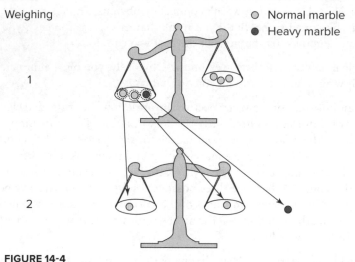

FIGURE 14-4

> **PROBLEM** *Now generalize your solution. What is the minimum number of weighings to find a heavy marble among* n *marbles?*

This is the part where the interviewer determines whether you hit on the preceding solution by luck or because you really understand it. Think about what happens after each weighing. You eliminate two-thirds of the marbles and keep one-third. After each weighing you have one-third as many marbles as you did before. When you get down to one marble, you've found the heavy marble.

Based on this reasoning, you can reformulate the question as, "How many times do you have to divide the number of marbles by 3 before you end up with 1?" If you start with three marbles, you divide by 3 once to get 1, so it takes one weighing. If you start with nine marbles, you divide by 3 twice, so it takes two weighings. Similarly, 27 marbles require three weighings. What mathematical operation can you use to represent this "How many times do you divide by 3 to get to 1" process?

Because multiplication and division are inverse operations, the number of times you must divide the number of marbles by 3 before you end up with 1 is the same as the number of times you have to multiply by 3 (starting at 1) before you get to the number of marbles. Repeated multiplication is expressed using exponents. If you want to express multiplying by 3 twice, you can write 3^2, which is equal to 9. When you multiply twice by 3, you get 9 — it takes two weighings to find the heavy marble among nine marbles. In more general terms, it takes i weighings to find the heavy marble from among n marbles, where $3^i = n$. You know the value of n and want to calculate i, so you need to solve this for i. You can solve for i using logarithms, the inverse operation of exponentiation. If you take $\log_3$ of both sides of the preceding equation, you get $i = \log_3 n$.

This works fine as long as n is a power of 3. However, if n isn't a power of 3, then this equation calculates a noninteger value for i, which doesn't make much sense, given that it's extremely difficult to perform a fractional weighing. For example, if $n = 8$, as in the previous part of the problem, $\log_3 8$ is some number between 1 and 2 (1.893. . . to be a little more precise). From your previous experience, you know it actually takes two weighings when you have eight marbles. This seems to indicate that if you calculate a fractional number of weighings, you should round it up to the nearest integer.

Does this make sense? Try applying it to $n = 10$ to see whether you can justify always rounding up. $\log_3 9$ is 2, so $\log_3 10$ will be a little more than two, or three if you round up to the nearest integer. Is that the correct number of weighings for 10 marbles? For 10 marbles, you would start out with two groups of 3 and one group of 4. If the heavy marble were in either of the groups of 3, you could find it with just one more weighing, but if it turns out to be in the group of 4, you might need as many as two more weighings for a total of 3, just as you calculated. In this case the fractional weighing seems to represent a weighing that you might need to make under some circumstances (if the heavy marble happens to be in the larger group) but not others. Because you're trying to calculate the number of weighings needed to guarantee you can find the heavy marble, you must count that fractional weighing as a full weighing even though you won't always perform it, so it makes sense to always round up to the nearest integer. In programming, the function that rounds up to the nearest integer is often called *ceiling*, so you might express the minimum number of weighings needed to guarantee you find the heavy marble among n marbles as *ceiling*($\log_3(n)$).

> **NOTE** *For the group of 4 (out of the total of 10 marbles), you would divide the 4 marbles into two groups of 1 and one group of 2. If the heavy marble happened to be in the group of 2, you would need one more weighing (the third weighing) to determine which was the heavy marble. A fractional weighing may also represent a weighing that will always be performed but won't eliminate a full 2/3 of the remaining marbles. For example, when $n = 8$, the fractional weighing represents the weighing needed to determine which marble is heavier in the case in which the heavy marble is known to be in the group of 2 after the first weighing. In any case, it must be counted as a full weighing, so rounding up is appropriate.*

This is another example of a problem designed such that the wrong solution occurs first to most intelligent, logically thinking people. Most people find it quite difficult to come up with the idea to use three groups, but relatively easy to solve the problem after that leap. It's not an accident that this problem begins by asking you to solve the case of eight marbles. As a power of 2, it works cleanly for the incorrect solution, but because it's not a power (or multiple, for that matter) of 3, it's a little messy for the correct solution. People generally get the correct answer more quickly when asked to solve the problem for nine marbles. Watch out for details like this that may steer your thinking in a particular (and often incorrect) direction.

This problem is a relatively easy example of a whole class of tricky problems involving weighing items with a two-pan scale. For more practice with these, you can work out the solution to the preceding problem for a group of marbles in which one marble has a different weight, but you don't know whether it's heavier or lighter.

Number of American Gas Stations

> **PROBLEM** *How many gas stations are there in the United States?*

Clearly this is an estimation problem. Although it would probably be faster and more accurate to search for the figure on the Internet, you won't get credit for that.

As with any estimation problem, the key is connecting the unknown quantity you're trying to estimate to quantities that you know or can make a reasonable guess at. Often you can establish these connections by considering the interactions between the things you quantify. In this case, cars are filled with gas at gas stations, so it seems reasonable that the number of gas stations in a nation would be related to the number of vehicles. You probably don't have any better idea of how many vehicles there are in the US than you do the number of gas stations, but vehicles have to be driven by people, so you can connect the number of vehicles to the population.

You might know that the population of the United States is something just upwards of 300 million. (If not, you could estimate this, too. For instance: There are at over a billion people in China, and there are about 10 million people in New York. The US is much smaller than China, but must be much bigger than New York, so the population is probably at least 100 million.) Try taking the population as a starting point.

Not everyone has a car, so suppose there are 150 million cars on the road. But there are also commercial vehicles to consider, say one commercial vehicle for every passenger car, for a total of 300 million vehicles. You can determine the number of gas stations from this figure by estimating how many vehicles a gas station can serve.

You can base the estimation of the number of vehicles served by a gas station on your own experiences. In our experience, it takes about 6 minutes to fill up a car. We go to the gas station about once a week, and there are usually two other cars there. Assuming this is average for Americans, each gas station services about 30 cars an hour. Suppose a gas station were open 12 hours a day, 7 days a week: That would be 84 hours a week. 84 is a difficult number for mental arithmetic, and in reality, a gas station is probably open more than 12 hours a day, so estimate that the average gas station is open 100 hours a week. That means it services 3,000 cars a week.

If every vehicle goes to the gas station about once a week and each station sees 3,000 vehicles a week, there must be approximately 100,000 gas stations in the United States. Figures estimated like this are not precise, but they are typically within an order of magnitude — that is, in this case we can be fairly confident that there are more than 10,000 gas stations and fewer than 1,000,000. In fact, in 2008 the United States Census Bureau put out a press release stating that there were 116,855 gas stations in the United States in 2006.

It's much more important that you can form a reasonable framework for the estimation and rapidly work through the calculations than that you accurately estimate the statistic.

For more practice, try estimating the number of kindergarten teachers in your state, the circumference of the earth, and the weight of a ferryboat.

SUMMARY

You'll probably encounter a brainteaser or two during the interview process, even if they're not directly related to your programming skills. Some interviewers use these kinds of problems to see your thought processes at work and determine how well you can think outside the box.

Brainteasers come in many different forms, but the obvious answer is almost invariably wrong. Start by verifying your assumptions to make sure you're solving the right problem. Don't be intimidated by the problem — break it into pieces, simplify the problem, and solve specific cases to find the general solution. Beware of simple problems because they're trickier than they seem. If you don't have all the facts you need, make reasonable estimates based on prior knowledge and experience.

Always think out loud and explain to the interviewer what you're doing and the reasoning behind your decisions. Focus on the problem and keep working; it's your thought processes that count the most here, not the answer.

15

Graphical and Spatial Puzzles

Many brainteasers are graphical in nature or involve spatial thinking. All the techniques you've used on nongraphical puzzles are still applicable, but with these problems you have another very powerful technique available to you: diagrams.

DRAW IT FIRST

The importance of drawing diagrams cannot be overstated. Consider that although humans have been using written language and mathematics for only a few thousand years, they have been evolving to analyze visual problems (for example, can that rhinoceros catch me before I get to that tree?) for millions of years. Humans are generally much better suited to solving problems presented in pictures than those presented in text or numbers. As the saying goes, "a picture is worth a thousand words." This maxim also applies to technical interviews.

> **NOTE** *Whenever possible, draw a picture.*

In some cases, the "actors" in these brainteasers are static, but more often they change or move. When this is the case, don't draw just one picture, draw many pictures. Make a diagram for each moment in time for which you have information. You can often gain insight by observing how the situation changes between each of your diagrams.

> **NOTE** *If the problem involves motion or change, draw multiple pictures of different points in time.*

Most graphical problems are two-dimensional. Even when a problem involves three-dimensional objects, the objects are often constrained to the same plane, enabling you to simplify the problem to two dimensions. It's much easier to diagram two dimensions than three, so don't work in three dimensions unless you must.

If the problem is fundamentally a three-dimensional problem, assess your relative abilities with drawing and visualization before proceeding. If you're not good at drawing, your diagram of a three-dimensional problem may do more to confuse than elucidate. On the other hand, if you're a good artist or drafter, but have trouble with visualization, you may be better off with a diagram. Whatever approach you take, try to attack spatial problems spatially, not with computation or symbolic mathematics.

> **NOTE** *Visualization may be more appropriate than diagramming for three-dimensional problems, but in either case, attack the problem spatially.*

GRAPHICAL AND SPATIAL PROBLEMS

Diagramming and visualization are the keys to solving the following brainteasers.

Boat and Dock

> **PROBLEM** *You are sitting in a small boat, holding the end of a rope. The other end of the rope is tied to the top of a nearby pier such that it is higher above the water than your end of the rope. You pull on the rope, causing your boat to move toward the pier, stopping directly underneath the pier. As you pull on the rope, which of the following is faster: the speed the boat moves across the water or the speed the rope moves through your hands?*

You should begin this problem by drawing a diagram, both to ensure you understand the scenario and to get you started on the solution. The edge of the pier, the water, and the rope form the legs of a right triangle, as shown in Figure 15-1. To facilitate further discussion, these segments are labeled A, B, and C, respectively.

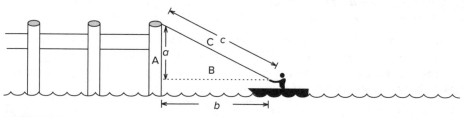

FIGURE 15-1

Here you have something familiar but with an unusual twist. You've probably worked with right triangles *ad nauseam* in your math classes, but those were static shapes. This triangle is collapsing. Be wary of this difference. Although it seems minor, it may be enough to make the wrong answer seem intuitively correct.

Given your experience with right triangles, you may decide to attack this problem mathematically. You need to determine whether side B or side C gets shorter more quickly as the boat moves. Put another way, for a given change in the length of B, what is the change in the length of C?

How might you calculate this? A derivative gives you the ratio of rates of change between two variables. If you calculated the derivative of C with respect to B and it were greater than 1, you would know that the rope was moving faster; conversely, if it were less than 1, the boat must have moved faster.

This is a good point at which to stop and consider where you've been and where you're going. You can set up an equation relating B and C using the Pythagorean theorem. It looks as if this method will eventually lead you to the correct answer. If you're good at math and comfortable with calculus, this may even be the best way to proceed. The apparent need for calculus, however, should serve as a warning that you may be missing an easier way to solve the problem.

Try returning to the original diagram and taking a more graphical approach. What other diagrams might you draw? Because you don't know the boat's initial distance from the pier or how high the pier is, all diagrams of the boat in motion are effectively equivalent. What about when the boat stops under the pier, as shown in Figure 15-2? That would be different; you no longer have a triangle because the rope hangs down the side of the pier.

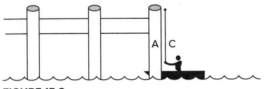

FIGURE 15-2

How far does the boat travel, and how much rope is hauled in between the times shown in the two figures? Because you aren't given any numbers, call the initial lengths of sides A, B, and C lowercase *a*, *b*, and *c*, respectively. When the boat is under the pier, side B has a length of 0, so the boat has moved through a distance of *b*. The rope, on the other hand, started with a length of *c*. In the second diagram, a length of rope equal to *a* is still out of the boat, so the total amount hauled in is *c* − *a*.

Because these distances were covered in the same time, the greater distance must have been covered at a higher speed. Which is greater: *c* − *a* or *b*? Recall from geometry that the sum of the lengths of two sides of a triangle must always be greater than the length of the third. For example, *a* + *b* > *c*. (If you think about this, it makes intuitive sense. Suppose one side were longer than the other two put together. There would be no way to arrange the sides so that they meet at three vertices because the shorter two sides are too short to span the distance from one end of the long side to the other.) Subtracting *a* from both sides gives *b* > *c* − *a*. The boat traveled a greater distance, so it was moving faster across the water than the speed of the rope through your hands.

For the mathematically curious, pick up the calculus where you left it, to show that you can determine the solution using that method. From the Pythagorean theorem, $c^2 = a^2 + b^2$. Use this to calculate the derivative of *c* with respect to *b*:

$$c = \sqrt{a^2 + b^2}$$

$$\frac{dc}{db} = \frac{1}{2}(a^2 + b^2)^{-\frac{1}{2}}(2b) \quad = \quad \frac{b}{\sqrt{a^2 + b^2}}$$

b is positive, so when $a = 0$, the final expression is equal to 1. When a is greater than 0, as in this problem, the denominator is greater than the numerator, and the expression is less than 1. (In case you've been out of a math class for too long, the numerator is the expression above the fraction bar, and the denominator is the expression below it.) This means that for a given infinitesimal change in b, there is a smaller change in c, so the boat is moving faster.

This problem belongs to a curious class of puzzles that seem to be more difficult when you know more mathematics, which are particularly devilish in interviews. Because you expect difficult questions and you may be a little nervous, you're unlikely to stop and ask yourself whether there's an easier way.

One of the nastiest examples of this type of problem involves two locomotives, heading toward each other at 10 mph. When the locomotives are exactly 30 miles apart, a bird sitting on the front of one locomotive flies off at 60 mph toward the other locomotive. When it reaches the other locomotive, it immediately turns around and flies back to the first. The bird continues like this until, sadly, it is smashed between the two locomotives as they collide.

When asked how far the bird traveled, many calculus students spend hours trying to set up and sum impossibly difficult infinite series. Other students who have never heard of an infinite series might instead determine that it took the locomotives 1.5 hours to close the 30-mile gap, and that in that time a bird traveling 60 mph would have traveled 90 miles.

Counting Cubes

> **PROBLEM** *Imagine a cubic array made up of a 3-by-3-by-3 arrangement of smaller cubes so that the array is three cubes wide, three cubes high, and three cubes deep. How many of the cubes are on the surface of the cubic array?*

For this problem, it may help to picture a Rubik's Cube, as shown in Figure 15-3.

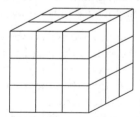

FIGURE 15-3

This is a spatial visualization problem. Different people find different techniques useful in visualization, so this discussion presents a variety of approaches. The hope is that you can find at least one of them useful. You can try to draw a diagram, but because the problem is in three dimensions, you may find your diagram more confusing than helpful.

One way you might try to solve this problem is by counting the cubes on each face of the array. A cube has six faces. Each face of the cubic array has nine cubes (3×3), so you might conclude that there are 6 × 9 = 54 cubes on the surface. But there are only 3 × 3 × 3 = 27 cubes total, so it's obviously not possible for twice that many to be on the surface. The fallacy in this method is that some cubes are on more than one face — for example, the corner cubes are on three faces. Rather than try to make complicated adjustments for cubes that are on more than one face, you should look for an easier solution.

A better way to attack this problem is to count the cubes in layers. The array is three cubes high, so there are three layers. All the cubes on the top layer are on the surface (nine cubes). All the cubes of the middle layer except for the center cube are on the surface (eight cubes). Finally, all the cubes on the bottom layer are on the surface (nine cubes). This gives a total of 9 + 8 + 9 = 26 cubes on the surface.

The preceding method works, but perhaps a better way to find the solution is to count the cubes that are not on the surface and then subtract this number from the total number of cubes. Vivid, specific objects are often easier to visualize than vague concepts — you may want to imagine the cubes on the surface to be transparent red and the non-surface cubes to be bright blue. Hopefully, you can visualize only one bright blue cube surrounded by a shell of red cubes. Because this is the only cube that isn't on the surface, there must be 27 – 1 = 26 cubes on the surface.

> **PROBLEM** *Now imagine that you have a 4-by-4-by-4 cubic array of cubes. How many cubes are on the surface of this array?*

As the number of cubes increases, the accounting necessary for the layer approach becomes more complicated, so try to solve this by visualizing and counting the cubes that are not on the surface.

The nonsurface cubes form a smaller cubic array within the larger array. How many cubes are in this smaller array? Your initial impulse may be that there are four cubes in the array; if so, consider whether it's possible to arrange four cubes into a cubic array. (It isn't.) The correct answer is that the nonsurface cubes form a 2 × 2 × 2 array of eight cubes. There are a total of 4 × 4 × 4 = 64 cubes, so there are 64 – 8 = 56 cubes on the surface.

> **PROBLEM** *Generalize your solution to an n-by-n-by-n cubic array of cubes. In terms of n, how many cubes are on the surface?*

Now that you can't explicitly count the cubes, the problem starts to get a little more interesting. You know that there are n^3 cubes total. If you can calculate the number of cubes that aren't on the surface, you can also calculate the number that are on the surface. Try to visualize the situation, mentally coloring the surface cubes red and the interior cubes blue. What does it look like? You should see a cubic array of blue cubes surrounded by a one-cube-thick shell of red cubes. If you can determine the size of the smaller array, you can calculate the number of cubes it contains. Because the smaller array fits entirely within the larger one, it must be fewer than n cubes across, but how many fewer?

Visualize a single line of cubes running all the way through the array. The line would be n cubes long. Because the shell of red surface cubes is one cube thick, both the first and last cubes would be red, and all the other cubes would be blue. This means there would be $n - 2$ blue cubes in the row, so the array of interior cubes is $n - 2$ cubes across. It's a cubic array, so its height and depth are the same as its width. Therefore, you can calculate that there are $(n - 2)^3$ cubes that are not on the surface. Subtracting this from the total number of cubes gives you $n^3 - (n - 2)^3$ cubes on the surface. Test this formula using the cases you've already worked out by hand: $3^3 - (3 - 2)^3 = 26$; $4^3 - (4 - 2)^3 = 56$. It looks as if you have the answer for this part, but you're not done yet.

> **PROBLEM** *A cube is an object that measures the same distance across in three perpendicular directions in a three-dimensional space. A four-dimensional hypercube is an object that measures the same distance across in four perpendicular directions in a four-dimensional space. Calculate the number of 4-D hypercubes on the surface of an* n-by-n-by-n-by-n *hypercubic array of 4-D hypercubes.*

The fun starts here. This began as a visualization problem, but taking it to four dimensions makes it difficult for most people to visualize. Visualization can still be helpful, though. You might find the following device useful.

People often represent time as a fourth dimension. The easiest way to visualize time in a concrete fashion is to imagine a strip of film from a movie. Each frame in the filmstrip represents a different time, or a different location along the fourth dimension. To fully represent four dimensions, you must imagine that each frame consists of a full three-dimensional space, not two-dimensional pictures as in an actual filmstrip. If you can visualize this, you can visualize four dimensions.

Because a hypercube measures the same distance in each direction, the filmstrip representing the hypercubic array in this problem is n frames long. In each of the frames, you see an $n \times n \times n$ array of cubes, just as in the previous part of the problem. (The cubes in each frame are actually hypercubes because their existence in the frame gives them a duration of one frame, or a width of one unit in the time (fourth) dimension. However, it may be easier to think of them as normal 3-D cubes when trying to visualize a single frame.) This means there are $n \times n^3 = n^4$ hypercubes in total. For color, the arrays you see in the middle frames of the filmstrip look just like the array from the previous part of the problem — a red shell surrounding a blue core.

All the cubes in the first and last frames are on the surface in the fourth dimension because they are at the ends of the filmstrip. All the cubes in these frames are red. In other words, there are $n - 2$ frames that have blue cubes, and each of these frames looks like the array from the previous part of the problem.

Multiplying the number of frames with blue cubes by the number of blue cubes in each frame gives $(n - 2)(n - 2)^3 = (n - 2)^4$, the total number of blue hypercubes. Subtracting from the previous result yields $n^4 - (n - 2)^4$ hypercubes on the surface of the hypercubic array.

> **PROBLEM** *Generalize your solution to* i *dimensions. How many hypercubes are there on the surface of an* n-by-n-by-n-by- ... -by-n *(*i *dimensions) hypercubic array of* i *dimensional hypercubes?*

You're almost there. At this point you may find it helpful to extend the device you've been using for visualization into many dimensions, or you may find it easier to dispense with visualization and solve the problem using patterns and mathematics. The following discussion examines both methods.

Visualizing a filmstrip gave you four dimensions, but there's no reason to limit yourself to a single filmstrip. If you imagine lining up n filmstrips side by side, you have five dimensions: three in each frame, one given by the frame number, and one more given by the filmstrip that holds the frame. Each of these filmstrips would look just like the filmstrip from the four-dimensional case, except for the rightmost and leftmost filmstrips. These two filmstrips would be surface filmstrips in the fifth dimension, so all the cubes in each of their frames would be red. You can further extend this to six dimensions by imagining a stack of multiple layers of filmstrips.

Beyond six dimensions, it again becomes difficult to visualize the situation (you might think of different tables, each holding stacks of layers of filmstrips), but the device has served its purpose in illustrating that dimensions are an arbitrary construction — there is nothing special about objects with more than three dimensions.

Each dimension you add gives you n copies of what you were visualizing before. Of these, two of the copies are always entirely on the surface, leaving $n - 2$ copies in which there are blue interior cubes. This means that with each additional dimension, the total number of hypercubes increases by a factor of n and the number of nonsurface hypercubes increases by a factor of $n - 2$. You have one of each of these factors for each dimension, giving you a final result of $n^i - (n - 2)^i$ hypercubes on the surface of the array.

Alternatively, you might take a pattern-based approach and note that you raised both parts of the expression to the power of 3 in the three-dimensional case and to the power of 4 in the four-dimensional case. From this you might deduce that the exponent represents the number of dimensions in the problem. You might check this by trying the one- and two-dimensional cases (a line and a square), where you would find that your proposed solution appears to work. Thinking about it mathematically, when you have n hypercubes in each of i directions, it seems reasonable that you would have a total of n^i hypercubes; for the same reason, raising $(n - 2)$ to the ith power also seems to make sense. This isn't a proof, but it should be enough to make you confident that $n^i - (n - 2)^i$ is the right answer.

It's interesting to look at the progression of the parts of this problem. The first part of the problem is quite easy. Taken by itself, the last part of the problem would seem almost impossible. Each part of the problem is only a little more difficult than the preceding, and each part helps you gain new insight, so by the time you reach the final part, it doesn't seem so insurmountable. It's good to remember this technique. Solving simpler, easier, more specific cases can give you insight into the solution of a more difficult, general problem, even if you aren't led through the process explicitly as you were here.

The Fox and the Duck

PROBLEM *A duck, pursued by a fox, escapes to the center of a perfectly circular pond. The fox cannot swim, and the duck cannot take flight from the water. (It's a deficient duck.) The fox is four times faster than the duck. Assuming the fox and duck pursue optimum strategies, is it possible for the duck to reach the edge of the pond and fly away without being eaten? If so, how?*

The most obvious strategy for the duck is to swim directly away from where the fox is standing. The duck must swim a distance of r to the edge of the pond. The fox, meanwhile, has to run around half the circumference of the pond, a distance of πr. Because the fox moves four times faster than the duck, and $\pi r < 4r$, it's apparent that any duck pursuing this strategy would soon be fox food.

Think about what this result tells you. Does it prove that the duck can't escape? No, it just shows that the duck can't escape using this strategy. If there weren't anything else to this problem, it would be a trivial geometry exercise — not worth asking in an interview — so this result suggests the duck can escape, you just don't know how.

Instead of focusing on the duck, try thinking about the fox's strategy. The fox will run around the perimeter of the pond to stay as close to the duck as possible. Because the shortest distance from any point inside the circle to the edge lies along a radius, the fox will try to stay on the same radius as the duck.

How can the duck make life most difficult for the fox? If the duck swims back and forth along a radius, the fox can just sit on that radius. The duck could try swimming back and forth across the center point of the pond, which would keep the fox running as the duck's radius repeatedly switched from one side of the pond to the other. However, consider that each time the duck crosses the center point, he returns to the problem's initial configuration: He is in the center and the fox is at the edge. The duck won't make much progress that way.

Another possibility would involve the duck swimming in a circle concentric with the pond, so the fox would have to keep running around the pond to stay on the duck's radius. When the duck is near the edge of the pond, the fox has no trouble staying on the same radius as the duck because they are covering approximately equal distances and the fox is four times faster. However, as the duck moves closer to the center of the pond, the circumference of its circle becomes smaller and smaller. At a distance of ¼ r from the center of the pond, the duck's circle is exactly four times smaller than the circumference of the pond, so the fox can just barely stay on the same radius as the duck. At any distance less than ¼ r from the center, the fox must cover more than four times the distance that the duck does to move between two radii. That means that as the duck circles, the fox starts to lag behind.

This strategy seems to give the duck a way to put some distance between it and the fox. If the duck swims long enough, eventually the fox will lag so far behind that the radius the duck is on will be 180 degrees from the fox; in other words, the point on the shore closest to the duck will be farthest from the fox. Perhaps this head start would be enough that the duck could make a radial beeline for the shore and get there ahead of the fox.

How can the head start be maximized? When the duck's circle has a radius of ¼ r the fox just keeps pace with it, so at a radius of ¼ r minus some infinitesimal amount ε, the duck would just barely pull ahead. Eventually, when it got 180 degrees ahead of the fox, it would be ¾ $r + \varepsilon$ from the nearest point on the shore. The fox, however, would be half the circumference of the pond from that point: πr. In this case, the fox would have to cover more than four times the distance that the duck does (¾ $r \times 4 < \pi r$), so the duck could make it to land and fly away, as shown in Figure 15-4.

You might want to try to work out the solution to a similar problem: This time, the fox chases a rabbit. They are inside a circular pen from which they cannot escape. If the rabbit can run at the same speed as the fox, is it possible for the fox to catch the rabbit?

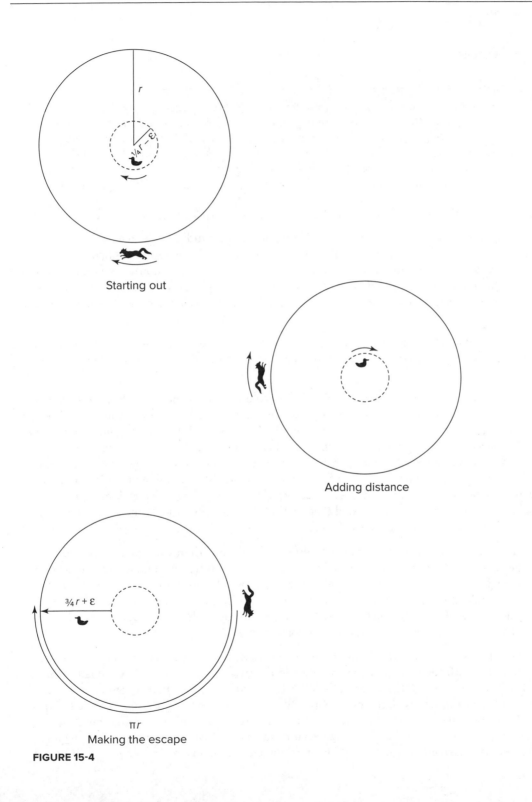

Starting out

Adding distance

Making the escape

πr

FIGURE 15-4

Burning Fuses

> **PROBLEM** *You are given two fuses and a lighter. When lit, each fuse takes exactly 1 hour to burn from one end to the other. The fuses do not burn at a constant rate, though, and they are not identical. In other words, you may make no assumptions about the relationship between the length of a section of fuse and the time it has taken or will take to burn. Two equal lengths of fuse do not necessarily take the same time to burn. Using only the fuses and the lighter, measure a period of exactly 45 minutes.*

One of the difficult parts of this problem is keeping firmly in mind that the length of a piece of fuse has nothing to do with the time it takes to burn. Although this is stated explicitly in the problem, constant rates and relationships between time and distance are so familiar that it can be easy to fall into the trap of trying to somehow measure a physical length of fuse. Because the burn rate is unknown and variable, the only useful measure is time. Mindful of this, you can begin to solve the problem.

The materials and actions available to you are fairly circumscribed in this problem. In such a case, it can be useful to begin by considering all possible actions and then identify which of these possible actions might be useful.

There are two locations where you can light the fuses: at an end or somewhere that is not an end (in the middle). If you light one of the fuses at an end, it will burn through in 60 minutes. That's longer than the total length of time you need to measure, so it probably isn't directly useful. If you light a fuse in the middle, you end up with two flames, each burning toward a different end of the fuse. If you were extremely lucky, you might light the exact center (in burn time; it might not be the physical center) of the fuse, in which case both flames would extinguish simultaneously after 30 minutes. It's much more likely that you would miss the center of the fuse, giving you one flame that went out sometime before 30 minutes and a second that continued burning for some time after. This doesn't seem like a reliable way to make a measurement.

When you lit the fuse in the middle, you got a different burn time than when you lit the end. Why is this? Lighting the middle of the fuse created two flames, so you were burning in two places at once. How else might you use two flames? You've seen that lighting the middle of the fuse is problematic because you don't actually know where (in time) you're lighting. That leaves the ends of the fuse. If you light both ends of the fuse, the flames will burn toward each other until they meet and extinguish each other after exactly 30 minutes. This could be useful.

So far, you can measure exactly 30 minutes using one fuse. If you could figure out how to measure 15 minutes with the other fuse, you could add the two times to solve the problem. What would you need to measure 15 minutes? Either a 15-minute length of fuse, burning at one end, or a 30-minute length of fuse burning at both ends would do the trick. Because you're starting with a 60-minute length of fuse, this means you need to remove either 45 or 30 minutes from the fuse. Again, this must be done by burning because cutting the fuse would involve making a physical (distance) measurement, which would be meaningless. Forty-five minutes could be removed by burning from both ends for 22.5 minutes or one end for 45 minutes. Measuring 22.5 minutes seems an even harder problem than the one you were given; if you knew how to measure 45 minutes you'd have solved the problem, so this possibility doesn't look particularly fruitful.

The other option is removing 30 minutes of the fuse, which could be done by burning from both ends for 15 minutes or one end for 30 minutes. The need to measure 15 minutes returns you to the task at hand, but you do know how to measure 30 minutes: Exactly 30 minutes elapse from lighting both ends of the first fuse until the flames go out. If you light one end of the second fuse at the same moment you light both ends of the first, then you'll be left with 30 minutes of fuse on the second fuse when the first fuse is gone. You can light the other end (the one that isn't already burning) of this second fuse as soon as the first goes out. The two flames burning on the 30-minute length of fuse extinguish each other after exactly 15 minutes, giving you a total of 30 + 15 = 45 minutes.

Escaping the Train

> **PROBLEM** *Two boys walking in the woods decided to take a shortcut through a railroad tunnel. When they had walked two-thirds of the way through the tunnel, their worst fears were realized. A train was coming in the opposite direction, nearing the tunnel entrance. The boys panicked and each ran for a different end of the tunnel. Both boys ran at the same speed, 10 miles per hour. Each boy escaped from the tunnel just at the instant that the train would have squashed him into the rails. Assuming the train's speed was constant, and both boys were capable of instantaneous reaction and acceleration, how fast was the train going?*

At first, this seems like a classic algebraic word problem, straight out of your high school homework. When you begin to set up your x's and y's, however, you realize you're missing a lot of the information you would expect to have in a standard algebra rate problem. Specifically, although you know the boys' speeds, you don't have any information about distances or times. Perhaps this is more challenging than it first appeared.

A good way to start is by drawing a diagram using the information you have. Call the boys Abner and Brent (A and B to their friends). At the moment the problem begins, when the boys have just noticed the train, the train is an unknown distance from the tunnel, heading toward them. A and B are both in the same place, one-third of the tunnel length from the entrance closest to the train. A is running toward the train and B away from it, as shown in Figure 15-5.

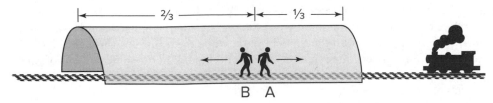

FIGURE 15-5

The only additional information you have is that both boys just barely escape. Try drawing diagrams of the moments of their escapes. A is running toward the train and has only one-third of the tunnel to cover, so he'll escape before B. Because he reaches the end of the tunnel at the last possible instant, he and the train must be at the end of the tunnel at the same time. Where would B be at this time? A and B run at the same speed; A moves one-third of the length of the tunnel before escaping, so B must also have run one-third of the length of the tunnel. That would put him one-third of the way from the end of the tunnel he's headed for, as shown in Figure 15-6.

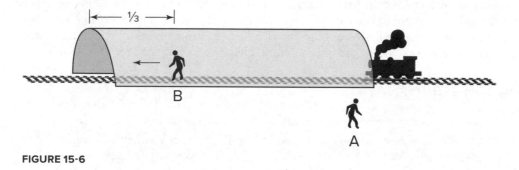

FIGURE 15-6

Now diagram B's escape. The train has come all the way through the tunnel, and both it and B are right at the end of the tunnel. (A is somewhere outside the other end of the tunnel, counting his blessings.) Figure 15-7 shows this situation.

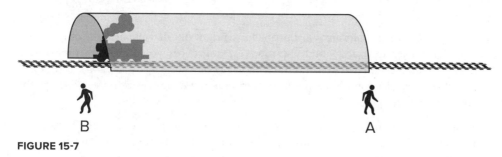

FIGURE 15-7

None of these diagrams seem particularly illuminating on their own. Because you need to determine the speed of the train, you should look at how it moves — how its position changes between your three diagrams. Between the first and second diagrams, A and B each run one-third of the length of the tunnel, while the train moves an unknown distance. No help there. Between the second and third diagrams, B again runs one-third the tunnel length, while the train runs through the whole tunnel. Therefore, the train covers three times more distance than B in the same amount of time. This means the train must be three times as fast as B. B can travel 10 miles per hour, so the train moves at 30 miles per hour.

SUMMARY

Many brainteasers are graphical in nature and serve to test your spatial thinking. You need to apply the general brainteaser guidelines from the previous chapter to these kinds of questions, but often the correct answer is evident only when you try to visualize the problem. Don't underestimate the power of diagrams!

16

Knowledge-Based Questions

Knowledge-based questions vary greatly in frequency from interview to interview. Some interviewers do not ask knowledge-based questions, whereas others focus solely on them. Interviewers often ask these questions when a whiteboard or paper isn't available, such as at lunch, or when they are satisfied with your coding ability and want to test your general computer knowledge.

PREPARATION

Knowledge-based questions generally come from two sources: what you said on your résumé and your answers to questions earlier in the interview.

Questions drawn from your résumé are usually short and simple — just long enough to verify that you actually know the technologies you claim to have used. It's a good idea to review your résumé prior to your interview to make sure you're prepared to answer questions about *every* item on the résumé, no matter how small. Some interviewers even go through your résumé and ask you general questions about each item — "What is X?" and "What have you done with X?" For example, if you put SOAP on your resume, be prepared for the questions "What is SOAP?" and "What have you done with SOAP?" If you can't intelligently answer either question, you should remove the SOAP reference from your résumé.

> **NOTE** *Be prepared to answer questions about everything on your résumé.*

In a similar vein, be careful with what you say during the interview. The interviewer may want some more in-depth explanation of technologies and techniques you mentioned, just to ascertain how deep your knowledge goes. Sometimes the questioning seems quite innocent. If you say you "started programming in Java several years ago," don't be surprised if the interviewer asks you what version of Java you started with. If all you did initially was read a book about Java 1.4 and didn't do any real programming until Java 6 was released, don't say you started with Java 1.4.

If you do, you won't have a satisfactory answer for a question like "*What new feature in Java 5 did you like the best?*" — a reasonable question given all the changes to the language that were introduced with version 5 (including generics, autoboxing, and for-each loops). Be truthful and accurate about your background so your answers don't trip you up later.

As a general rule, any concept you bring up in your discussion of a programming problem is fair game for follow-up questions. Use this to your advantage by introducing topics that you're comfortable with and (when possible) avoiding topics you don't know well. For instance, if you mention that a particular algorithm may be inefficient because it has poor locality of reference, an obvious follow up question is, "What is locality of reference and how does it affect performance?" If you have a good answer for this, you look like a superstar who understands the nuances of algorithms and programming. On the other hand, even if your comment about the algorithm is correct, if you can't at least define the term you just used, it seems like you're repeating something you memorized but don't understand.

PROBLEMS

It would be impossible to cover every conceivable area of computer knowledge that could appear on a résumé or in an interview. Instead, this chapter provides a sample of knowledge-based questions. These questions focus on system-level issues, trade-offs between various methods of programming, and advanced features of languages. All these topic areas make sense from the interviewer's perspective. A candidate who claims to know a lot about computers but who isn't aware of basic performance issues of data structures, networks, and architecture is likely to make poor design decisions that may be expensive to fix later. Furthermore, many job assignments are not as specific as "Implement this algorithm in this language," but may be more along the lines of "We have this problem that we need solved." A strong candidate understands the trade-offs between various solutions and knows when to use each one.

Interviewers prefer specific, detailed descriptions to general answers. For example, suppose you are asked, "What is AJAX?" One general answer is, "It stands for *asynchronous JavaScript and XML.*" Although this answer is technically correct, it doesn't demonstrate that you actually understand what AJAX programming is about and why it has become so popular. A better answer would be "AJAX, which is short for asynchronous JavaScript and XML, is an architectural style for building interactive web applications in which code to perform tasks such as interface updates and input validation are implemented on the client in JavaScript and data exchanges with the server occur in the background over HTTP. XML was originally the preferred format for returning data to the client for processing, but many applications have shifted to other formats, like JSON. Applications built using AJAX don't suffer the frustrating delays in user interface response that are common in conventional web applications." It seems clear which answer is better.

> **NOTE** *Offer specific and thorough responses.*

One final note: The answers presented here have been researched and polished by several people over an extended period of time. In many cases they also include detailed explanations and examples. As a candidate answering a question in an interview, you would not be expected to provide such a detailed response. Any well-organized answer that hits most of the points in these solutions would probably be considered excellent.

C++ versus Java

> **PROBLEM** *What are the differences between C++ and Java?*

C++ and Java are syntactically similar. Java's designers intended this to make it easy for C++ developers to learn Java. Apart from this similarity, Java and C++ differ in a variety of ways, largely because of their different design goals. Security, portability, and simplicity were of paramount importance in the design of Java, whereas C++ is more concerned with performance, backward compatibility with C, and programmer control. Java is compiled to virtual machine byte-code and requires a virtual machine to run; C++ is compiled to native machine code. This gives Java greater potential for portability and security. Historically, this has also made Java slower than C++, but with just-in-time compiler techniques in modern virtual machines, performance is often comparable.

C++ is an approximate superset of C and maintains features such as programmer-controlled memory management, pointers, and a preprocessor for backward compatibility with C. In contrast, Java eliminates these and other error-prone features. Java replaces programmer memory deallocations with garbage collection. Java further dispenses with C++ features, such as operator overloading and multiple inheritance. (A limited form of multiple inheritance can be simulated in Java using interfaces.) These choices are seen by some to make Java a better choice for rapid development and for projects where portability and security are important.

In Java, all objects are passed by reference, whereas in C++, the default behavior is to pass objects by value. Java does not perform automatic type casting like C++; though newer Java features, such as generics and autoboxing, handle many common cases of type casting. In Java, all methods are virtual, meaning the implementation for a method is selected according to the type of the object as opposed to the type of the reference. In C++, methods must be explicitly declared as virtual. Java has defined sizes for primitive data types, whereas type sizes are implementation-dependent in C++.

In situations in which there is legacy C code and a great need for performance, C++ has certain benefits, especially when low-level system access is required. In situations in which portability, security, and speed of development are emphasized, Java (or a similar language such as C#) may be a better choice.

Friend Classes

> **PROBLEM** *Discuss friend classes in C++ and give an example of when you would use one.*

The `friend` keyword is applied to either a function or a class. It gives the `friend` function or `friend` class access to the private members of the class in which the declaration occurs. Some programmers feel this feature violates the principles of object-oriented programming because it allows a class to operate on another class's private members. This violation can, in turn, lead to unexpected bugs when a change in the internal implementation of a class causes problems with the friend class that accesses it.

In some cases, however, the benefits of a `friend` class outweigh its drawbacks. For example, suppose you implemented a dynamic array class. Imagine that you want a separate class to iterate through your array. The iterator class would probably need access to the dynamic array class's private members to function correctly. It would make sense to declare the iterator as a `friend` to the array class. The workings of the two classes are inextricably tied together already, so it probably doesn't make sense to enforce a meaningless separation between the two.

Java and C# do not support the concept of `friend` classes. The closest match these languages have to `friend`s is to omit the access modifiers, thereby specifying "default" access (in Java) or use the "internal" access modifier (in C#) for member data. However, this makes every class in the package (Java) or assembly (C#) equivalent to a `friend`. In some cases, it may be possible to use a nested class to accomplish a similar design to that achieved with `friend` classes in C++.

Argument Passing

PROBLEM *Consider the following C++ function prototypes for a function,* `foo`, *which takes an object of class* `Fruit` *as an argument:*

```
void foo(Fruit bar);        // Prototype 1
void foo(Fruit* bar);       // Prototype 2
void foo(Fruit& bar);       // Prototype 3
void foo(const Fruit* bar); // Prototype 4
void foo(Fruit*& bar);      // Prototype 5
```

For each prototype, discuss how the argument will be passed and what the implications would be for a function implemented using that form of argument passing.

In the first prototype, the object argument is passed by value. This means that `Fruit`'s copy constructor would be called to duplicate the object on the stack. The compiler will create a default member by member copy constructor if `Fruit` doesn't have an explicit one defined; this may lead to bugs if `Fruit` contains pointers to resources it owns, such as dynamically allocated memory or file handles. Within the function, `bar` is an object of class `Fruit`. Because `bar` is a copy of the object that was passed to the function, any changes made to `bar` will not be reflected in the original object. This is the least efficient way to pass an object because every data member of the object must be copied into a new copy of the object.

For the second prototype, `bar` is a pointer to a `Fruit` object. This is more efficient than passing by value because only the address of the object is copied onto the stack (or possibly into a register), not the object itself. Because `bar` points at the object that was passed to `foo`, any changes made through `bar` are reflected in the original object.

The third prototype shows `bar` being passed by reference. This case is similar to the second: It involves no copying of the object and allows `foo` to operate directly on the calling function's object. The most obvious difference between a function using a reference and one using a pointer is syntactic. A pointer must be explicitly dereferenced before member variables and functions can be accessed, but members can be accessed directly using a reference. Therefore, the arrow operator (->) is usually used to access members when working with pointers, whereas the dot operator (.) is used for references. A subtler but more important difference is that the pointer may not point at a `Fruit`; the pointer version of `foo` could be passed a null pointer. In the implementation using references, however, `bar` is guaranteed to be a reference to a `Fruit`. (Although it's possible for the reference to be invalid.)

In the fourth prototype, `bar` is passed as a constant pointer to the object. This has the performance advantages of passing pointers, but `foo` is prevented from modifying `bar`. Only methods declared as `const` can be called on `bar` from within `foo`, which prevents `foo` from modifying `bar` indirectly.

In the final case, `bar` is a reference to a pointer to a `Fruit` object. As in the second case, this means that changes made to the object are seen by the calling function. In addition, because `bar` is a reference to a pointer, not merely a pointer, if `bar` is modified to point to a different `Fruit` object, the pointer in the calling function is modified as well.

Macros and Inline Functions

> **PROBLEM** *In C++ and C99, compare and contrast macros and inline functions.*

Macros are implemented with simple text replacement in the preprocessor. For example, if you define the macro:

```
#define AVERAGE(a, b) ((a + b) / 2)
```

then the preprocessor replaces any occurrences of `AVERAGE(foo, bar)` in your code with `((foo + bar) / 2)`. You commonly use macros in places where the thing that you're substituting is ugly and used often enough that it warrants abstraction behind a pretty name, but is too simple to be worth the overhead of a function call.

Inline functions are declared and defined much like regular functions. Unlike macros, they are handled by the compiler directly. An inline function implementation of the `AVERAGE` macro would look like

```
inline int Average(int a, int b)
{
    return (a + b)/2;
}
```

From the programmer's perspective, calling an inline function is like calling a regular function. Just as for a regular function, you must specify the argument and return types for an inline function, which is not necessary (or possible) for the macro. This can be both an advantage and a disadvantage: The inline function has better type safety, but you can use a single definition of the macro for any type that has addition and division operators defined. A templated inline function would avoid the need to write a separate definition for each argument type, at the expense of increased complexity. From the compiler's perspective, when it encounters a call to an inline function, it writes a copy of the compiled function definition instead of generating a function call. (Technically, when a programmer specifies a function as inline the compiler interprets this as a suggestion — it may or may not actually inline the function depending on its calculations of what will yield the best performance.)

Both inline functions and macros provide a way to eliminate function call overhead at the expense of program size. Although inline functions have the semantics of a function call, macros have the semantics of text replacement. Macros can create bugs due to the unexpected behavior of text replacement semantics.

For example, suppose you had the following macro and code:

```
#define CUBE(x) x * x * x

int foo, bar = 2;
foo = CUBE(++bar);
```

You would probably expect this code to set bar to 3 and foo to 27, but look at how it expands:

```
foo = ++bar * ++bar * ++bar;
```

because of this, bar is set to 5 and foo is set to an undefined value larger than 27 (for example, 80 with one version of the GNU C++ compiler). If CUBE were implemented as an inline function, this problem wouldn't occur. Inline functions (like normal functions) evaluate their arguments only once, so any side effects of evaluation happen only once.

Here's another problem that stems from using macros. Suppose you have a macro with two statements in it like this:

```
#define INCREMENT_BOTH(x, y) x++; y++
```

If you favor leaving off the curly brackets when there's only one statement in the body of an if statement, you might write something like this:

```
if (flag)
    INCREMENT_BOTH(foo, bar);
```

You would probably expect this to be equivalent to:

```
if (flag) {
    foo++;
    bar++;
}
```

Instead, when the macro is expanded, the if binds to just the first statement in the macro definition, leaving you with code equivalent to:

```
if (flag) {
    foo++;
}
bar++;
```

An inline function call is a single statement, regardless of how many statements there are in the body of the function, so this problem would not occur.

A final reason to avoid macros is that when you use them, the code that is compiled is not visible in the source. This makes debugging macro-related problems particularly difficult. Macros are included in C++ and C99 largely for compatibility with older versions of C; in general it's a good idea to avoid macros and opt for inline functions.

Inheritance

PROBLEM *Assume you have the class hierarchy shown in Figure 16-1.*

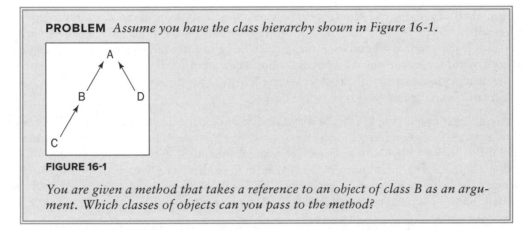

FIGURE 16-1

You are given a method that takes a reference to an object of class B as an argument. Which classes of objects can you pass to the method?

Clearly, you can pass B because that's exactly what the method takes. You can't possibly pass D because it may have totally different characteristics than B. A is the parent class of B. Consider that a child class is required to implement all the methods of the parent, but the parent does not necessarily have all the methods of a child. Thus, the parent class, A, cannot be passed to the method. C is the child class of B and is guaranteed to have all the methods of B, so you can pass C to the method.

Garbage Collection

PROBLEM *What is garbage collection? What are some of the different implementations of garbage collection, and what are the trade-offs between them?*

Garbage collection is the process by which memory that is no longer in use is identified and reclaimed. This reclamation occurs without programmer assistance. C#, Java, Lisp, and Python are examples of languages with garbage-collection facilities.

Garbage collection provides several advantages over having a programmer explicitly deallocate memory. It eliminates bugs caused by dangling pointers, multiple deallocation, and memory leaks. It also promotes greater simplicity in program and interface design because the complicated mechanisms traditionally used to ensure that memory is properly freed are unnecessary. In addition, because programmers don't have to worry about memory deallocation, program development proceeds at a more rapid pace.

Garbage collection is not without its disadvantages. Garbage-collected programs often run more slowly because of the overhead needed for the system to determine when to deallocate and reclaim memory that is no longer needed. In addition, the system will occasionally over-allocate memory and may not free memory at the ideal time.

One method of garbage collection is *reference counting*. This involves tracking how many variables reference an object. Initially, there will be one reference to a piece of memory. The reference count increases if the variable referencing it is copied. When a variable referencing an object changes value or goes out of scope, the object's reference count is decremented. If a reference count ever goes to 0, the memory associated with the object is freed: If there are no references to the object, then the object (and hence its memory) is no longer needed.

Reference counting is simple and relatively fast. Memory is freed and becomes available for reuse as soon as it is no longer referenced, which is usually an advantage. However, simple implementations have difficulty with circular references. Consider what happens in the case of a circular linked list with nothing external pointing to it. Every element in the list has a nonzero reference count, yet the memory isn't referenced by any object outside the list itself. Thus, the memory could safely be deallocated, but simple reference-based garbage collection won't free it.

Weak references — references that are not included in an object's reference count — provide one means to deal with this problem. If every cycle of references in a data structure contains a weak reference, then you can reclaim the structure when you lose the last external reference. For example, consider a doubly linked list: In a simple reference counting system, every pair of adjacent elements form a cycle, so the list isn't reclaimed even when it's no longer externally referenced. If all the "previous" references are defined as weak references, then when there are no external references to the list, the head element's reference count becomes 0, and it is deallocated. This causes a cascading deallocation along the list as deallocation of each element sets the reference count of the next element to 0. This style of garbage collection is available in recent versions of C++ as `std::shared_ptr` and `std::weak_ptr`.

A second method of garbage collection is known as a *tracing garbage collector*. Under this scheme, memory that is no longer referenced remains allocated until it is identified and deallocated during a garbage collection cycle. This has the advantages of handling cyclical data structures and avoiding the overhead of incrementing and decrementing reference counts. The simplest implementation of a tracing garbage collector is called *mark and sweep*. Each cycle involves two passes. In the first pass, the memory manager marks all objects that can be accessed by any thread in the program. In the second pass, all unmarked objects are deallocated, or swept away. Mark and sweep requires that all execution threads are suspended during garbage collection, which results in unpredictable pauses during program execution. Most modern tracing garbage collectors, including those in the Java Virtual Machine and the .NET Common Language Runtime that C# uses, employ a more complex scheme called *tri-color marking*, which doesn't require suspending execution. (Although it doesn't eliminate the computational overhead of garbage collection cycles.)

32-Bit versus 64-Bit Applications

> **PROBLEM** *What's the difference between a 32-bit application and a 64-bit application? Which is faster?*

These terms refer to the size of the memory addresses and general-purpose registers that an application uses. A 64-bit application requires a 64-bit processor and a 64-bit operating system to run. Most 64-bit systems are also capable of running 32-bit applications in a compatibility mode.

Memory address size is the most important difference between 32- and 64-bit applications. Use of 64-bit memory addresses allows a process to address a theoretical maximum of 2^{64} = 16 exabytes of memory, a dramatic increase from the 2^{32} = 4 gigabytes of memory to which a 32-bit process is limited. Many modern computers have more than 4 gigabytes of physical memory, so a 64-bit application may be faster because it can keep more data in memory, reducing slow disk access. The expanded 64-bit address size also makes memory-mapped files more practical, which may allow for more efficient file access than traditional APIs. In addition, 64-bit arithmetic may be faster because of the larger register size. (Although many "32-bit" processors have extensions that allow for 64-bit arithmetic.)

On the other hand, 64-bit memory addresses mean that all pointers require twice as much memory to store. For data structures that employ pointers (or references, which use pointers behind the scenes), this means that the same structure requires more memory in a 64-bit application than a 32-bit application. More important, any given system has the same fixed-size processor cache whether running 32-bit or 64-bit applications. Because the 64-bit data structures are larger, less of them fit in cache, so there are likely to be more cache misses in which the processor must wait for values to be accessed from main memory (or higher cache levels).

Because some aspects of a 64-bit application lead to higher performance and others lead to lower performance, some codes may run faster as 32-bit and others run faster as 64-bit.

From a practical perspective, one of the most common 64-bit architectures in use today is the AMD/Intel x86-64. When processors of this architecture run in 64-bit mode, several features unavailable in 32-bit mode are activated, including an additional eight general purpose registers. These features typically improve performance enough to compensate for any losses due to increased pointer size. Therefore, 64-bit applications are almost always faster than 32-bit applications on these chips, but this is particular to the x86-64 architecture and is not a general feature of trade-offs between 32- and 64-bit applications.

Network Performance

> **PROBLEM** *What are the two major issues in networking performance?*

Any network can be measured by two major characteristics: latency and bandwidth. *Latency* refers to the time it takes a given bit of information to get from one point to another on the network.

Bandwidth refers to the rate at which data moves through the network once communication is established. The perfect network would have infinite bandwidth and no latency.

A pipe is a useful analog for a network. The time it takes for a molecule of water to go through the whole pipe is related to the length; this is analogous to the latency. The width of the pipe determines the bandwidth: how much water can pass in a given time.

Informally, people often talk about the "speed" of a network as if it's a single quantity, but a network may have good performance by one measure and poor performance by the other. For example, satellite-based data services frequently have high bandwidth but also high latency.

Depending on the application the network is used for, either bandwidth or latency may be the most important factor. For example, telephone calls over a network (such as Voice over IP) are sensitive to latency, which causes irritating delays that lead to people accidentally talking over each other, but telephony requires relatively little bandwidth. On the other hand, streaming HD video requires a network with fairly high bandwidth, but the latency affects only the time between requesting the stream and the start of the video, which is usually of little concern.

Web Application Security

> **PROBLEM** *Consider the following line of code, taken from the login routine of a web-based application:*
>
> ```
> result = sql.executeQuery("SELECT uid FROM Users WHERE user = '" +
>                   username + "' AND pass = '" + pword + "';");
> ```
>
> username *and* pword *are strings returned from a form on the application's login page. Based on this code, what security problems do you see with this application? What techniques would you use to fix them?*

This code constructs a SQL query by concatenating strings provided by the user. If the username and password match a row stored in the database, then the user id is returned to allow access to that account. Because these strings come from an untrusted source, they open this application to attack by *SQL injection.* Consider how this application would behave if a malicious user entered a username of admin' OR 'A' = 'A and a random password string (for example, xyz). After concatenation, the query string becomes

```
SELECT uid FROM Users WHERE user = 'admin' OR 'A' = 'A' AND pass = 'xyz';
```

which returns the user id for the administrative account even if the password doesn't match, allowing the malicious user to log in as the administrator. There are many variations on this attack, depending on the goal of the attacker and the form of the query being attacked, but they all stem from the same issue: data from an untrusted source compiled or interpreted in an executable context. It's easy to forget that SQL is a programming language (a limited, domain-specific language, but a programming language nonetheless). Concatenating user data directly into a query essentially gives the user some ability to modify part of the source code of your application — clearly not a good security practice.

There are two ways to fix this problem: Filter the data so that it can be trusted, or avoid putting the data in an executable context.

Filtering the data involves searching the string returned from the user for potentially problematic patterns and either escaping or deleting them. For example, the preceding example would fail if, prior to constructing the query, the application either removed all instances of ' or escaped them by changing them to ''.

This type of approach to security is called *blacklisting*. The problem with blacklisting is that you can block only forms of attacks that you know about. There are a large number of ways to construct a SQL injection, and new forms are frequently invented. Many of the more complex forms are specifically designed to evade filters by using unusual encodings for strings that appear benign when filtered but are later translated into malicious form by other layers of the application stack. To maintain security with a filtering approach, the filter must detect all forms of attack, known and yet to be invented, and must be applied to every piece of untrusted data the application receives; the odds of this are poor.

A better approach is to avoid putting the data in executable context. You can achieve this through the use of prepared statements. A *prepared statement* is a SQL query that has placeholders to identify the locations that are filled with data when the query executes. The statement is compiled before data are bound to the placeholders. When the prepared statement executes, compilation has already taken place, so any potentially executable SQL strings in the data can't affect the structure or intent of the query. Prepared statements also improve performance when queries execute more than once because instead of parsing, compiling and optimizing the query for each execution, this process is performed only once. A reimplementation of this code with prepared statements might look like:

```
sql = db.prepareStatement("SELECT uid FROM Users WHERE user = ? AND " +
                          "pass = ? ;");
sql.setString(1, username);
sql.setString(2, pword);
result = sql.executeQuery();
```

There's one more problem with this application. The password string that the user enters is compared directly to the `pass` column. This suggests that the passwords are stored as *cleartext*: the same string that the user enters. Passwords stored this way are a major security risk. If an attacker obtains the contents of the `Users` table, it's trivial to use the data to log in as any user. Worse yet, because many users have the same passwords across multiple sites, the attacker may be able to impersonate your users elsewhere.

The solution to this problem is to use a *cryptographic hash*. A cryptographic hash is a function that takes an arbitrary input string and produces a fixed length *fingerprint* or *digest* string. The function has the property that, given the digest, it is computationally infeasible to compute either the original input or another input that would produce the same digest. Some commonly used cryptographic hash functions are *MD5* (now obsolete due to security flaws), *SHA-1* (security questionable), and *SHA-256* (a good choice for new applications). Instead of storing the cleartext password, the cryptographic hash function is applied to the password and the resulting digest value is stored in the database. On subsequent login attempts, the password is again hashed, and if the digest values are the same, it's safe to assume that the password is correct.

With hashed passwords, an attacker who obtains the contents of the `Users` table won't be able to use the data to log in directly because it doesn't contain the passwords. The attacker can still use the data to try to determine the passwords by brute-force guessing. Well-designed applications take several steps to make this more difficult. If the hash function is applied to the passwords directly, then a given password will have the same digest value for any user in the system. The attacker can compute the digest for each guess once and compare it against every account; the attacker can even compare the stored password digests to a large set of precomputed digests of common passwords — called a *rainbow table* — to rapidly test a large number of password guesses.

To prevent this, you should always salt cryptographic hashes. A *salt* is a random string of characters selected for each user that is concatenated with the password before hashing. You store the salt in cleartext, so its value would be known to the attacker, but because the salt is different for each user, the attacker must attack each user's password separately rendering rainbow tables useless.

Another technique commonly used to make cracking passwords more difficult is iteration of the hash: repeated application of the hash function with the output of one round becoming the input of the next. This increases the cost (time) of computing the hash. With an appropriately chosen number of iterations, computation of the iterated hash once for each login has a negligible performance impact on the web application, but the cost of computing it millions or billions of times to crack passwords is infeasible.

Cryptography

> **PROBLEM** *Discuss the differences between symmetric key cryptography and public key cryptography. Give an example of when you would use each.*

Symmetric key cryptography, also called *shared key cryptography,* involves two people using the same key to encrypt and decrypt information. *Public key cryptography* makes use of two different keys: a public key for encryption and a private key for decryption. Symmetric key cryptography has the advantage that it's much faster than public key cryptography. It is also generally easier to implement and usually requires less processing power. On the downside, the two parties sending messages must agree on the same private key before securely transmitting information. This is often inconvenient or even impossible. If the two parties are geographically separated, then a secure means of communication is needed for one to tell the other what the key will be. In a pure symmetric key scenario, secure communication is generally not available. (If it were, there would be little need for encryption to create another secure channel.)

Public key cryptography has the advantage that the public key, used for encryption, does not need to be kept secret for encrypted messages to remain secure. This means public keys can be transmitted over insecure channels. Often, applications use public key cryptography to establish a shared session key and then communicate via symmetric key cryptography using the shared session key. This solution provides the convenience of public key cryptography with the performance of shared key cryptography.

Both public key and symmetric key cryptography are used to get secure information from the web. First your browser establishes a shared session key with the website using public key cryptography.

Then you communicate with the website using symmetric key cryptography to actually obtain the private information.

Hash Tables versus Binary Search Trees

> **PROBLEM** *Compare and contrast a hash table and a binary search tree. If you were designing the address book data structure for a mobile device with limited memory, which one would you use?*

A hash table does one thing well. It stores and retrieves data quickly (in $O(1)$ or constant time in the average case). However, its uses beyond this are limited.

A binary search tree can insert and retrieve in $O(\log(n))$. This is fast, though not as fast as a hash table's $O(1)$. However, a binary search tree also maintains its data in sorted order.

In a mobile device, you want to keep as much memory as possible available for data storage. If you use an unordered data structure such as a hash table, you need additional memory to sort the values, as you undoubtedly want to display the values in alphabetical order. Therefore, if you use a hash table, you must set aside memory for sorting that could otherwise be used as storage space.

If you use a binary search tree, you won't have to waste memory or processing time on sorting records for display. Although binary tree operations are slower than hash table operations, a device like this is unlikely to have more than approximately 10,000 entries, so a binary search tree's $O(\log(n))$ lookup will be fast enough. For these reasons, a binary search tree is better suited for this kind of task than a hash table.

SUMMARY

Knowledge-based questions are an easy way for interviewers to assess your familiarity and experience with the programming languages and techniques they expect you to know based on the requirements for the job and what's in your résumé. Be sure you have a good grasp of the fundamental knowledge you'll need for the job for which you're applying.

17

Nontechnical Questions

Non-technical questions are an important part of the job interview process. Some of these questions are asked early in the process to determine whether your experience, education, and goals make you appropriate for the job in question — there's no point to proceed with the technical interviews if you're not the kind of candidate the company is looking for.

Other questions are asked after the technical interviews are over and the company is considering making you an offer. Although you won't get an offer on the strength of your nontechnical answers alone, a poor performance on nontechnical issues can lose you an offer you otherwise might have received.

> **NOTE** *Non-technical questions are important! Treat them that way.*

Non-technical questions are challenging because often no right or wrong answers exist. Different people can have different answers to the same question.

Most interviewing books discuss how to effectively answer all kinds of nontechnical questions. Rather than rehash what these books say, this chapter focuses on the nontechnical questions that are particularly common in programming interviews.

WHY NON-TECHNICAL QUESTIONS?

Many nontechnical questions are asked to assess a candidate's experience and ability to fit in with other employees.

Experience includes your work history and your knowledge. Questions about your experience must be answered carefully and completely to allay any doubts about your ability to perform the job.

For example, suppose you're asked the question, "Have you ever programmed for Linux?" Your interviewer has seen your résumé, so she probably has a good idea that you haven't. In effect, the interviewer is saying, "We use Linux — can you do the job even though you've never used it?" Don't lie, but don't answer "No" if you can avoid it. Instead, emphasize a similar strength: "I haven't used Linux specifically, but I have done UNIX development." Even if you don't have similar or related experience, you can still emphasize your strengths: "I don't know Linux well, but I'd like to learn it. I'm used to learning new things and I pick them up quickly. For instance, I published my first Android app only four weeks after I started learning the API." Pay attention to the job description when it's explained to you. Emphasize any similar and relevant experience that makes you a strong candidate.

Fit is the other key theme of nontechnical questions. *Fit* refers to how well you can adapt to the organization and become a contributing member. Most people think this just means being a nice person, but that is only half the picture. You must be good at working with others.

For example, suppose you say, "At my last job, I designed and implemented a system to move our HR information gathering to the web all by myself." This may sound like a positive comment, but it can set off alarms about whether you can and will work with other people. Therefore, you must emphasize the team concept. If you took the lead that's definitely a point in your favor, but be sure to present it as leading a team, not as working in isolation. Describe how you want to be part of a great team and a contributing team player. Everyone likes hearing the word team — everyone.

> **NOTE** *Many nontechnical questions are designed to ensure that you have relevant experience and can fit in with the existing team.*

Not all nontechnical questions deal with experience and fit. Some of the questions are practical. If the job is located in the San Francisco area and you reside elsewhere, relocation (or telecommuting) needs to be discussed.

QUESTIONS

When reading the sample questions and following discussions, try to compose your own answer. Think of how you would respond to such a question and what points you would want to emphasize in different situations. (It's much easier to think of an answer now than when you're in front of an interviewer.) Don't be afraid to refine your response if you find that it isn't effective. Finally, make sure that every response positions you as a valuable employee.

"What Do You Want to Do?"

Always pay attention to who asks this question. If it's a human resource representative scheduling interviews, be honest and tell him what you want to do. The HR rep can generally use this information to set up interviews with appropriate groups.

If you're asked this question by a technical interviewer, watch out! If you answer this question poorly, you won't get an offer. These interviewers ask this question partly to discover your goals and ambitions. If you want to do something different from the available job, your interviewer will probably decide that you should look for a different job.

If you want the job, make sure you indicate that you're interested in doing it, sound sincere, and give a reason. For example, you could say, "I've always been interested in systems-level programming and really enjoy it, so I'm hoping to join a large company and do systems-level work." Or you could say, "I want to do web programming so that I can show my work to my friends. I'm hoping to do this at a startup like yours where my web server experience can help the company grow."

Sometimes, you may not know what specific job you're interviewing for. Some companies hire software engineers and match them to jobs after they've been hired. In these cases, you can always fall back on describing the company you're applying to as the ideal company for you. This will be easier and more effective if you've done at least a little bit of research about the company before your interview — the Internet is your friend! Mention that you're hoping to do development that's exciting and provides a lot of opportunity to contribute and learn. You can say that you see the work as just one part of the package; other important parts are the team and the company. This sort of response shows that you have your act together and prevents you from talking your way out of a job.

There is a fine line between sounding enthusiastic and seeming dateless and desperate. No one wants an employee who has been rejected by everyone else. Make sure your answer never sounds like you'd be happy to take any sort of job the company would be willing to offer. This sort of response virtually guarantees nothing more than a thank-you-for-coming-in letter.

If you know exactly what you want to do and wouldn't accept any other kind of job, don't talk yourself up for a job you'd never accept. This approach may prevent you from getting some job offers, but they aren't jobs that you want. One advantage to expressing exactly what you want to do is that even if you don't begin the day interviewing with an interesting group, you may end the day interviewing with such a group.

One final note on answering this question: It's a good opportunity to mention that you want to work with a great team — don't pass it up. Make sure that being a member of a great team comes across as one of your priorities.

"What Is Your Favorite Programming Language?"

This may seem like a technical question, and there are certainly technical aspects to it. You want to give specific, technical reasons why you like any language that you mention, but there is also a hidden nontechnical agenda in this question. Many people develop an almost-religious attachment to certain languages, computers, or operating systems. These people can be difficult to work with because they often insist on using their favorites even when they are ill-suited to the problem at hand. You should be careful to avoid coming across as such a person. Acknowledge that there are some tasks for which your favorite language is a poor choice. Mention that you are familiar with a range of languages and that you believe that no one language is a universal solution. It's important to pick the best tool for the job.

This advice holds for other "favorites" questions, such as "What is your favorite kind of computer?" or "What is your favorite operating system?"

"What Is Your Work Style?"

This question usually indicates that the company you're interviewing with has an unorthodox work style. For example, it may be a startup requiring long hours in cramped conditions or a larger company that's just beginning a new project. Or perhaps it is a fervent believer in the two-person team programming model. In any case, know what your work style is and make sure it's compatible with the company's.

"What Can You Tell Me About Your Experience?"

This question is one that everyone should practice and have an answer for. Make sure your answer highlights specific achievements and be enthusiastic as you talk about your projects. Enthusiasm is extremely important!

Talk not only about the factual aspects of your previous assignments, but also about what you learned. Talk about what went right but also what went wrong. Describe positive and negative experiences and what you learned from each of them.

Keep your response to approximately 30–60 seconds, depending on your experience. Again, be sure to practice this ahead of time.

"What Are Your Career Goals?"

This question gives you a chance to explain why you want this job (apart from the money) and how you see it fitting into your overall career. This is similar to the question about what you want to do. The employer is concerned that you may not want to do the job. In this case, it's because the job may not fit your career goals. That's not good for you or the company.

It's certainly okay to be uncertain about what you want to do — many people are. Try to have at least a general idea of where you see yourself going. Your answer might be as simple as, "I'm hoping to work in development for a while and work on some great projects. Then, I'm looking to go into project management. Beyond that, it's hard to say." This answer shows motivation and convinces the employer that you'll succeed on the job.

"Why Are You Looking to Change Jobs?"

Interviewers generally want to know what you don't like to do. Clearly, you don't like your last job or you would probably still be there. In addition, there's a fear that you may be trying to cover a weakness that caused you to leave your last job. Answer this question by citing a change in environment, factors out of your control, or a weakness that the interviewer already knows. Following are some examples:

➤ **A change in environment:** "I've worked in a large company for 5 years and experienced the software development process for a mature product. I no longer want to be a number in a large company. I want to join a startup and be a key person from the ground up and watch something grow." Or you could answer: "I worked at a startup that didn't have its act together. Now I want to work at a company that does."

➤ **Factors out of your control:** "My current company has given up on the project I've been working on, and they're trying to relocate me to something that I don't find interesting." Or you could respond, "My company was acquired, and the whole atmosphere has changed since then."

➤ **A weakness that the interviewer already knows:** "My last job required extensive systems-level programming. I was way behind everyone else on that topic, and I don't find that sort of work exciting. I'm much more interested in doing web programming, which I do have experience in."

One final note: even though money can be a good reason to change jobs, don't cite it as a primary reason. Perhaps your current employer doesn't consider you valuable enough to pay you more, and you don't want a potential employer to agree with that assessment.

"What Salary Are You Expecting?"

This question may appear in any context. It's most common, though, either at the initial screening or when the company has decided to make you an offer. If it's asked at the beginning, the employer may want to know if it's even worth talking to you, given your salary expectations, or the employer may genuinely have no idea what the position should pay. It is generally considered wise to put this question off as long as possible. It is not in your interest to discuss numbers until you've convinced the potential employer of your value. If you can't escape this question in the early stages of an interview, try to give a range of salaries with the amount that you want at the low end. This gives you good bargaining room later.

If you're asked the question near the end of the process, this can only indicate good things. If the interviewer has no interest in hiring you at this point, he won't bother asking this question. Generally, larger companies have less latitude in compensation packages than smaller companies. If you're asked this question, it probably indicates the company is willing to negotiate. Realize that companies are often unaware of how to make a competitive offer that works for you. This is your chance to tell them how to do exactly that:

➤ **Do your homework.** If you find that people with similar jobs in your area make $60,000–$75,000 a year, you're probably not going to make $100,000 a year. Make sure your salary expectations are realistic.

➤ **Never undersell yourself.** If you're looking for an annual salary of $70,000, don't tell an employer that you're looking for approximately $60,000 a year with the hope that the employer will, for some reason, offer more. If you lowball yourself, an employer will happily hire you at the lower salary.

➤ **Consider carefully what you want in a total compensation package.** You may be graduating from college and want a signing bonus to offset the costs of finding an apartment, moving, and placing deposits. Or you may be looking to join a startup offering generous stock options and slightly lower salaries. In any case, figure out exactly what you're looking for in terms of bonuses, benefits, stock options, and salary.

In general, try not to tip your hand too early when answering this question. The person with more information generally does better in a negotiation. Instead of answering a question about salary directly, ask what range the interviewer is prepared to offer. There are four possible answers to your question:

➤ **The range may be about what you expected.** In this case, you can usually gain a slightly higher salary with a simple technique. Start by not being too excited — stay cool. Next, say that you had a similar but slightly higher range in mind, setting your minimum at the maximum of the offered range. For example, if the employer says, "We're expecting to pay $60,000 to $65,000," you should respond, "That seems about right. I'm looking to make $65,000 to $70,000 and hoping for the high end of that range." Finally, negotiate in a professional manner until you agree on a number with the interviewer; you'll probably receive an offer between $63,000 and $68,000.

➤ **The negotiator starts with a range higher than you expected.** This is great!

➤ **The negotiator may not answer your question.** He may give a response such as "We have a wide range of salaries depending on the applicant. What were you expecting?" This response is actually quite favorable because it indicates that he has the authority to pay you a competitive salary. The response shows that the negotiator is willing to negotiate, but it also indicates that you may be subject to some hardball negotiating skills.

Bearing in mind that negotiation will follow, respond with one number, the high end of your range. This gives you room to negotiate and still receive a favorable offer. For example, if you're expecting between $65,000 and $70,000, say, "I'm expecting $70,000 a year." Presenting it like this leaves the other negotiator less room to lowball you than if you give a range. Avoid weaker expressions like "I'm hoping for...." or "I'd really like...." The negotiator may accept your number, or may try to negotiate a slightly lower salary. If you remain professional and negotiate carefully, your final salary should fall within your desired range. Alternatively, the negotiator may respond by telling you that the company has a substantially lower range in mind. In this case, your response should be the same as in option four, which is described next.

➤ **The offer may be less than you expected.** This is the most difficult position for negotiations, but you still may get what you want. Re-emphasize your skills and state the salary range you were expecting. For example, if you were offered a salary of $45,000 but were expecting $60,000, you may say, "I have to admit I'm a little disappointed with that offer. Given my extensive experience with web development and the contributions I can make to this company, I'm expecting a salary of $60,000." The negotiator may need time to get back to you, which is perfectly fine. If the negotiator doesn't increase the offer after hearing your range, he will often cite one of the following three reasons, none of which you should accept.

1. **That amount wasn't budgeted.** The budget may be a constraint on the company, but it shouldn't be a constraint on your salary. If the company wants you, it will find the money and a way around this artificial barrier. If the company truly can't find the money, it's such a cash-strapped, close-to-death organization that you probably don't want to work there. You can politely and diplomatically explain that the salary you're proposing is the fair value for an employee with your skills and experience, and that you hope they can rework their budget to reflect that.

2. **Similar employees at the company don't make that much.** It doesn't matter what the company pays other employees. That's between the company and those employees. Other employees shouldn't determine your compensation. You can respond by saying, "I wasn't aware that my compensation would be tied to other employees' compensations. I'm looking for a package commensurate with my skills of X and believe that $Y is such a package."

3. **Your experience doesn't warrant such a salary.** If you've done your homework, you know your experience and skills do warrant such a salary and the company is trying to lowball you. Simply reemphasize your skills and explain that, after doing your research, you know your desired salary is indeed the competitive market salary. The company may realize it is out of touch with the market and increase its offer.

If the negotiator does not increase the offer but you still want the job, you have two last-ditch tactics.

➤ **You can say that you're tempted to take the job, but that you'd like a salary review in 6 months to discuss your performance and compensation.** You generally have a much stronger hand before you join a company, so you shouldn't expect miracles. Most negotiators, however, will grant this request. Make sure you get it in writing if you go this route. Keep in mind that your employer can easily give you a salary review and still not give you a raise no matter how well you've performed. If you're not going to be happy with the possibility of either leaving the job or keeping the lower salary in 6 months, it may be best to keep looking now.

➤ **Try to negotiate other parts of the package.** For example, you may ask for additional vacation days, flex hours, or a signing bonus.

Here are a few final thoughts on the salary issue:

➤ **Some people are too embarrassed or shy to talk about salary.** You should realize that you're already looking to engage in a business relationship, and salary is just one more part of the picture. No employer expects you to work for free, and there's no reason you should act as if compensation isn't important. Even while recognizing this, many people find negotiations uncomfortable and unpleasant. If you feel this way, keep in mind that your total time spent negotiating is unlikely to be more than a few hours. A few hours of discomfort is a small price to pay for several thousand extra dollars in your pocket every year you work for the company.

➤ **Many negotiators cite factors such as benefits or work style to draw you to a company.** These factors may be important reasons to join a company, and you'd certainly want all the benefits spelled out. These perks, though, are generally not negotiable. Don't bother discussing non-negotiable factors in a negotiation, and don't get sidetracked if your negotiator mentions them.

"What Is Your Salary History?"

This is a different question from what you expect to make. In this case, the negotiator wants to know your previous salary — most likely to use this as a guide to determine your offer. If this question is raised (unless you were happy with your previous salary), politely answer that you expect compensation appropriate for the new job and responsibilities and that the compensation that you received for a different set of tasks isn't relevant. In addition, resist any temptation to inflate your old salary because you may be asked to back up any claim with pay stubs or other proof.

"Why Should We Hire You?"

This question implies that there's no obvious reason why you're qualified for the job. Clearly, you have skills and experience that make you qualified; otherwise, the interviewer wouldn't be talking to you. In these instances, avoid becoming defensive and reciting your résumé to list your qualifications. Instead, keep things positive by talking about why you want to work at the company and why the job is a good match for your skills. This response shows you can handle criticism and may deflect your interviewer.

"Why Do You Want to Work for This Company?"

When you get this question, you're actually being asked, "What do you know about our company?" Most employers would prefer to hire someone who is excited about working for them rather than someone who is willing to take any job he or she can get. If you don't know enough about the company to describe something about the company that makes you want to work there, it makes it quite clear you're in the latter category.

To avoid appearing uninterested or unexcited, do enough research on the company you're interviewing with to have a good answer to this question. Aim for an answer that's specific enough to show you know something about the company but not so specific that you limit your opportunities. For instance, "Because I like to program" is too general because it could apply to any software company, but "I think product X has the most exciting technology in the world and can't imaging working on anything else" may not improve your chances if they were planning to assign you to product Y.

"Do You Have Any Questions for Me?"

Conventional wisdom has always said to ask a question because it shows enthusiasm. Nothing spoils a good interview, though, like asking a stupid question right at the end. Asking a contrived question just because you feel you should won't count in your favor.

A thoughtful and articulate question can tell you a lot about the company and impress your interviewer. Often, your interviewer doesn't tell you what she does. This is a good time to ask. It lets you know more about what you would potentially be doing and shows genuine interest in the person. In addition, if the interviewer mentioned anything during the interview that sounded interesting, ask for more detail about it. This can yield further insight into your potential future employer.

Finally, if you don't have questions, you can make a joke of it. You could say, "Gee, I know that I'm supposed to ask a question, but the people I interviewed with this morning answered all my questions. I guess you're off the hook!"

SUMMARY

Non-technical questions are just as important as the technical ones. Although good answers to non-technical questions won't get you hired if you bomb the technical part of the interview, bad answers can definitely preclude a job offer. Treat these questions with the respect they deserve.

APPENDIX

Résumés

Whether you have a contact in the industry, are going through a company's recruiting process, or are using a headhunter, everyone will ask to see your résumé. Your résumé convinces people that you have relevant skills and talents and are worth consideration as a candidate. A good résumé is a necessary — but not sufficient — condition to get hired. If the people who read your résumé don't find the relevant information they're looking for, they'll move on to the next job candidate. This is why it's so important that your résumé doesn't sell you short.

THE TECHNICAL RÉSUMÉ

Technical résumés are written differently than the non-technical résumés described in most résumé books. Non-technical jobs generally have some latitude in terms of necessary skills, but technical jobs usually require a specific skill set. Employers aren't interested in talking to candidates who don't have the necessary skills for the job. This means that technical résumés generally require more specific information than non-technical résumés.

A Poor Example

The example in this section starts with an extreme case of a poor résumé from a junior developer. Hopefully, no real résumé would ever be this bad, but the steps taken to improve such an extreme case are relevant to almost anyone's résumé. Figure A-1 shows the sample résumé before improvements.

George David Lee

Current Address:
18 CandleStick Drive #234
San Mateo, CA 94403
650-867-5309
george@windblown.com

Permanent Address:
19 Juniata Dr.
Gladwyne, PA 19035
610-221-9999
george@my_isp.com

Objective: I am looking to join a growing and dynamic company. I am specifically interested in working for a company which provides interesting work and career opportunity. I am also interested in an organization which provides the opportunity for me to grow as an employee and learn new skills. Finally, I am interested in companies in the high-tech space that are looking to hire people.

Information:

- Citizenship: United States of America
- Birthdate: April 18, 1988
- Place of Birth: Denver, Colorado, USA
- Hometown: Philadelphia, Pennsylvania, USA
- Social Security Number: 078-05-1120
- Marital Status: Divorced

Work History:

June 2011-Present, Programmer

Windblown Technologies, Inc., San Francisco, California

I was part of a large group that moved old legacy applications from old computers like DEC Alpha to newer computers made by Intel and used lots of new technologies and languages to do this. The advantages to our clients was that new computers are cheaper than old computers and they don't break as much. This way, it makes sense for them to have us do this. I did a portion of the programming on the new machines, but also had to work with the old machines. Our clients were able to see substantial cost savings as a result of our project. The group got quite good at moving these things and I was part of six projects in my time here. Another big project involved a lot of web stuff where I had to use a database and some other neat technologies. I am leaving because our current projects have not been very intresting and I feel like I am no longer learning anything here.
Reference: Henry Rogers
Windblown Technologies, Inc.
1818 Smith St. Suite #299
San Francisco, CA 94115
415-999-8845
henry@windblown.com

FIGURE A-1

May 2011-June 2011

BananaSoft Inc. Developer of apps., San Francisco, California
This job didn't really work out and I left really soon. All I did was work on some HTML programming which was never used.

No Reference

January 2010-May 2011

F=MA computing corp. Engineer, Palo Alto, California

My role here was to work with a group of people on our main project. This project centered around developing a piece of software that allowed you to figure out dependencies between clients and servers. The advantages of this device are that you can more quickly debug and maintain legacy client/server devices. This was an exciting and interesting position. The reason that I left was because my boss left and the company brought in a different boss who didn't know what he was doing.
Reference: Angelina Diaz
1919 44th St.
Palo Alto, CA 94405
650-668-9955
Angelina.diaz@fma.com

June 2010 – December 2010

I did not have a job during this time because I spent it traveling around Europe after college. I traveled through:
- **England**
- **France**
- **Germany**
- **Czech Republic**
- **Ireland**
- **Italy**
- **Spain**

September 2006 – June 2010

UCLA Housing and Dining Student Food Server, Los Angeles, California

My responsibilities included preparing dinner for over 500 students in the Walker Dining Commons. I started out as a card swiper for the first year. Later, I started to cook food and spend one year as a pasta chef. After working as a Pasta chef, I spend the last two years overseeing the salad production. I left this job because I graduated from college.
Reference: Harry Wong
UCLA Housing and Dining

FIGURE A-1   *continues*

(continued)

1818 Bruin Dr.
Los Angeles, CA 91611
310-557-9988 extension 7788
hwong@dining.ucla.edu

June 2005-September 2005 and June 2004 – September 2004

AGI Communications, Intern, Santa Ana, California

Learned how to work in a large company and be part of a dynamic organization. Worked on a project for the human resources department which they eventually scrapped even after I had worked on it for two summers.
Reference: Rajiv Kumar
AGI Communications
1313 Mayflower St. Suite #202
Santa Ana, CA 92610
rajiv@agi.com

June 2002 – September 2002

Elm St. Ice cream shop, Senior Scooper, Bryn Mawr, Pennsylvania

My responsibilities included serving ice cream to customers, dealing with suppliers and locking up. After one month, I was promoted to senior scooper meaning that I got to assign people tasks.
Education:
University of California Los Angeles, Los Angeles, CA 2006-2010.
Bachelors of Science in Computer Systems Engineering, GPA 3.1 / 4.0
Member of Kappa Delta Phi Fraternity

Abraham Lincoln High School, Rosemont, PA 2002-2006, GPA 3.4/4.0

- Chess club president
- 11th grade essay contest award winner
- 3 Varsity letters in Soccer
- 2 Varsity letters in Wrestling

Hobbies:

- Partying
- Hiking
- Surfing
- Chess

Additional References are available upon request.

Sell Yourself

Most of this résumé's problems result from a single fundamental error: Lee wrote his résumé to describe himself, not to get a job. Lee's résumé is much more an autobiography than it is a sales pitch for him and his skills. This is a common problem. Many people believe their résumé should describe everything they've ever done. That way, a potential employer can carefully read all the information and make an informed decision regarding whether to grant an interview. Unfortunately, it doesn't work this way. Employers have a large number of résumés to evaluate (most of them from people not well qualified for the job) in addition to all their other work. As a result, they spend little time on each résumé they read. Your résumé must be a marketing tool that sells you and convinces an employer that you're valuable — quickly. When you keep this idea in mind, most of the other problems become self-evident.

> **NOTE** *Write your résumé to sell yourself.*

Keep It Short

Lee's résumé has a number of other common problems. One of the biggest is length. An interviewer may receive 50 résumés for an opening. From previous experience, he knows that the vast majority of the candidates are probably not appropriate for the job. The interviewer will have time to speak with only four or five of the candidates and so must eliminate 90 percent of the applicants based on their résumés. Interviewers don't carefully read through each résumé; they quickly scan it to determine whether they can find any reason to keep it. The one question going through the interviewer's mind is, "What can this person do for me now?" Your résumé must look so good that the interviewer can't possibly risk passing on you. An interviewer won't wait long to throw out a résumé. If he doesn't see anything compelling after 15 or 20 seconds of looking at the résumé's first page, the résumé won't make it any further.

Despite the need to make an impression, avoid the temptation to lie or add items you're unfamiliar with. Inflating your résumé can create a variety of problems. First, many interviewers will ask you about every item on your résumé; if you clearly aren't familiar with something, it calls your entire résumé into question. Second, if you claim knowledge of a wide variety of technologies outside your experience, an interviewer may not even have to talk to you to figure out that you're lying. Finally, if you throw in a grab bag of random buzzwords that don't follow any particular theme, you may appear to be a jack-of-all-trades and master of none. The net result is that your résumé becomes a hindrance to you getting a job, instead of a tool that helps you.

Keep your résumé as short as possible. If you have less than 5 years of experience, one page is sufficient. More experienced job hunters can use two pages. Under no circumstances should any résumé exceed three pages; if it does, you're writing a *curriculum vitae (CV)*, not a résumé. In the United States, a CV is appropriate only for jobs in academia, which follow a completely different interview and hiring process than this book describes. Some hiring managers for international positions may expect a lengthier résumé, along the lines of a CV.

> **NOTE** *Keep your résumé short. Make every word count.*

List the Right Information

Contentwise, Lee's résumé is not "buzzword-compliant" — it doesn't mention technologies by name. This is a big problem because many companies use automated systems that look for certain keywords to flag promising résumés. For example, when a position requires a "Java developer with XML experience," the system selects all résumés with the words "Java" and "XML." Other companies file résumés by skills, but the result is the same. Because Lee's résumé is short on buzzwords, it is unlikely to even make it into the stack of résumés that an interviewer sees. He should list all software products, operating systems, languages, technologies, and methodologies that he has used. He should also list any other relevant topics he has experience with — for example, security algorithms or network protocols. Lee should then categorize his skills by topic, as shown in Figure A-2.

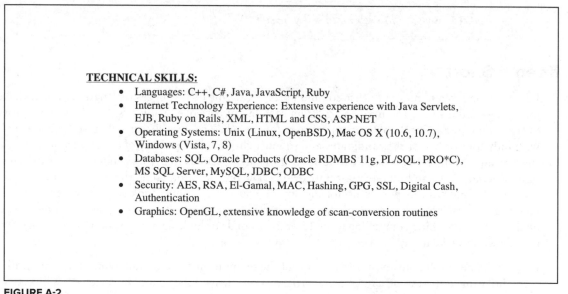

TECHNICAL SKILLS:
- Languages: C++, C#, Java, JavaScript, Ruby
- Internet Technology Experience: Extensive experience with Java Servlets, EJB, Ruby on Rails, XML, HTML and CSS, ASP.NET
- Operating Systems: Unix (Linux, OpenBSD), Mac OS X (10.6, 10.7), Windows (Vista, 7, 8)
- Databases: SQL, Oracle Products (Oracle RDMBS 11g, PL/SQL, PRO*C), MS SQL Server, MySQL, JDBC, ODBC
- Security: AES, RSA, El-Gamal, MAC, Hashing, GPG, SSL, Digital Cash, Authentication
- Graphics: OpenGL, extensive knowledge of scan-conversion routines

FIGURE A-2

When you list specific products in your résumé, include version numbers to show that you're up to date with the latest-and-greatest technologies if you have experience with the most recent version of the product. On the other hand, if your experience is with older or outdated versions, it's better to omit the version numbers. Most version numbers are omitted from the examples shown here because they would be obsolete by the time you read this, but your résumé should be updated much more frequently than a book. Always keep your résumé updated with your most recent experiences.

> **NOTE** *Explicitly list your skills by name on your résumé.*

Be Clear and Concise

Lee's résumé also needs to be formatted more cleanly. In its current form, it uses too many fonts, formats, and lines. This is generally annoying — some would say it makes his résumé look like a ransom note. It can also cause problems for an automated scanning system. Choose a standard font such as Times New Roman, and stick with it throughout the résumé.

Lee's content is difficult to read, rambling, and unfocused; it doesn't describe his contributions and doesn't sell him as a valuable employee. This is especially true regarding his work experience. First, Lee should reorganize his content into bulleted lists. These are faster to read than descriptions in paragraph form, and they make it easier for an interviewer to absorb more in less time. This increases the chances that Lee's résumé will be one of the few that the interviewer decides to act on.

Lee's descriptions should be more focused. His descriptions don't clearly state exactly what he did. He describes what the team did and the general company focus, but not his role, which is the most important part of selling himself as a good candidate. Each item in his work history should read like a description of his accomplishments in the job, not like a job description for the position. He should also use action verbs such as *implemented*, *designed*, *programmed*, *monitored*, *administered*, and *architected* to describe his contributions. These should describe specific actions, such as "designed database schema for Oracle 11g database and programmed database connectivity using Java threads and JDBC." When possible, he should quantify his tasks and describe the results of his work. For example, he could write "administered network of 20 Linux machines for Fortune 100 client, resulting in $1 million in revenues annually." This is a good sell job because it answers the question, "What can you do for me right now?" One caveat is to make sure that any metrics you give are impressive. If your metrics don't work in your favor, omit them.

Another part of focusing the content is to decide the order in which to list responsibilities for a certain job. Generally, you want to list responsibilities from most impressive to least impressive. However, make sure that you get the main point across first. For example, if you did both sales and development at a job, you may have some impressive sales, some impressive development work, and a few less-impressive sales. If you want to emphasize that you were successful in sales, you should list all your sales work first, followed by all your development work. In addition, make sure your points follow a coherent order. This often means grouping items by topic area, even if it causes them to deviate slightly from a strict ranking by importance.

Many people have trouble selling themselves in their résumés. Often, this happens because they feel that they have to be modest and avoid boasting. As a result, many job applicants end up underselling themselves. Don't lie, but do put the most impressive slant on whatever you have done. Remember, your résumé is your personal advertisement; employers will read it with an understanding of that context. If you have trouble saying nice things about yourself, ask a friend for help.

> **NOTE** *Present your experience in bulleted lists and cast it in the best possible light.*

Relevant Information Only

Lee's résumé also includes irrelevant items that take up valuable space. One of the first items an interviewer reads about Lee is that he's a citizen of the United States and was born in Denver. Even though his citizenship or residence status may be important later in the game, when a job offer is about to be made, none of this information will convince an interviewer that he's the person for the job and just wastes valuable space. (Again, international job applications are different and may require this kind of citizenship information.) Other irrelevant information includes his birthdate, hometown, Social Security number, marital status, hobbies, and travel history — information that doesn't make him a more attractive candidate.

Lee's use of the word "I" is unnecessary because the résumé is obviously about him. He shouldn't bother to mention references either. Interviewers won't check references until they're about to make an offer, so it's pointless to put them on your résumé. He doesn't even need to include "References are available upon request" because that's always implicit. Similarly, a résumé is not the place to mention why he left earlier jobs. This question is likely to come up in interviews, and it's a good idea to have a strong, positive response prepared, but it doesn't belong on a résumé. Lee's middle name should also be omitted unless he usually goes by George David.

Finally, omit any additional information that makes you a less-attractive candidate. For example, don't put something on your résumé such as "looking for half-time position until graduation in June, and then conversion to full time." Most interviewers would pass over someone like this and look for someone available full time instead. However, if the interviewer speaks with you and is impressed, it's a different story.

Lee needs to look at his résumé and focus all necessary information to make it as short and useful as possible. Every word must count. For example, he can start with his address information. He should give only one e-mail address and phone number. It's extremely unusual for a potential employer to contact you via postal mail, so the mailing addresses aren't necessary. Lee also lists too much information about his high school accomplishments. Old awards, accomplishments, or job tasks that are not relevant to your current job search should generally be omitted. Any job that you left more than 10 years ago or is totally unrelated to the job that you're currently seeking should be mentioned only briefly. For example, Lee goes into too much detail about his work at the ice cream shop and the dining hall. It's fine to mention this employment, but he won't get a programming job based on his ice cream scooping ability. He should provide only relevant job data. Lee should also omit the job that he held for 2 months because it will count against him. Finally, Lee's objective statement doesn't add anything. Everyone is looking for an "interesting" job with a "dynamic" company. His objective statement should briefly state what sort of job he wants, such as "software engineer" or "database programmer."

> **NOTE** *Include only relevant information.*

Use Reverse Chronological Ordering

After improving the résumé's content, Lee needs to decide how to order his information most effectively. One obvious way to do this is chronologically. In this case, Lee would start out with his high school education, then his job at the ice cream shop, then college, and so forth. A reader could easily follow Lee's experience throughout his life. Even though this is a consistent ordering, it is a poor choice. Always put the most compelling reason for you to be considered for a job first, at the top of the résumé. Interviewers start reading résumés from the top, so you want to put your best, most relevant stuff first, where it can convince the interviewer to read the rest of the résumé. After that first reason, continue to follow a clear and concise organization that spells out your qualifications. The end of the résumé is for the least-impressive information. Your most recent experiences are more relevant than your earliest experiences, so where you do use chronological ordering, put things in reverse order.

In Lee's case, his most impressive asset is undoubtedly his skills. He has a wide range of relevant skills. He should begin his résumé with these skills. Next, Lee should list either his work history or education. Early in your career you should generally put your education first, especially if you went to an impressive school. Later, put your experience first. In Lee's case, it's a toss-up as to whether to list his education or his work experience next. He's right on the cusp of when he should switch from listing education first to work history first. Lee did graduate from an impressive school not too long ago, and he has held several jobs since then, none of them for very long. Therefore, there's probably a slight advantage to listing his education before his work history. In Lee's case, his education is a single item. If he had more than one degree, he would put the most impressive one (usually a post-graduate or university degree) first.

Always Proofread

Lee also needs to proofread his résumé better. For example, he spelled "interesting" as "intresting" and used "spend" when he should have used "spent." Mistakes make you look careless and unprofessional. Many people stop reading a résumé as soon as they find a single mistake. At the very least, mistakes make you a weaker candidate. The only way to avoid mistakes is to proofread. Proofread over and over and over. Then, let the résumé sit for a while, come back to it, and proofread some more. It's also a good idea to ask a trusted friend to proofread for mistakes. While your friend is reading your résumé, ask whether she thinks any sections are unclear, has a recommendation on how to improve your résumé, or thinks you could do a better job selling yourself. Your friend's reactions may give you a clue about how your résumé will appear to an interviewer.

One final matter concerns printing your résumé. Usually, you will submit your résumé electronically and printing won't be an issue. If you print out your résumé, there's no need to use special paper or have your résumé professionally printed. Résumés are often photocopied, scanned, faxed, and written on, making fancy paper and printing a wasted expense. A laser printer and simple white paper will suffice.

The Improved Example

Following all the preceding recommendations, Lee's improved résumé appears in Figure A-3.

George Lee
650-867-5309
george@my_isp.com

<u>OBJECTIVE</u>: Developer

<u>TECHNICAL SKILLS</u>:

- Languages: C++, C#, Java, JavaScript, Ruby
- Internet Technology Experience: Extensive experience with Java Servlets, EJB, Ruby on Rails, XML, HTML and CSS, ASP.NET
- Operating Systems: Unix (Linux, OpenBSD), Mac OS X (10.6, 10.7), Windows (Vista, 7, 8)
- Databases: SQL, Oracle Products (Oracle RDMBS 11g, PL/SQL, PRO*C), MS SQL Server, MySQL, JDBC, ODBC
- Security: AES, RSA, El-Gamal, MAC, Hashing, GPG, SSL, Digital Cash, Authentication
- Graphics: OpenGL, extensive knowledge of scan-conversion routines

<u>EDUCATION</u>:

University of California Los Angeles, 2006-2010.
BS, Computer Systems Engineering, GPA 3.1 / 4.0

<u>EXPERIENCE</u>:

6/11–
Present

Developer and Consultant, Windblown Technologies, Inc., San Francisco, California

- Lead developer on four projects generating $1 million in revenues.
- Ported 100,000-line enterprise payroll application from DEC Alpha to commodity Intel servers.
- Designed database schema for Oracle 11g database; programmed database connectivity using Java threads and JDBC.
- Architected Web tracking application to monitor packages for shipping firm using JSP, JDBC, and an Oracle 11g database.
- Wrote front-end Java Servlet code to allow an airline to securely communicate with its suppliers via the Internet.

1/10–5/11

F=MA Computing Corp. Server-side Engineer, Palo Alto, California

- Improved on Internet order procurement performance by 25 percent using JBoss, Java EJB, and Oracle 11g.
- Developed TCP/IP stack tracer to find client/server dependencies.
- Created Web-based reporting system using Ruby on Rails and MySQL.
- Wrote C# application to monitor mission-critical systems and notify administrators in case of failure.
- Ported Windows NT-based automobile production monitoring agent to Linux.

6/05–9/05

AGI Communications, Santa Ana, CA, Developer

- Developed HR time tracking system

9/06–6/10

UCLA Housing and Dining Student Food Server

FIGURE A-3

This résumé describes the experiences and skills of the same person, but the presentation is entirely different — now Lee looks like someone worth calling for an interview.

Managers and Senior Developers

Although the same ideas that improved Lee's résumé will also improve a senior job candidate's résumé, there are some additional issues to consider. Senior people generally have some management responsibility, and it's important that their résumés show they are capable of this task. For example, consider the résumé presented in Figure A-4 for a senior manager, Sam White. As you read through his résumé, think about which of the techniques that benefited Lee's résumé could also be helpful for White.

White's résumé has the same major problem as Lee's first résumé. It is an autobiography, not a marketing tool. This structural problem is evident from the beginning, where he gives a brief timeline of his life over the past 30 years. Writing an autobiography is a common problem for senior people with impressive credentials. Many senior people mistakenly believe that if they describe their accomplishments, interviews will follow. In fact, regardless of the applicant's seniority, the only question going through an interviewer's mind is "What can you do for me now?" In many ways, focus is even more important for a more senior job because you need to make a greater impression in just as little time.

Many of the specific problems with this résumé are the same as with Lee's initial résumé. It's too long — White should cut his résumé to no more than two pages and strive for one and a half. White should also arrange his descriptions in bulleted lists so that they are easier to read.

However, White's main content problem is that his résumé doesn't sell him for the sort of job he's trying to get. White spends a lot of time describing various job tasks that are clearly junior tasks. Senior positions generally require some management and have less emphasis on technical skills. The ability to perform junior tasks won't get you an interview for a job that requires senior skills. When applying for a senior position, stress your management skills and experience more than your technical skills or achievements in junior positions.

White also needs to show positive results from his past leadership. In this vein, it is necessary to both describe the experience and quantify the result. For example, White's résumé mentions "management and maintenance of web development effort for both U.S. and Canadian sites." This is an impressive achievement, but the size of the undertaking is not clear; nor is it clear whether the project was a success. The description in White's résumé leaves open the possibility that the project was a total failure and he is being forced to resign in disgrace or that the project was trivial and consisted of posting a few documents to a web server. White should quantify the results of his work whenever possible. For example, he could state, "Managed team of 7 in developing and maintaining U.S. and Canadian websites. Sites generate 33 million hits and $15 million annually."

White is looking for a job that is heavy on project management and lighter on skills. He should deemphasize his "flavor of the month" buzzwords and emphasize his experience. He may even want to eliminate his technology skills inventory to make sure the reader doesn't think he's applying for a less-senior position.

White's revised résumé appears in Figure A-5. Notice how the résumé explains his accomplishments much more clearly and does a much better sell job. White becomes someone who a company couldn't afford not to interview.

Samuel Thomas White
3437 Pine St.
Skokie, IL 60077
813-665-9987
sam_white@mindcurrent.com

Statement:

Over the past 3 decades my career has evolved from a lab technician to Web project manager. During that time, I spent some time away and earned my Ph.D. in physics. I have taught college computer science off and on for over 18 years and published numerous journal publications. I have spent the past four years as a project manager overseeing a large Web application development.

At the present, I am actively pursuing MSCE certification to better architect the necessary solutions. I have completed introductory hands-on courses in Networking Fundamentals, Windows Server 2008, and SQL Server. I am taking continuing education courses in management and in other advanced technology topics. Last March, I attended my company's manager seminar conference.

Brief Computer History:

1987: Completed dissertation, moved to Chicago

1987: I received my first personal computer. I wrote a program that implemented a rudimentary tax calculator.

1988: I started to consult for a living. I was independent and worked primarily on assembly programming.

1989: Formed my company, Big Dipper Consulting. Worked on a variety of projects ranging from network debugging tools to graphics chip optimizations.

1994: My first trip on the Web with NCSA Mosaic. I knew that this would be big. I started out running simple static pages, then moved onto CGI scripting. I have been on the forefront of Web technologies and have fulfilled numerous consulting contracts and led many development efforts.

Work History:

CorePlus Corporation
11/2009 -- Present   Senior Web Manager

Responsibilities include: management and maintenance of Web development effort for both U.S. and Canadian sites, management for network redesign, establishing and implementing protocols, migrating from Windows XP to Windows 7, leading security audit using cutting-edge tools and managing 12 employees, providing 24/7 access for both internal deployment and overseas operations, establishing procedures to ensure constant monitoring during non-working hours in case of failures, upgrading all software as new software is released and determined to be stable, ordering computers for both everyday (e-mail, Web), development and travel, establishing proper backup procedures, evaluating different vendors' software packages for current needs and anticipating future needs in both infrastructure and licenses.

Pile-ON Technologies
11/2005 -- 8/2009   Senior Web Developer

Responsibilities included: designing a UNIX-based Web development environment, installing necessary software including web server, development tools and source control, integrating legacy z/OS applications using IMS hierarchical databases to work with Web services that get and set the necessary information, selecting third-party screen scraping products to receive necessary information from legacy system, implementing security procedures to prevent denial of service, spoofing and other attacks, managing three junior developers and ensuring coordination and timeliness of efforts, verifying cross Web-browser compatibility for all Web design efforts, purchasing necessary infrastructure to ensure robustness against all possible problems, built in redundancy, hiring and building development team, reporting directly to the Senior VP of engineering, coordinating with customer support, upgrading network to include newest and fastest solutions, working with consultants to integrate new products.

Athnorn Inc.
6/2000 -- 11/2005   Senior Engineer, MIS

Responsibilities began by working as a C++ developer working on client/server application and doing some system administration tasks such as ensuring network reliability and integration between onsite and offshore developers. Promoted to senior engineer after two years. Additional responsibilities included designing enterprise-wide source control system and development environment spanning multiple sites, enabling connections via a VPN, managing a team of 5 developers and coordinating with marketing to ensure timeliness and quality of product, worked with contractors to implement third-party development products, evaluated and selected various vendors solutions, traveled to Europe, Japan, and the Middle East to meet with clients and assess future needs and problems, worked on moving several products to Linux based environment, designed system to allow synchronous development across multiple time zones, attended company management philosophy seminar, attained certification in advanced use of all products, ensured compliance with corporate standards, worked with customer support to respond to common problems.

Detroit Motor Company
Corp. of Engineers
1/2000 -- 5/2000   Contract Programmer Analyst

Four-month contract position which involved substantial modifications and enhancements to existing database program. This included custom generation of reports, additional ways to add information to database, and integration with existing products to achieve common functionality and data change. Also created files which allowed for much faster uploading and downloading of information. Also provided help with the LAN and WAN, technical support and full documentation of existing system. Worked on integration with legacy applications as well.

Tornado Development Corp.
6/1998 -- 10/1999   Contract Programmer

Responsible for planning, development and the administration of NetBSD file servers. Used Oracle and SQL to do a variety of tasks mostly having to do with order tracking and HR tasks such as payroll and employee benefits. Worked to provide technical support for all users on various types of platforms. Additionally installed and maintained a variety of common applications and was responsible for troubleshooting when problems occurred.

Garson and Brown, Attorneys at Law
6/1995-5/1998   Computer Engineer

FIGURE A-4   *continues*

(continued)

Responsibilities include troubleshooting, maintenance, repair, and support of LAN/WAN networks, often had to use telephone and troubleshoot problems with novice user, updated all company software including Novell, Windows and other third-party proprietary products, designed and installed LAN in office place, maintained LAN and was responsible for new users, provided all support and coordinated with vendors

Hummingbird Chip Designs
5/1990-6/1995   Chip Tester

Responsibilities included testing all chip designs thoroughly using a variety of third-party products that ensured reliability and yield, worked with consultants to attain knowledge using third-party testing products, wrote scripts that automated repetitive tasks, reported potential problems to developers, coordinated all yield test efforts, worked with customer service to verify customer problems, was a liaison between customer support and development

EDUCATION

Indiana University, Bloomington, IL, 1976-1980 BA in Physics

Junior Year Electronics Award Winner

Member of Lambda, Alpha, Nu Fraternity

Member of junior varsity fencing team

University of Wisconsin, Madison, Wisconsin, 1980-1987 PhD in Physics

Doctoral Thesis Work on Molecular Structure of Molybdenum compounds when exposed to intense laser bursts of varying frequencies.

Skills: Attended technical courses for Microsoft Windows XP, 7 and Server 2003, Extensive experience with TCP/IP protocols, security protocols including SSL and PGP, HP Openview, Java, VB, VBScript, ActiveX, ASP, IIS, Apache, Netscape Enterprise Server, FoxPro, IMS, SQL Relational databases including Oracle, Informix, Sybase, DB2 and SQL server, UNIX system administration (Irix and Linux), z/OS, C, C++, Network Architect, Shell Scripting, CGI scripting, HTML, DHTML, repairing printers

Hobbies:

Barbershop Quartet, Golf, Tennis, Frisbee

Horseback Riding, Walking, Swimming

Reading, Traveling, Cake Decorating

Other:

Conversant in Spanish

Citizen of the United States of America

References available upon request.

FIGURE A-4

Sam White
813-665-9987
sam_white@mindcurrent.com

Objective: Senior Manager in Internet Development

Experience:
11/09–present **CorePlus Corporation, Director of Web Development, Santa Rosa, CA**
- Managed team of seven in developing and maintaining U.S. and Canadian websites. Sites generate 33 million hits and $15 million annually.
- Led team of three system administrators to implement full network redundancy, perform a security audit, develop backup procedures, and upgrade hardware and software for an 800-computer Linux and Windows network.
- Evaluated all major systems purchases.
- Purchased $400,000 of software and professional services after evaluation of seven packages and three firms, leading to 20 percent faster customer service response times.
- Hired four developers and managed staff of seven with 100 percent retention.
- Selected contractors to migrate web servers from Windows to Linux. Migration occurred one month ahead of schedule and 20 percent under budget.

11/05–8/09 **Pile-ON technologies, Senior Web Developer, San Jose, CA**
- Designed UNIX Web development environment and supervised team of five in implementation of web log visualization tools. Tools have generated $5 million.
- Evaluated and selected more than $200,000 of software and services to supplement web logs development efforts.
- Developed feature set for $7 million product based on interviews with 20 clients.
- Wrote 100,000-line C++ libraries used by three products with similar database access patterns.
- Recruited and trained two junior developers.

6/00–11/05 **Athorn Inc., Lead Engineer, Fremont, CA**
- Coordinated five developers in on-time six-month project to develop client/server application enabling department store cash registers to update central databases in real time. Product has 50,000 users.
- Met with clients to determine future feature sets for cash register clients.
- Implemented VPN between San Francisco Bay Area office and New York City office.
- Selected, installed, and supported internal enterprisewide source control used by 30 developers on 10 projects.

FIGURE A-5 *continues*

(continued)

6/98–5/00	**Contract Programmer**
	• Upgraded network systems at Detroit Motors, Inc.
	• Installed and designed database applications for Tornado Development Corp.
6/95–5/98	**Garson and Brown, Attorneys at Law, Computer Engineer, Palo Alto, CA**
5/90–6/95	**Hummingbird Chip Designs, QA Tester, San Jose, CA**

Education:

University of Wisconsin, Madison, Wisconsin, Ph.D. in Physics, 1980–87
- Doctoral thesis work on molecular structure of molybdenum under multifrequency laser excitation.

Indiana University, Bloomington, Indiana, B. A. in Physics, 1980

Other:

- Fluent in Spanish

FIGURE A-5

This revamped résumé is a much more effective marketing tool for White.

Tailor the Résumé to the Position

When you send someone your résumé, you usually know something about the job you're applying for. When you do, you can give yourself an additional advantage by creating a new version of your résumé targeted specifically to that particular job. Remember, your résumé is your advertisement — just as television advertisers run different advertisements of the same product for different audiences, you want to sell yourself in the way that's going to be most effective for each opening.

Start with the general version of your résumé that you've developed using the preceding techniques. Now review your résumé, putting yourself in the position of the hiring manager who will be reading it. Your résumé should already sell you as a great programmer — does it also sell you as the best programmer for this particular position? Some specific things to consider:

➤ **Emphasize the most relevant skills and experience.** Items that are irrelevant to one job may be vital to another: Revise your résumé to highlight the things that make you the best candidate for the position.

➤ **Make your objective statement match the job description.** If your résumé tells the employer that the job you're looking for is not the one they're hiring for, you're not going to get an interview.

➤ **Use the terminology of the job description.** If there are multiple synonymous terms for your skills or experience, try to incorporate the terms you see in the job description into your résumé. This way your résumé appears appropriate for the position even to someone in HR who doesn't understand technology and might otherwise screen it out.

Keeping many versions of your résumé up to date is difficult, so usually the best strategy is to have one general version of your résumé that you keep updated and then adapt this version for each job application on a case-by-case basis. Remember to proofread carefully each time you adapt it! The general version is also useful when you need to provide a résumé but you don't have information about the position, or the résumé may be used for multiple job openings (such as when working with a headhunter).

SAMPLE RÉSUMÉ

The two résumés presented so far cover many of the cases you're likely to encounter when you write your résumé. You may find it helpful to see more examples of good résumés for different sorts of people to get a feel for how to write an effective résumé. The remaining portion of this appendix presents three résumés of people with different experience searching for different kinds of technical jobs, as shown in Figures A-6, A-7, and A-8. As you look at the résumés, notice what content stands out and how this helps sell the person as a potentially valuable employee.

Jenny Ramirez
jramirez7@mit.edu
227-886-4937

EDUCATION:

9/08–6/12   **Massachusetts Institute of Technology, Cambridge, MA.**
BS, Electrical Engineering, (GPA 3.7/4.0)
- Focus in databases and security
- National Merit Scholar, Phi Beta Kappa

EXPERIENCE:

6/11–8/11   **E-Commerce Developer, WebWorks Corporation, Huntington Beach, CA.**
Implemented search feature for Fortune 500 company's Internet storefront using ASP.NET and MS SQL Server.
Designed sample projects, using Oracle, MySQL, and MS SQL Server to demonstrate performance trade-offs to clients.
Made initial contact with two companies that became clients and resulted in $80,000 in revenues.
Wrote three proposals that were accepted, leading to $200,000 in revenues.

6/10–9/10   **Web Software Developer, The Aircraft Tech., Renton, WA.**
Designed, researched, and implemented a database solution to improve tracking and reporting of employee accomplishments.
Designed and implemented web services to dynamically report web server statistics.

1/10–6/10   **Computer Instructor, MIT Computer Science Department**

9/09–6/10   **Deans Tutor, MIT School of Engineering**

TECHNICAL SKILLS:
- Languages: C, C++, Java, Ruby
- Internet Technologies: Java Servlets, ASP.NET, Ruby on Rails, HTML, and CSS
- Systems: Linux, Windows Vista and 7
- Databases: SQL, MS SQL Server, Oracle, and MySQL

LANGUAGES:

Fluent in French, proficient in German

FIGURE A-6

Mike Shronsky
352-664-8811
mike_s227@warmmail.com

<u>Objective</u>: Software Engineer in Web Development

<u>Work Experience</u>:
5/10–present **Warner Tractors Manufacturers, Albuquerque, NM, Software Engineer**
- Created AJAX interface to allow customers to compare tractor models.
- Wrote Java servlets to generate dynamic web content from Oracle database.
- Implemented reporting and monitoring for SOAP-based web services system.
- Wrote SQL queries and designed database schema for Oracle database.
- Researched and selected development environment of Linux, Eclipse, Apache, and Tomcat.

7/08–4/10 **Problems Solved, Inc., Albuquerque, NM, Programmer**
- Incorporated focus group input into redesign of order tracking UI to improve workflow efficiency by 20 percent.
- Wrote 160 pages of product documentation for order tracking application.
- Analyzed product performance by writing PowerShell scripts.
- Wrote C# application to test web server responses for clients.

5/06–7/08 **Hernson and Walker Insurance Agents, Austin, TX, Network Engineer**
- Maintained network, ordered systems, and implemented data tracking system.

<u>Technical Skills</u>:
- Languages: Java, JavaScript, C#
- Databases: Oracle, MS SQL Server, MySQL
- Systems: Windows (Vista, 7, and Server 2008), Linux
- Web Skills: JSP, Apache, IIS, Tomcat

<u>Education</u>: Harcum College, Ardmore, PA, 2008, BA in management

FIGURE A-7

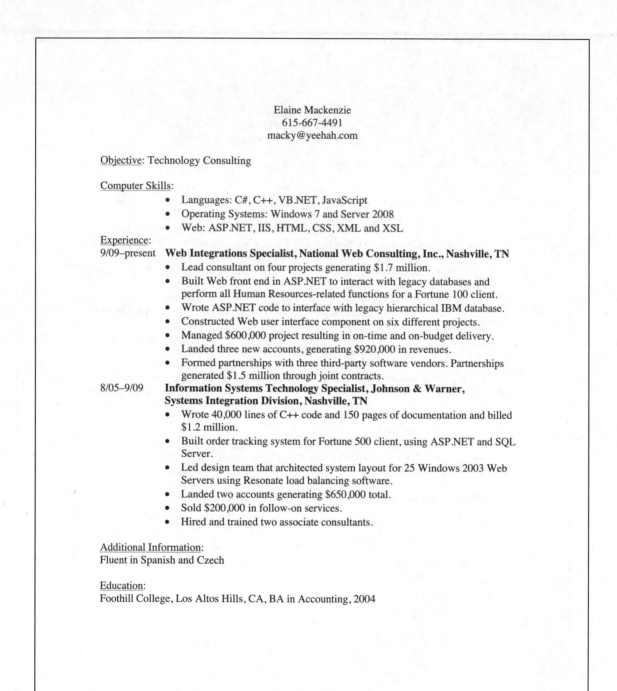

Elaine Mackenzie
615-667-4491
macky@yeehah.com

<u>Objective</u>: Technology Consulting

<u>Computer Skills</u>:

- Languages: C#, C++, VB.NET, JavaScript
- Operating Systems: Windows 7 and Server 2008
- Web: ASP.NET, IIS, HTML, CSS, XML and XSL

<u>Experience</u>:

9/09–present **Web Integrations Specialist, National Web Consulting, Inc., Nashville, TN**

- Lead consultant on four projects generating $1.7 million.
- Built Web front end in ASP.NET to interact with legacy databases and perform all Human Resources-related functions for a Fortune 100 client.
- Wrote ASP.NET code to interface with legacy hierarchical IBM database.
- Constructed Web user interface component on six different projects.
- Managed $600,000 project resulting in on-time and on-budget delivery.
- Landed three new accounts, generating $920,000 in revenues.
- Formed partnerships with three third-party software vendors. Partnerships generated $1.5 million through joint contracts.

8/05–9/09 **Information Systems Technology Specialist, Johnson & Warner, Systems Integration Division, Nashville, TN**

- Wrote 40,000 lines of C++ code and 150 pages of documentation and billed $1.2 million.
- Built order tracking system for Fortune 500 client, using ASP.NET and SQL Server.
- Led design team that architected system layout for 25 Windows 2003 Web Servers using Resonate load balancing software.
- Landed two accounts generating $650,000 total.
- Sold $200,000 in follow-on services.
- Hired and trained two associate consultants.

<u>Additional Information</u>:
Fluent in Spanish and Czech

<u>Education</u>:
Foothill College, Los Altos Hills, CA, BA in Accounting, 2004

FIGURE A-8

Conclusion

There's no denying it: Programming interviews are stressful. Not only because they're so intense, but because there's a lot at stake. You may have all the required skills, education, and experience on paper, but the hiring decision comes down to your performance during the technical interviews.

With the preparation this book has provided, you can go into your interviews with confidence: You know what to expect, you've practiced the techniques you need to solve the problems, and you know what to do when you get stuck. This gives you a significant edge over the candidates who are nervous and uncomfortable with the programming interview process.

Interview preparation isn't something you do once and never return to; it's an on-going process. Don't stop preparing after you put down this book!

- ➤ **Read about programming.** Stay current with the latest ideas, technologies, and trends in computing.

- ➤ **Keep practicing.** A web search with the phrase "technical interview questions" will list a number of sites with questions similar to those found in this book. Answers aren't usually provided, but even if they are, it's better to work through the problems yourself.

- ➤ **Get on our mailing list.** Visit http://www.piexposed.com to join our mailing list to get updates, additional interview tips, and articles.

- ➤ **Use our smartphone app.** We've prepared a simple, useful smartphone app to help you through the interview process. You can find links to it at http://www.piexposed.com.

After you land your dream programming job, let us know — we love to hear our readers' success stories! Use the contact form on the website or send your note to authors@piexposed.com. We hope you've found our book so helpful that you'll want to recommend it to your friends so that they can get great jobs, too.

Keep developing and practicing your problem-solving skills. They help at every stage of your career. Keep learning!

INDEX

schema
    relational database table definitions, 177
    in SQL database, 179
screening interviews, 12–13
search algorithms
    BFS (breadth-first search), 66
    DFS (depth-first search), 67
search engine optimization (SEO), managing
    online profile, 7
searches
    applying recursion to binary search,
        111–113
    binary search trees. *See* BSTs (binary search
        trees)
security, Web application security, 248
SELECT statement, SQL statements, 179–
    180, 182
selection sort
    determining best sorting algorithm,
        132–134
    implementing a stable version, 134–136
    overview, 126–127
selling yourself, in your résumé, 269
semaphores
    busy waiting problem and, 151
    thread synchronization and, 146–147
senior developers, résumé for, 276–282
SEO (search engine optimization), managing
    online profile, 7
SHA cryptographic hashes, 249
shared key (symmetric) cryptography, 250–251
sharing resources
    semaphores locking, 147
    threads and, 145
shift operators, bitwise operators, 194
simplification, as problem-solving
    technique, 209–210
Simula language, in history of OOP, 159
Singleton pattern
    applying, 172–175
    deferred initialization, 172–175

implementing, 172
overview of, 169
singly linked lists
    for finding *m*th to last element in, 50 52
    finding/fixing bugs in, 48–50
    overview of, 32–33
    tracking head element of, 34–36
"Six Degrees of Kevin Bacon" game, 79–82
skill set
    developing marketable skills, 5–6
    listing the right information in résumé, 270
    reversing chronological order in
        résumé, 273
    tailoring résumé to the position, 282
Smalltalk language, in history of OOP, 159
social networks
    job market and, 3
    managing online profile, 7
software architecture, know your aptitudes and
    likes, 2
software development firms, outsourcing risk
    and, 4
sorting
    algorithms for, 125–126
    determining best sorting algorithm,
        132–134
    implementing a stable version of selection
        sort algorithm, 134–136
    insertion sorts, 127–128
    merge sorts, 130–131
    multi-key sort problem, 137–138
    optimizing quicksort algorithm, 139–142
    overview, 125
    pancake sort problem, 142–144
    quicksort algorithm, 128–130
    selection sorts, 126–127
    stabilizing a sort routine, 138–139
    stack implementation in linked lists, 38–43
    summary, 144
spatial brainteasers. *See* graphical/spatial
    brainteasers